AURORA LEIGH

ELIZABETH BARRETT BROWNING (born 1806) was the eldest of the twelve children of the heir to a Jamaican plantation fortune. She grew up on her family's estate in Herefordshire, where from an early age she read widely, studied Greek, and wrote poetry. From 1821 she was in delicate health, living for prolonged periods as a near invalid. She moved with her family to London in 1835. By the time she met Robert Browning ten years later, she had been a publishing poet for twenty-five years and had gained a considerable reputation. Her love affair with Browning is recorded in their voluminous correspondence of 1845–6 and in her *Sonnets from the Portuguese* (published in 1850). Despite her father's interdiction, she married Browning in 1846. The couple immediately left for the continent, eventually settling in Florence, where her only child was born in 1849. *Casa Guidi Windows* (1851) and *Poems before Congress* (1860) reflect her intense involvement in Italian life and politics. *Aurora Leigh*, her major poetic achievement, was finally completed and published in 1856. Barrett Browning died in Florence in 1861 and was buried in the Protestant Cemetery there.

KERRY MCSWEENEY is Molson Professor of English at McGill University in Montreal. His publications include *Tennyson and Swinburne as Romantic Naturalists*, *Four Contemporary Novelists*, *Moby-Dick: Ishmael's Mighty Book*, *George Eliot (Marian Evans): A Literary Life*, monographs on *Middlemarch* and Ralph Ellison's *Invisible Man*, and editions of the critical writings of Angus Wilson and Carlyle's *Sartor Resartus* (World's Classics).

D1110226

THE WORLD'S CLASSICS

ELIZABETH BARRETT BROWNING

Aurora Leigh

——

Edited with an Introduction and Notes by
KERRY McSWEENEY

Oxford   New York
OXFORD UNIVERSITY PRESS

Oxford University Press, Walton Street, Oxford OX2 6DP

Oxford New York Toronto
Delhi Bombay Calcutta Madras Karachi
Kuala Lumpur Singapore Hong Kong Tokyo
Nairobi Dar es Salaam Cape Town
Melbourne Auckland Madrid
and associated companies in
Berlin Ibadan

Oxford is a trade mark of Oxford University Press

Editorial material © Kerry McSweeney 1993

First published as a World's Classics paperback 1993

British Library Cataloguing in Publication Data
Data available

Library of Congress Cataloging in Publication Data
Browning, Elizabeth Barrett, 1806–1861.
Aurora Leigh / Elizabeth Barrett Browning ; edited with an
introduction and notes by Kerry McSweeney.
p.   cm.—(The World's Classics)
Includes bibliographical references.
I. McSweeney, Kerry, 1941– . II. Title. III. Series.
PR4185.A2M38 1993 821'.8—dc20 92–28006
ISBN 0–19–282875–4

3 5 7 9 10 8 6 4

Printed in Great Britain by
BPC Paperbacks Ltd
Aylesbury, Bucks

ACKNOWLEDGEMENTS

SEVERAL colleagues and former colleagues helped me in various ways: Ron Reichertz, John Ripley, and Kate Shaw at McGill University; Catherine Harland, Peter Sabor, and Mel Wiebe at Queen's University. I am also grateful to Susanne McSweeney, Nicholas Temperley of the University of Illinois, my research assistants Roy Carpenter and Rory Leitch, Maria De Souza of the McGill Library, the librarians of the Beinecke Library of Yale University, and Samantha Webb and the other members of my 1991–2 graduate seminar in Victorian poetry. Variant readings from the Wellesley manuscript of *Aurora Leigh* are included by permission of the English Poetry Collection, Wellesley College Library; those from the Houghton manuscript by permission of the Houghton Library of Harvard University. It is a pleasure to acknowledge once again the financial assistance of the Social Sciences and Humanities Research Council of Canada.

CONTENTS

CONTENTS

INTRODUCTION

I

In the 1840s and 1850s English poets and critics were much concerned with the question of the proper subject-matter of poetry and with the relationship of poetry to contemporary life. In 1842, for example, John Stirling complained in the *Quarterly Review* that little 'has been done towards the poetic representation of our time'. Earlier in the century there had been the narrative poems of George Crabbe and Byron's *Don Juan*, that 'splendid attempt at a creative survey of modern life'. But while the early Victorian age was 'full of great though conflicting energies [and] seething with high feelings', so far no poetic mind had found 'in this huge, harassed, and luxurious national existence the nourishment, not the poison, of creative art'. The possibilities were immense, Stirling claimed, and there was no telling 'what poetry might be in our time and land, if a man of the highest powers and most complete cultivation exercised the art among us'.[1]

Matthew Arnold, on the other hand, felt that poetry and contemporary life were immiscible. In 1849 he urged his friend Arthur Hugh Clough to

Reflect . . . in spite of all the nonsense some people talk, how deeply *unpoetical* the age and all one's surroundings are. Not unprofound, not ungrand, not unmoving:—but *unpoetical* . . . My dearest Clough these are damned times—everything is against one—the height to which knowledge is come, the spread of luxury, our physical enervation, the absence of great *natures*, the unavoidable contact with millions of small ones, newspapers, cities, light profligate

---

[1] *Victorian Scrutinies: Reviews of Poetry, 1830–1870*, ed. Isobel Armstrong (London, 1972), 132, 130, 133, 125.

friends, moral desperadoes like Carlyle, our own selves, and the sickening consciousness of our difficulties.[2]

In his Preface to *Poems* (1853) Arnold quoted a particular example of the nonsense some people talked: the opinion of a periodical critic that 'the poet who would really fix the public attention must leave the exhausted past, and draw his subjects from matters of present import, and *therefore* both of interest and novelty'. Arnold branded this view 'completely false';[3] but despite his exhortations, his friend was not so sure. In the same year Clough observed in a review article principally concerned with Arnold's own metrical compositions that while 'poems after classical models, poems from Oriental sources, and the like, have undoubtedly a great literary value . . . there is no question, it is plain and patent enough, that people much prefer *Vanity Fair* and *Bleak House*'. For poetry 'to be widely popular, to gain the ear of multitudes', Clough thought it would have to deal 'more than at present it usually does, with general wants, ordinary feelings, the obvious rather than the rare facts of human nature . . . the actual, palpable things with which our every-day life is concerned'.[4]

The two principal poets of the period reacted in different ways to this debate. Robert Browning stayed in Italy both physically and imaginatively, and did not heed the plea that Charles Kingsley made in 1850, that he leave that 'effete and enervated' land and cast 'all his rugged genial force into the questions and the struggles of that mother-country to whom . . . he owes all his most valuable characteristics'.[5] Tennyson, on the other hand, made several extremely interesting efforts to accommodate his poetic gifts to contemporary subject-matter: his 'English Idyls', published in *Poems* (1842); *The Princess* (1847), his book-length 'medley' on the 'Woman

[2] *Letters of Matthew Arnold to Arthur Hugh Clough*, ed. H. F. Lowry (Oxford, 1932), 99, 111.
[3] *On the Classical Tradition*, ed. R. H. Super (Ann Arbor, Mich., 1960), 3.
[4] *Victorian Scrutinies*, 154–5.
[5] Boyd Litzinger and Donald Smalley (eds.), *Browning: The Critical Heritage* (London, 1970), 147–8.

Question'; and his 'monodrama', *Maud* (1855). Younger poets made equally energetic attempts to represent aspects of the age: Clough's *The Bothie of Toper-na-fuosich* (1848) and *Amours de Voyage* (1858); Coventry Patmore's *The Angel in the House* (1854–63); and George Meredith's *Modern Love* (1862). But the most ambitious effort was made not by a younger poet and not by a man (as Stirling had presumed would be the case). It was made by Elizabeth Barrett Browning, who was Tennyson's senior by three years and her husband's by six.

II

Given the circumstances of her life, one would hardly have expected Barrett Browning to be the person to supply the fullest poetical representation of the early Victorian age. Her childhood and adolescence had been passed on her family's estate in Herefordshire, and from her sixteenth year illness had caused her to live as a semi-invalid. One of her early letters to Robert Browning, written in March 1845, shows that she was keenly aware of the disadvantages of her position:

I have lived only inwardly ... Before this seclusion of my illness, I was secluded still—& there are few of the youngest women in the world who have not seen more, heard more, known more, of society, than I, who am scarcely to be called young now. I grew up in the country ... had no social opportunities ... had my heart in books & poetry ... & my experience, in reveries ... And do you also know what a disadvantage this ignorance is to my art—Why, if I live on & yet do not escape from this seclusion, do you not perceive that I labour under signal disadvantages ... that I am, in a manner, as a *blind poet*? Certainly, there is a compensation to a degree. I have had much of the inner life—& from the habit of selfconsciousness of selfanalysis, I make great guesses at Human Nature in the main. But how willingly I would as a poet exchange some of this lumbering, ponderous, helpless knowledge of books, for some experience of life & man ... [6]

---

[6] *Letters of Robert Browning and Elizabeth Barrett Barrett, 1845–1846*, ed. Elvan Kintner (Cambridge, Mass., 1969), i. 41.

No wonder that her poetic output during the previous quarter-century had been untinged by contemporary life and had drawn both its inspiration and its subject-matter from books and reveries. Her poetic début was *The Battle of Marathon*, a four-book epic in the manner of Pope's translation of Homer, privately printed in 1820, when she was only 14. It was followed six years later by *An Essay on Mind*, the model this time being Pope's *Essay on Man*. A translation of Aeschylus' *Prometheus Bound* appeared in 1833, followed five years later by *The Seraphim, and Other Poems*, a volume filled with angels, wandering souls, proud knights, and lovelorn maidens. It included a preface describing the contents as 'religious in their general character', and the author as feeling intensely 'the sublime uses of poetry, and the solemn responsibilities of the poet'. The title poem was in two parts: the scene of the first was 'the outer side of the shut Heavenly Gate'; that of the second, 'Mid-air, above Judaea'. The two-volume *Poems* of 1844 offered more of the same. The collection's principal poem, *A Drama of Exile*, was described by Edgar Allan Poe as 'a medley of metaphysical recitatives sung out of tune, at Adam and Eve, by all manner of inconceivable abstractions'. As for Eve, the central character, 'she is a mystical something or nothing, enwrapped in a fog of rhapsody about Transfiguration, and the Seed, and the Bruising of the Heel, and other talk of a nature that no man ever pretended to understand in plain prose'.[7] Two of the 1844 *Poems*, however, did point in a new direction. Railways are mentioned in 'Lady Geraldine's Courtship: A Romance of the Age' (as they are in its model, Tennyson's 'Locksley Hall'); and while 'The Cry of the Children' is worked up from books, the books are parliamentary reports concerning the employment of children in the mines and factories of early Victorian England.

The movement away from reverie and towards the contemporary world was greatly accelerated by Elizabeth's love affair

---

[7] *Essays and Reviews*, ed. G. R. Thompson (New York, 1984), 122, 118.

with Robert Browning, which culminated in their marriage in 1846 and the beginning of a new life in Italy. Barrett Browning had finally escaped from her 'seclusion'; she was able to replace reveries with personal experience and observation, and to break away completely from the 'pedantic study of false models' that Poe had identified as the principal contaminant of her 'happy audacity of thought and expression never before known in one of her sex'.[8] *Sonnets from the Portuguese*, for example, which was written in 1845–6, is a generically innovative work that comes directly out of intense personal experience, and displays a self-conscious awareness of its freshness ('I [had] lived with visions for my company | Instead of men and women'). *Casa Guidi Windows* (1847, 1851) is a poem of personal impressions of contemporary life—albeit of the life of Tuscany and the political situation there. And *Aurora Leigh*, her next major effort and principal poetic achievement, is both a penetrating study of the inner life of a nineteenth-century woman and a vividly coloured representation of the age.

III

Even before she met her future husband, Barrett Browning had begun to think about writing a long poem 'comprehending the aspect and manners of modern life, and flinching at nothing of the conventional'. After all, she reflected in October 1844, 'a true poetical novel—modern, and on the level of the manners of the day—might be as good a poem as any other, and much more popular besides'.[9] Later that year she continued her ruminations:

people care for a story—there's the truth! . . . where is the obstacle to making as interesting a story of a poem as of a prose work . . . Conversations & events, why may they not be given as rapidly & passionately & lucidly in verse as in prose . . . You see nobody is offended by my approach to the conventions of vulgar life in 'Lady

[8] Ibid. 141.
[9] *Letters*, ed. Frederic G. Kenyon (London, 1898), i. 204.

Geraldine'—and it gives me the courage to go on, & touch this real everyday life of our age, & hold it with my two hands. I want to write a poem of a new class, in a measure—a Don Juan, without the mockery & impurity . . . under one aspect,—& having unity, as a work of art,—& admitting of as much philosophical dreaming & digression (which is in fact a characteristic of the age) as I like to use.

In the winter of 1844–5 Barrett Browning had an intention, but she did not yet have a plan. She first needed a story, which had to be of her own devising so that she could develop it as she liked: 'A few characters—a simple story—& plenty of room for passion & thought—*that* is what I want . . . & am not likely to find easily.'[10] This proved to be the case; it was only in early 1853 that she had a story in hand and was able to begin composing. 'The poem I am about', she wrote in April of that year, 'will fill a volume when done. It is . . . written in blank verse, in the autobiographical form; the heroine, an artist woman—not a painter, mind. It is intensely modern, crammed from the times (not the 'Times' newspaper) as far as my strength will allow.'[11]

The story she devised is indeed simple, and concerns only a few characters. Aurora Leigh, the first-person narrator, recounts her development as a person and a poet from birth to the age of 30. Her early life is spent in Italy. She loses her Italian mother at the age of 4, and is 13 when her English father dies and she is sent back to England to live in the country with her utterly conventional aunt. On her twentieth birthday she is proposed to by her cousin Romney Leigh, heir to the family estates, who urges her to give up her poetic ambitions and join him in fighting the evils of the age. She refuses his offer, claiming for herself as a woman an equal right to vocational fulfilment, and insisting that the poet's work is at least as important to society as the reformer's.

---

[10] *Letters of Elizabeth Barrett Browning to Mary Russell Mitford*, ed. Meredith B. Raymond and Mary Rose Sullivan (Winfield, Kan., 1983), iii. 49.
[11] Ibid. ii. 112.

After her aunt's death, Aurora moves to London to live on a small legacy and make her way in the literary world. Some years later she is visited by Lady Waldemar, who asks her help in preventing Romney, whom Lady Waldemar wants for herself, from marrying a seamstress named Marian Erle as a way of calling attention to the need to bridge the chasm between the rich and the poor. Aurora visits Marian's slum dwelling and learns the unfortunate young woman's life story. On their wedding day Marian leaves Romney waiting at the altar and disappears. Two years later, Aurora, now a successful poet, decides to return to Italy. *En route*, she lingers in Paris, where she comes upon Marian and her baby and learns of her recent misadventures. She takes the unwed mother and her child with her to Italy; the three live quietly outside Florence until the arrival of Romney, who is much changed by the failure of his socialist schemes, precipitates the resolution of the plot.

Strictly speaking, Barrett Browning's 'story' may be said to be her own. But it is only to be expected that a major work by so bookish an author would have a considerable number of intertextual connections with antecedent works—both poems and prose fictions. The former include *Don Juan*, which Barrett Browning herself cited as a precedent, and two poems of Tennyson's—though they were more important as stimuli or negative exempla than as models. 'Locksley Hall' (1842) was 'passionate and *full*'; but 'there is no story, no *manners*, no modern allusion, except in the grand general adjuration to the "Mother-age"'.[12] As for *The Princess*, in a letter of January 1846 Barrett Browning reported the news that Tennyson 'is writing a new poem—he has finished the second book of it—and it is in blank verse & a fairy tale, & called the "University", the university-members being all females . . . I dont know what to think—it makes me open my eyes. Now isn't the world too old & fond of steam, for blank verse poems, in ever so many books, to be written on

[12] Ibid. i. 204.

the fairies?' It was inevitable that when she read the finished poem, she would profess herself 'to be a good deal disappointed'.[13] But while Barrett Browning was let down by Tennyson's fantastications, she could hardly have failed to notice that *The Princess* explores the relation of sexual love, marriage, and the nurturing of children to the intellectual and vocational aspirations of nineteenth-century women,[14] and that Tennyson's views on the subject were in essential agreement with her own.

Another important poetic presupposition was Wordsworth's *The Prelude* (1850), his book-length autobiographical account in blank verse of the growth of a poet's mind and imagination from childhood to maturity. (At the beginning of *Aurora Leigh* the Wordsworthian point of reference is signalled by Barrett Browning's appropriation of the powerful image in the ninth section of Wordsworth's 'Immortality' ode—the human life-cycle as a journey inland from the shores of the oceanic infinite, of which the adult traveller retains a felt sense.) Both *The Prelude* and *Aurora Leigh* tell of the early loss of first the mother and then the father; of the substitution of a natural bond for the maternal one; of early poetic aspirations and self-doubts; and of the growing assurance of vocation. Both detail the failure of radical hopes for social reform; and both end with their subjects, now in their fourth decade, reaffirming their faith in poetry as a force for good in individual human lives. There are, to be sure, significant differences between Wordsworth's male and Barrett Browning's female *Künstlerroman*: the emphasis in the latter on the poet's dependence on human love, for example, has no parallel in *The Prelude*'s account of the development of a poet who was early 'taught to feel, perhaps too much, | The self-sufficing power of Solitude'. But this and other features of Barrett Browning's 'Prelude' come into sharper

[13] *Letters of . . . Elizabeth Barrett Barrett*, i. 427; *Letters*, i. 367.
[14] On this aspect of *The Princess*, see Elaine Jordan, *Alfred Tennyson* (Cambridge, 1988), ch. 3.

focus when viewed through the lens of Wordsworth's ante-cedent text.

When she searched English poetic history for female antecedents, Barrett Browning was forced to lament: 'I look everywhere for grandmothers and see none.' In her view, Joanna Baillie (1762–1851) was 'the first female poet in all senses in England'.[15] Barrett Browning was a sensitive and discriminating reader of the two principal female poets of the next generation, Felicia Hemans (1793–1835) and Letitia Elizabeth Landon (1802–38). But while both these writers influenced her thinking about the distinctive vocational and emotional vicissitudes of the female poet, neither's work was helpful in her attempt to write a long poem of a new class. What *was* extremely helpful was the work of a number of nineteenth-century female novelists. Jane Austen, however, was not one of them—for reasons that are indicative of the idealizing propensities of Barrett Browning's high Victorian aesthetic even when the artistic medium is realistic:

She is perfect in what she attempts . . . but the excellence lies, I do hold, rather in the execution than the aspiration. It is a narrow, earthly, & essentially unpoetical view of life: it is only half a true view. Her human creatures never look up; and when they look within it is not deeply . . . Conventional Life is not the Inward Life . . . and a writer who is not one-sided, must comprehend *both* in his view of Humanity. Jane Austen is one-sided—and her side is the inferior & darkest side. God, Nature, the Soul . . . what does she say, or suggest of these?[16]

Madame de Staël's *Corinne* (1807), which she had read three times by her mid-twenties, was much more to Barrett Browning's taste. There are close similarities between *Aurora Leigh* and de Staël's digressive, idea-laden novel, in which (it has been said) the modern woman makes her first appearance in literature. Born of an Italian mother and a British father, Corinne lives in Italy until early adolescence, when she is

[15] *Letters*, i. 232, 230.
[16] *Letters . . . to Mary Russell Mitford*, ii. 238.

taken to a country house in England where she is taught to be a conventional gentlewoman and where she comes to realize that her vocation is to be an artist. Late in the novel she returns to Italy in sorrow. Like Aurora, she lives in the country outside Florence brooding on the knowledge (in her case, not erroneous) that someone she cares for deeply has married someone else.

The novels of George Sand were also favourite reading-material, and not without reason did one of the reviewers of *Aurora Leigh* complain that the heroine had been 'made to resemble too closely some of the female portraits' of the French novelist.[17] In *Consuelo*, for example, which Barrett Browning described as 'a sort of rambling Odyssey, a female Odyssey, if you like',[18] the title character is a woman artist who is eloquently insistent on her right to liberty as a condition of her art. And there were the novels of Charlotte Brontë. *Jane Eyre* and *Villette* were both admired by Barrett Browning, and anyone familiar with the former will not fail to be struck by the resemblances between Romney Leigh and St John Rivers, and by the fact that Romney is made to suffer the fates of both Rivers (rejection) and Rochester (blinding).

There are also intertextual connections between *Aurora Leigh* and novels by what may be called Barrett Browning's literary fathers and brothers. Chief among them was Balzac, 'a writer of most wonderful faculty—with an overflow of life everywhere—with the vision & the utterance of a great seer'. Who else, she remarked of the author of *Le Cousin Pons*, 'could have taken such a subject, out of the lowest mud of humanity, and glorified and consecrated it?'[19] Another French novelist she much admired was Eugène Sue, whose *Les Mystères de Paris*, read for the second time in the early 1850s, was 'a work of genius & power' despite its extravagances and impurities, and from whose virtuous heroine the

---

[17] W. E. Aytoun, *Blackwood's Edinburgh Magazine*, 81 (1857), 33.
[18] *Letters of . . . Elizabeth Barrett Barrett*, i. 160.
[19] Ibid. ii. 663; *Letters*, i. 442.

essential features of Marian Erle seem to have been drawn.[20]
And she was also impressed by the fiction of Edward Bulwer
Lytton, whose 'splendid' *Ernest Maltravers* was a story of the
present day, having, as its author explained, 'the philosophical
design, of a moral education or apprenticeship', and exploit-
ing the recognition that 'so much not hitherto said might be
conveyed with advantage through the lips or in the life of an
imaginary writer of our own time'.[21]

During the composition of *Aurora Leigh*, which extended
from the late winter of 1853 to the summer of 1856, Barrett
Browning struggled to amalgamate her diverse materials, to
control the centrifugal tendencies of her imagination, and to
accommodate thematic imperatives that became insistent
during the process of composition. The intensity of her
engagement is instanced in a letter of March 1855:

Between five & six thousand lines written, & more still to write—
Blank verse—Why not?—An autobiography of a poetess—not me
. . . opposing the practical & the ideal lifes & showing how the
practical & real (so called) is but the eternal evolution of the ideal &
spiritual—that it is from *inner to outer* . . . whether in life, morals, or
art—A good deal, in this relation, upon the social question, &
against the socialists—A good deal, in fact, about everything in the
world & beyond—taken from the times, 'hot and hot—' I rather
took fright at [Dickens's] 'Hard Times', as Robert told me from a
review (we neither of us have seen the book) that it treated of an
opposition of the Real & Ideal—But upon consideration I took
breath & courage—because it is *impossible* that Dickens & I could
walk precisely the same ground—If we did, there would be still,
'badger's foot' and 'ourangontang's',—distinct enough. 'The Devil,'
you say—*Don't*—I believe my book will be clear enough,—& alive
enough, even if the story may be wanting in 'rapidity'—There are
characters—talks.[22]

---

[20] *Letters . . . to Mary Russell Mitford*, ii. 385.

[21] Ibid. i. 55; 'Preface to the Edition of 1840', *Ernest Maltravers* (London,
n.d.), pp. viii, ix.

[22] Quoted in James Borg, 'The Fashioning of Elizabeth Barrett Browning's *Aurora Leigh*' (Ph.D. diss. Northwestern, 1979), 166–7.

And in February 1856 she reported herself to be 'in a plague
of industry . . . It's a sort of *furia!*', as she struggled to finish
the enormous work into which she had put so much 'of
myself . . . of my soul, my thoughts, emotions, opinions'.[23]

IV

Aurora Leigh is made up of a large number of ingredients
held together by the creative *furia* of the author. The poem is
a self-confident bravura performance, and it is the performance itself, rather than any single ingredient, that is its most
striking feature. *Aurora Leigh* unscrupulously mixes genres
(novel, autobiography, social satire, tract for the times, treatise
on poetics, theodicy), subjects (geographically ranging from
the slums of London to the New Jerusalem), and themes
(sexual, vocational, aesthetic, social, religious), and holds
them all suspended in a cornucopian fluency of discourse
that makes use of what Hippolyte Taine, an early admirer of
the poem, described as 'a system of notation . . . created from
instant to instant, out of anything and everything'.[24] This
description nicely captures the breathless, hit-or-miss feel of
the narration, which can quickly modulate from dialogue to
description to 'some chromatic sequence of fine thought'
leading to an 'unconjectured harmony' (iv. 1100–2). There
are many examples in the poem of what Virginia Woolf called
the 'lively and secular and satirical' play of Barrett Browning's
mind: 'her ardour and abundance, her brilliant descriptive
powers, her shrewd and caustic humour'.[25] A superb one-
line example is Aurora's description of her early unauthentic
poems as 'gasps of make-believe galvanic life' (iii. 249). A
more pyrotechnic notation is the description of the 'soul' as
not a clean white paper, but

> A palimpsest, a prophet's holograph
> Defiled, erased and covered by a monk's—

---

[23] *Letters*, ii. 225, 228.
[24] *Notes on England*, trans. Edward Hyams (London, 1957), 270.
[25] '*Aurora Leigh*', in *Collected Essays* (London, 1966), i. 213, 218.

> The apocalypse, by a Longus! poring on
> Which obscene text, we may discern perhaps
> Some fair, fine trace of what was written once,
> Some upstroke of an alpha and omega
> Expressing the old scripture.   (i. 826–32)

The worldly and satirical aspects of the poem (its *Don Juan* elements) are also instanced in the account of the conventional education of a young lady that Aurora's aunt imposes on her (Book I), the high society gossip in Saint James's church (Book IV), the extended rendering of Lord Howe's evening party (Book V), and the splendid characterizations of upper-class personages: the ostentatiously Catholic Sir Blaise Delorme, 'thirty five | And medieval' (v. 632–3); Lord Howe, the notional radical, whose socialist ideals do not keep him from living according to the aristocratic 'traditions of his kind' (iv. 712); and (best of all) the worldly Lady Waldemar, who is every bit Aurora's equal in intelligence, satiric bite, and scintillating figurative language.

Some of the early readers of *Aurora Leigh* were extravagant in their admiration. John Ruskin, for example, hailed it as the first 'perfect poetical expression of the Age', and told Robert Browning: 'I like it *all*, familiar parts and unfamiliar, passionate and satirical, evil telling and good telling, philosophical and dramatic—all.'[26] And at the end of the century Swinburne still vividly remembered the poem's initial impact:

The advent of *Aurora Leigh* can never be forgotten by any lover of poetry who was old enough at the time to read it . . . they were right in the impression that they never had read . . . anything in any way comparable with that unique work of audaciously feminine and ambitiously impulsive genius. It is one of the longest poems in the world, and there is not a dead line in it.[27]

The response of other readers, however, was more equivocal. Some judged the poem immoral and unfit for female

---

[26] *Works*, ed. E. T. Cook and Alexander Wedderburn (London, 1903–12), xxxvi. 247–8.

[27] *Complete Works*, ed. Edmund Gosse (London, 1925), xvi. 4.

perusal because of the references to prostitution and because of the story of Marian Erle, who is drugged, raped, and impregnated, but nevertheless remains essentially pure and a loving mother of her illegitimate child. Barrett Browning's response to such criticism was as unflinching as it is commendable: 'I don't like coarse subjects, or the coarse treatment of any subject. But I am deeply convinced that the corruption of our society requires not shut doors and windows, but light and air: and that it is exactly because pure and prosperous women choose to *ignore* vice, that miserable women suffer wrong by it everywhere.'[28] Another example of her humanitarian concern is the depiction of the London proletariat: the slum called Saint Margaret's Court; the appalling denizens of Saint Giles; the workers in a seamstress's shop, including Lucy Gresham, who dies squalidly in the bed she shares with her demented and paralytic grandmother. At the end of *The Princess*, Tennyson's narrator remarks that 'ourselves [we English] are full | Of social wrong'; but one would never have guessed this to be the case from anything that went before in his poem. The London of *Aurora Leigh*, on the other hand, comprehends the London of Engels's *The Condition of the Working Class in England* (1845), Dickens's *Bleak House* (1852–3), and Mayhew's *London Labour and the London Poor* (1861–2).

The periodical reviews of *Aurora Leigh* included appreciable amounts of negative criticism. Some of it was directed at the two principal non-title characters, Romney Leigh and Marian Erle, who were condemned as implausible creations, puppet-like embodiments of ideas and ideal values lacking distinctive voices. It is easy to understand these strictures: both Romney and Marian have character, but neither has personality. The former 'lives by diagrams, | And crosses out the spontaneities | Of all his individual, personal life | With formal universals' (iii. 744–7); the latter is self-effacing and without ego, as colourless as her physical appearance: 'not

[28] *Letters*, ii. 445.

white nor brown, | But could look either, like a mist that changed | According to being shone on more or less' (iii. 810–12). But both are thematically vital to the poem, and essential features of its representation of the age.

The major complaints of reviewers concerned the poem's style and its formlessness. The first of these was the target of W. C. Roscoe's animadversions in the *National Review*. Barrett Browning, he wrote, had the bad habit of poeticizing everything, and of maintaining an 'artificial heat' for this purpose. But her programmatic poetic excitement tended to manifest itself only in the poem's diction; there was no 'corresponding elevation in the structure of the metre, or the flow of the rhythm'. Moreover, there was frequently a discordance between matter and manner—for example, between a subject and the simile under which it was represented. Barrett Browning frequently made the error of carrying a figurative comparison one step too far—as when Aurora is describing the annotations in her father's books:

> *conferenda hæc cum his—*
> *Corruptè citat—lege potiùs*,
> And so on, in the scholar's regal way
> Of giving judgment on the parts of speech,
> As if he sat on all twelve thrones up-piled,
> Arraigning Israel.   (v. 1222–7)

The single word 'regal', Roscoe observed, was all that was needed; the last two lines were *de trop*.

These complaints are largely justified. Stylistic excesses can be an impediment to the reader's engagement with *Aurora Leigh*, though not everyone will agree that they comprise a 'fundamental deficiency' (Roscoe's phrase).[29] Of a passage in *The Princess* describing a Mechanics' Institute fête, Tennyson remarked that 'it was very difficult in blank verse to give descriptions . . . and at the same time to retain poetical elevation', and that 'the employment of rhyme would have

[29] *National Review*, 4 (1857), 241, 247, 242.

made it much easier'.[30] Where Tennyson is calculating and
qualitative, Barrett Browning is impetuous and quantitative.
A great deal of the blank verse of *Aurora Leigh* is distinctly
prosy and only nominally metrical. The author seems to have
felt that elevation could be achieved simply by the addition of
an endless stream of figurative ornamentation. The most
sympathetic way to regard this appliqué is to place it in the
context of Barrett Browning's extraordinarily energetic and
resourceful attempt to give poetical treatment to contemporary subjects. It is also helpful to notice that the narrator is
self-consciously aware of her predisposition to embellish-
ment. In Book II, for example, Aurora interrupts a descriptive
passage to exclaim:

> why, so, indeed,
> I'm writing like a poet, somewhat large
> In the type of the image, and exaggerate
> A small thing with a great thing, topping it.   (1168–71)

There is also narratorial self-consciousness in *Aurora Leigh*
concerning the poem's form. Henry James was not alone in
thinking that Barrett Browning's 'sense of the poetic form
was an absolute muddle';[31] it was presumably to pre-empt
such complaints that in Book V the author has Aurora ask
herself 'What form is best for poems?' The answer is to
'Trust the spirit . . . to make the form . . . Inward evermore |
To outward' (223–8). Prima facie, this might seem an
unsatisfactory rationale for solving the formal and composi-
tional problems presented by a book-length narrative poem.
Consider, for example, the insufficient attention given to the
difficulties of accommodating two generically different elements: a first-person retrospective account of inner development, and a presentation of modern life held together by a
love-plot. The mixture of these elements leads to confusing

---

[30] Quoted in *Poems of Tennyson*, ed. Christopher Ricks, 2nd edn. (London,
1987), ii. 187–8.
[31] *Literary Criticism: Essays on Literature, American Writers, English Writers*,
ed. Leon Edel (New York, 1984), 1229.

switches between retrospective and present-tense narration, and to a blurring of the distinction between the narrating self and the experiencing self. In the first four books the principal subject is Aurora's artistic development, and the narration is clearly retrospective. Beginning with Book V, however, the principal subject is the search for emotional fulfilment and the attainment of its prerequisite, self-knowledge. Here the mode of narration changes from authoritative retrospection to an immersion in events that presupposes no distance between character and narrator.

On the other hand, most readers of *Aurora Leigh* have been unaware of this discontinuity, and only one reviewer and two recent commentators seem to have noticed it.[32] This is surely because Aurora Leigh, as both character and narrator, is her same loquacious self throughout the poem, and in both the first four and the last five books is equally preoccupied with her own inner experience. That is to say, her subjectivity is predominant throughout the poem. In the early Victorian period the question of subjectivity as poetic subject-matter was as pressing as that of the relationship of poetry to contemporary life. In the 1830s Carlyle, Browning, and Tennyson had all felt impelled to announce the renunciation of subjectivity: 'Close thy *Byron*; open thy *Goethe*' was the imperative encapsulation of the spiritual progression of the central character of Carlyle's *Sartor Resartus*; 'I'll look within no more', announced the speaker of *Pauline*, Browning's first published poem; and the soul figure in Tennyson's 'Palace of Art' eventually comes to quit her enclosed art world and seek out 'a cottage in the vale'—though she says she may one day return to the palace with others when she has purged herself of the guilt of self-absorption. And in his 1853 Preface Arnold not only excoriated the view that the poet should take his subjects from contemporary life; he also anathematized the claim that 'A true allegory of the state of one's own mind

---

[32] See Alison Case, 'Gender and Narration in *Aurora Leigh*', *Victorian Poetry*, 29 (1991), 17–32.

in a representative history is perhaps the highest thing that one can attempt in the way of poetry.' The 'eternal objects of poetry' were rather those human actions that perennially appealed 'to the great primary human affections'.[33]

It might be thought that Victorian poems of contemporary life would be evidence of the decline of subjectivity as *materia poetica*. But this is by no means the case. Tennyson's 'Locksley Hall' and *Maud*, Clough's *Amours de Voyage*, Meredith's *Modern Love*, and *Aurora Leigh*: all these poems of contemporary life find their focal point and centre of interest in the intense and frequently incapacitating self-consciousness of the central character. This distinctive mixture of subjective and objective in mid-century poetry was cited by W. C. Roscoe as the reason for the unpopularity of the narrative poems of George Crabbe, 'the last great poet who made man and the lives of men the direct subject of his verse'. In 'modern poetry', Roscoe observed,

the concrete man and the actual life have been subordinated to, or displayed only to throw a more vivid light on, the elucidation of feelings and ideas; and often these have been simply the feelings and ideas of the poet himself—Modern poets are not simply lyrical; they do not utter themselves directly. They are contemplative, but contemplate themselves; they frame outward delineations, but use them as machinery for displaying the results of introspection. *Aurora Leigh* is a vivisection on the bookseller's counter.[34]

Barrett Browning flaunts the fact that her poem is a representation of 'this live, throbbing age'—that it is 'living art' presenting and recording 'true life' (v. 203, 221–2). But it is equally a Romantic autobiography dominated by the subjectivity of the title character. In Book V Aurora analyses the shortcomings of the drama of her day, and comes to the conclusion that one should not attempt to write for the stage,

---

[33] *On the Classical Tradition*, 8, 3–4.
[34] Arthur Pollard (ed.), *Crabbe: The Critical Heritage* (London, 1972), 396–7.

but rather 'take for a worthier stage the soul itself' (340). Commentators have rightly called attention to the similarities between this declaration and Robert Browning's 1835 Preface to *Paracelsus*, in which he speaks of not having recourse to the external machinery of the stage, but rather of writing poems that display action in character, not character in action. But these similar reorientations led the two poets in quite different directions. Browning exploited the potential of the dramatic monologue form with magnificent results. On the other hand, for Barrett Browning, who had long had the habit of self-consciousness, to take the 'soul itself' for the stage meant returning to the intense subjectivity of Romantic autobiographical poetry. This in turn entailed a high degree of self-reflexivity in the narrator of *Aurora Leigh*. A passage of several hundred lines at the beginning of Book V is only one of a number of places in the text where the subject of the poem is explicitly or implicitly the process of its composition. This narratorial self-consciousness is another important point of similarity between Barrett Browning's poem and Wordsworth's *The Prelude*; and the more one is attuned to this fundamental aspect of the presentation, the less apposite formalist criteria will seem.

V

For many late twentieth-century readers, the most compelling feature of *Aurora Leigh*, the first female *Künstlerroman*, is its representation of the inner life of a woman artist—including the 'heart's large seasons', when it 'hopes | And fears, joys, grieves, and loves', as well as the times when it feels 'all that strain | Of sexual passion' (v. 13–15). Certainly, some of the poem's most striking moments are those in which these seasons and strains are evoked: for example, the 'strange and melancholy walk' through the London streets that Aurora and Romney take in Book IV:

> The night came drizzling downward in dark rain,
> And, as we walked, the colour of the time,

> The act, the presence, my hand upon his arm,
> His voice in my ear, and mine to my own sense,
> Appeared unnatural.   (393–8)

Or Aurora's dreamy vision at the beginning of Book VIII, when Florence looked one evening

> As some drowned city in some enchanted sea,
> Cut off from nature—drawing you who gaze
> With passionate desire, to leap and plunge
> And find a sea-king with a voice of waves,
> And treacherous soft eyes, and slippery locks
> You cannot kiss but you shall bring away
> Their salt upon your lips.   (38–44)

As Dorothy Mermin observes, this 'strange and sexy' reverie immediately precedes the appearance of Romney, thus establishing Aurora 'as the speaking subject whose desire elicits its object'.[35]

Equally striking are the notations concerning the emotional needs of women artists. 'We women', observes Aurora in Book V, are too apt to depend on a single person:

> Which proves a certain impotence in art.
> We strain our natures at doing something great,
> Far less because it's something great to do,
> Than haply that we, so, commend ourselves
> As being not small, and more appreciable
> To some one friend.   (43–9)

In another place the subject is the competitive disadvantages of women's emotional make-up:

> So, hard for women to keep pace with men!
> As well give up at once, sit down at once,
> And weep as I do. Tears, tears! *why* we weep?
> 'Tis worth inquiry?—that we've shamed a life,
> Or lost a love, or missed a world, perhaps?
> By no means. Simply, that we've walked too far,

> Or talked too much, or felt the wind i' the east—
> And so we weep, as if both body and soul
> Broke up in water—this way.
>
> Poor mixed rags
> Forsooth we're made of, like those other dolls
> That lean with pretty faces into fairs.
> It seems as if I had a man in me,
> Despising such a woman. (vii. 202–14)

Or consider the lines in Book V evoking the loneliness of the unloved woman poet:

> How dreary 'tis for women to sit still
> On winter nights by solitary fires
> And hear the nations praising them far off,
> Too far! ay, praising our quick sense of love,
> Our very heart of passionate womanhood,
> Which could not beat so in the verse without
> Being present also in the unkissed lips
> And eyes undried because there's none to ask
> The reason they grew moist. (439–47)

This passage has great resonance: it recalls Felicia Hemans's plaintive lyric 'Woman and Fame'; Letitia Elizabeth Landon's two monodies on Mrs Hemans; and Barrett Browning's own poem of 1844, 'L. E. L.'s Last Question'. At the same time, the passage looks forward to Elizabeth Gaskell's biography of Charlotte Brontë, the title-page of which quotes its opening lines; to Christina Rossetti's 'L.E.L.' ('Whose heart was breaking for a little love' is the poem's epigraph); and to Emily Dickinson's cryptic poem (number 312 in her *Complete Poems*) on the death of Barrett Browning.

Almost all of the appreciable amount of critical attention that *Aurora Leigh* has received in the past twenty years has been from feminist critics. One commentator studied the intertextual connections between the poem and a variety of antecedent works, and concluded that Barrett Browning's text is 'radical and rupturing, a major confrontation of patriarchal attitudes unique in the imaginative literature of its

day'.[36] Another argued that the images and metaphors in
Aurora Leigh tell a different story from that of the narrative:
not the public story of a woman poet living in Victorian
society, but 'the inner story of such a woman's feelings about
herself, particularly about her femininity'. Barrett Browning
saw 'women's central problem as the antifeminine biases they
had themselves internalised'; the 'metaphorical language of
the poem' describes the process by which one woman freed
herself from these biases.[37] In this reading, certain features
of the text light up as never before: for example, Aurora's
description of how the portrait of her late mother appeared
to her younger self (i. 146–68). It was by turns 'Ghost, fiend,
and angel, fairy, witch, and sprite': a 'dauntless Muse', a
'dreadful Fate', a 'loving Psyche', Medusa, 'Our Lady of the
Passion', and a serpent woman. A male reviewer called this
description 'a perfect shoal of mangled and pompous sim-
iles';[38] but for present-day feminist commentators, the
description embodies 'all the patriarchal myths of female-
ness', and expresses 'the deep ambivalence' that the young
Aurora 'feels about being a woman'.[39]

Still other commentators have emphasized the mammo-
centric features of the poem—the abundant references to the
maternal nurturing power, to the 'mother's breasts | Which,
round the new-made creatures hanging there, | Throb lumi-
nous and harmonious like pure spheres' (v. 16–18)—and
have decoded the most astonishing passage in the entire
poem:

> Never flinch,
> But still, unscrupulously epic, catch
> Upon the burning lava of a song

[36] Cora Kaplan, Introduction to *Aurora Leigh, with Other Poems* (London, 1978), 35.

[37] Barbara Charlesworth Gelpi, '*Aurora Leigh*: The Vocation of the Woman Poet', *Victorian Poetry*, 19 (1981), 36.

[38] John Nichol, *Westminster Review*, 68 (1857), 401.

[39] Sandra M. Gilbert, 'From *Patria* to *Matria*: Elizabeth Barrett Browning's Risorgimento', *PMLA* 99 (1984), 195; Gelpi, '*Aurora Leigh*', 38.

> The full-veined, heaving, double-breasted Age:
> That, when the next shall come, the men of that
> May touch the impress with reverent hand, and say
> 'Behold—behold the paps we all have sucked!'
>
> (v. 213–19)

Here, it is said, the poet 'claims both biological and cultural authority to speak'; here she 'anticipates contemporary feminist aesthetics of the body', and boldly reclaims 'the epic tradition for woman'; here 'an uncompromising female poetics' is joined 'with lush erotic imagery. Lava is a precise image for something which takes sculptural shape naturally, like female art as Barrett Browning saw it.'[40]

The feminist rereading of *Aurora Leigh* over the past two decades deserves all the credit for having placed Barrett Browning's verse novel where it belongs: in the canon of major Victorian literary texts. After a point, however, because of its exclusive concentration on one feature of the poem, this revisionary enterprise begins to yield diminishing returns, and to blur rather than to sharpen the reader's perception of the text. One crucial point that can be lost sight of is that (like George Eliot) the author of *Aurora Leigh* did not espouse a feminist ideology and was not a feminist by either Victorian or present-day criteria. *Aurora Leigh* may tell the story of a woman's struggle to free herself from internalized anti-feminist biases and to find vocational fulfilment; but in the end Aurora comes to realize the value of being 'a woman, such | As God made women, to save men by love' (vii. 184–5). And while the poem may claim for women a distinctive biological and cultural authority to speak, what is enunciated is not a feminist vision. This is made clear by Deirdre David, who shows that the poem 'is a coherent expression of Barrett Browning's conservative political views,

[40] Rachel Blau DuPlessis, *Writing beyond the Ending: Narrative Strategies of Twentieth-Century Women Writers* (Bloomington, Ind., 1985), 85; Susan Stanford Friedman, 'Gender and Genre Anxiety: Elizabeth Barrett Browning and H.D. as Epic Poets', *Tulsa Studies in Women's Literature*, 5 (1986), 211; Helen McNeil, *Emily Dickinson* (London, 1986), 154.

with which her sexual politics are consistently coherent'. Its
'female imagery is employed to show that the "art" of the
woman poet performs a "service" for the patriarchal vision of
the apocalypse. Woman's talent is made the attendant of
conservative male ideals'; in the poem 'we hear a woman's
voice speaking patriarchal discourse—boldly, passionately,
and without rancour'; '*Aurora Leigh* is certainly confronta-
tional: its enemy, however, is not patriarchy but the middle-
class materialism which found a convenient ally in patriarchal
formations.' The passage in Book V (quoted above) about the
woman artist's unkissed lips 'implies that artistic creation is
unfulfilling to the woman poet unless she is sexually loved'.[41]

That is to say, the essential context in which *Aurora Leigh*
must be placed if it is to be understood and fully savoured is
not feminist; it is high Victorian. Like Carlyle and Ruskin,
the poet of *Aurora Leigh* is a cultural prophet inscribing a
secular scripture. She writes as one

> Of the only truth-tellers now left to God,
> The only speakers of essential truth,
> Opposed to relative, comparative,
> And temporal truths.   (i. 859–62)

Barrett Browning was a great admirer of Carlyle, and her
description of his work may serve equally well as a description
of her own in *Aurora Leigh*: she 'is not an originator, but a
renewer, although [her] medium is highly original'. Her aim
is to 'return to first principles of thought and first elements
of feeling . . . to dissolve from eye and ear the film of habit
and convention'.[42]

For Barrett Browning, poets are those who have had
conferred on them the 'sorrowful great gift . . . of a twofold
life' (v. 380–1). Their responsibility is to keep mankind aware

---

[41] *Intellectual Women and Victorian Patriarchy* (Ithaca, NY, 1987), 98, 157,
145, 151.
[42] *Complete Works*, ed. Charlotte Porter and Helen A. Clarke (New York,
1900), vi. 317.

of 'the truth which draws | Through all things upwards—that a twofold world | Must go to a perfect cosmos'. Poets must remain firmly grounded in the natural world, but they do so in order 'to reach | The spiritual beyond it'. Whoever separates the two (like the one-sided Jane Austen) 'In art, in morals, or the social drift, | Tears up the bond of nature and brings death . . . writes unreal verse . . . deals ignorantly with men, | Is wrong, in short, at all points' (vii. 761–9, 779–80). The most powerful symbol of the twofold life is Jesus Christ, of whose divinity Barrett Browning was in no doubt. Rather than any antecedent texts concerning women, it is the Bible, which she read daily over many years 'in as simple a spirit as I can' in order to acquire 'a stronger apprehension' of what she already knew,[43] that is the essential presupposition of *Aurora Leigh*, and far and away the most important literary influence.

The two biblical texts that meant most to her were Revelation, which is repeatedly alluded to throughout the poem, and the Gospel of John, in which she found 'a depth of Love everywhere—serene thro' its profundity'.[44] It is this same love, a 'sacramental gift | With eucharistic meanings' (i. 90–1), that is celebrated in *Aurora Leigh*. In its closing books the title character finally comes to see that her great failure in her first years of adult life had been not to realize the supreme value of love:

> Art is much, but love is more.
> O Art, my Art, thou'rt much, but Love is more!
> Art symbolises heaven, but Love is God
> And makes heaven. I, Aurora, fell from mine.
> I would not be a woman like the rest,
> A simple woman who believes in love
> And owns the right of love because she loves,
> And, hearing she's beloved, is satisfied
> With what contents God. (ix. 656–64)

[43] *Letters*, i. 159–60.
[44] *Letters . . . to Mary Russell Mitford*, ii. 63.

The highest expression of love was 'God's love'; next highest was 'the love of wedded souls' (ix. 881–2). A number of literary works published in the middle of the nineteenth century express confidence in the institution of marriage as the primary means to human fulfilment: *Jane Eyre, David Copperfield*, Gaskell's *North and South, The Princess*, Clough's *The Bothie*, and Patmore's *The Angel in the House* are all examples. But only the last of these comes close to matching the exalted status and divine aura with which marriage is invested in *Aurora Leigh*. As the Roman Catholic critic Richard Simpson complained in his review, wedded love is 'the key-note of Mrs Browning's poem': it is 'proclaimed to be the essence of Christianity' as well as 'the centre and *summum bonum* of humanity'.[45]

In Barrett Browning's view, the love of wedded souls was the visible analogue of the invisible love of God, the transcendent patriarch, on which it depended. Thus, the failure of Aurora and Romney to realize the supreme importance of love was also their failure to place themselves in God's hands. 'We surely made too small a part for God', observes Aurora (viii. 555); and Romney, his heroic socialist schemes having failed, finally learns to 'throw the remedy back on God' (viii. 701), to be content to work at doing the little good that he can, and to concentrate on individual rather than social improvement. God, love, duty, work, art, and the New Jerusalem are all celebrated in the rhapsodic finale of *Aurora Leigh*—a 250-line love-duet that Poe would doubtless have described as metaphysical recitatives sung out of tune.

VI

Fortunately, it is not necessary to share the transcendent spiritual vision of Barrett Browning in order to value *Aurora Leigh* highly, any more than it is necessary to share the ideology of feminist commentators in order to do so. Neither George Eliot nor Virginia Woolf, for example, held the

[45] *Richard Simpson as Critic*, ed. David Carroll (London, 1977), 79.

Christian vision of Barrett Browning; but that hardly kept them from greatly admiring her poetic representation of the age and from enjoying it enormously. In her notice in the *Westminster Review* Eliot spoke of the 'profound impression' that the poem had made on her:

Other poems of our own day may have higher finish, or a higher degree of certain poetic qualities; but no poem embraces so wide a range of thought and emotion, or takes such complete possession of our nature. Mrs Browning is, perhaps, the first woman who has produced a work which exhibits all the peculiar powers without the negations of her sex; which superadds to masculine vigour, breadth, and culture, feminine subtlety of perception, feminine quickness of sensibility, and feminine tenderness.

Six months later she was reading the poem 'for the third time with more enjoyment than ever'.[46] Virginia Woolf's twentieth-century assessment was more critical, but no less enthusiastic: 'Stimulating and boring, ungainly and eloquent, monstrous and exquisite, all by turns, it overwhelms and bewilders; but, nevertheless it still commands our interest and inspires our respect ... We laugh, we protest, we complain—it is absurd, it is impossible, we cannot tolerate this exaggeration a moment longer—but, nevertheless, we read to the end enthralled.'[47]

[46] *Westminster Review*, 67 (1857), 306; *Letters*, ed. Gordon S. Haight (New Haven, Conn., 1954–78), ii. 342.
[47] *Collected Essays*, i. 214, 218.

NOTE ON THE TEXT

The first edition of *Aurora Leigh* (dated 1857) was published in London by Chapman and Hall on 15 November 1856. The need for a second edition became apparent almost immediately, and on 2 December Robert Browning informed Edward Chapman that he could

> print tomorrow, if you please. There is nothing whatever to correct, that we are able to see at present, the book having been *settled* for some time to come while we were in London [during the summer and early autumn of 1856] for that purpose. My wife made up her mind to it as it *is*, and for the present . . . cannot reconsider the subject. All the 'modern' passages, illustrations, are vitally necessary, she thinks . . . and could not be detached without capital injury to the rest of the poem.[1]

Barrett Browning's letters, however, tell a somewhat different story. It is clear from her correspondence that as late as mid-June she was still struggling to finish her enormous poem, and that well into October she was reading proofs under great pressure. It is therefore not surprising that in February 1857 she told a correspondent:

> I certainly will, when the time comes, go over the poem carefully, and see where an offence can be got rid of without loss otherwise. The second edition was issued so early that Robert would not let me alter even a comma, would not let me look between the pages in order to [make] the least alteration. He said (the truth) that my head was dizzy-blind with the book, and that, if I changed anything, it would be probably for the worse; like arranging a room in the dark . . . Oh, that there are faults in the book, no human being knows so well as I; defects, weaknesses, great gaps of intelligence. Don't let me stop to recount them.[2]

[1] *New Letters*, ed. W. C. DeVane and K. L. Knickerbocker (New Haven, Conn., 1950), 96–7.
[2] *Letters*, ed. Frederic G. Kenyon (London, 1898), ii. 254–5.

Demand for *Aurora Leigh* remained high, and a third edition was in print by the middle of 1857. It was not until late the following year that the opportunity arose for Barrett Browning to correct the text of her poem. Chapman had decided to bring out a fourth edition in a new format, and on 7 October 1858 Robert Browning informed him that 'my wife wants particularly to change a word or two'.[3] Before her revisions were complete, however, Elizabeth had changed considerably more than a word or two. Early in January 1859 she told a correspondent:

Aurora Leigh I despatched to England [from Rome] by a queen's messenger three days since, all except the last two books which are not quite finished. I have worked hard at it as if my conscience were in my eyes and fingers bodily; and though probably I have not removed much which you wish away, I *have* put out a few expressions trenching on coarseness ... as far as I could, without affecting the life of my own conception.[4]

And on 7 January she gave a similar report in another letter: 'Very busy I have been ... having dizzied myself with the "ifs" and "ands", and done some little good I hope at much cost.'[5]

The 'fourth edition, revised', was published on 11 June 1859. Most of the 200 or so substantive changes in the 10,938 lines of the poem involved a single word or phrase. Some were clearly intended to mitigate the 'coarseness' of the first-edition text; others to make the poem more topical. The more significant of these changes are indicated in the notes. The vast majority of the alterations, however, were stylistic, affecting punctuation rather than the choice of words. Many commas were deleted; semi-colons were changed to commas or full stops; and many of the dashes,

[3] *New Letters*, 112.
[4] S. Musgrove, 'Unpublished Letters of Thomas De Quincey and Elizabeth Barrett Browning', *Auckland University College Bulletin*, English Series 7 (1954), 32–3.
[5] *Letters*, ii. 302.

ellipses, and exclamation marks with which the first edition was sprinkled were eliminated. The cumulative effect of these changes was to make the 1859 text seem less agitated and spasmodic than that of the first edition.

The fourth edition was the last to be seen through the press by the author, and thus represents her final intention for the poem. This is the text reproduced here. It has been set from a copy in the University of Illinois Library. Corrections in the author's hand in a presentation copy in the Beinecke Library, Yale University, have been consulted; obvious misprints have been silently corrected; punctuation and spelling have been made consistent and, in some cases, to conform with current usage (e.g. 'sat' for 'sate', 'today' for 'to-day'); and redundant commas preceding dashes and parentheses have been omitted.

The working manuscript of the poem is in the Wellesley College Library; a fair-copy transcription in the author's hand is in the Houghton Library, Harvard University. Like the substantive changes for the fourth edition, the changes in the Houghton manuscript for the first edition show the poet tempering the 'coarseness' of her text and increasing its topicality. The more significant of these are also indicated in the notes, as are a small selection of the variant readings in the Wellesley manuscript. A detailed account of the manuscripts is found in James Borg's dissertation, 'The Fashioning of Elizabeth Barrett Browning's *Aurora Leigh*' (Ph.D. diss. Northwestern, 1979); and Margaret Reynolds's edition of the poem (Athens, Oh., 1992); the publishing history of the poem is given in Warner Barnes's *A Bibliography of Elizabeth Barrett Browning* (Austin, Tex., 1967).

SELECT BIBLIOGRAPHY

Editions

The best edition of Barrett Browning's works is the six-volume *Complete Works*, ed. Charlotte Porter and Helen A. Clarke (New York, 1900; repr., 1973). Philip Kelley and Ronald Hudson's edition of *The Brownings' Correspondence* (Winfield, Kan., 1984–   ) will supersede earlier collections of her letters, of which the most important are: *Letters*, ed. Frederic G. Kenyon, 2 vols. (London, 1898); *Letters to her Sister, 1846–1859*, ed. Leonard Huxley (London, 1929); *Letters of Robert Browning and Elizabeth Barrett Barrett, 1845–1846*, ed. Elvan Kintner, 2 vols. (Cambridge, Mass., 1969); and *Letters of Elizabeth Barrett Browning to Mary Russell Mitford, 1836–1854*, ed. Meredith B. Raymond and Mary Rose Sullivan, 3 vols. (Winfield, Kan., 1983). There are facsimile editions of *Aurora Leigh* by Cora Kaplan (London, 1978) and Gardner B. Taplin (Chicago, 1979), and a critical edition by Margaret Reynolds (Athens, Oh., 1992).

Bibliography

Gardner B. Taplin, 'Elizabeth Barrett Browning', *Victorian Newsletter*, 13 (1958), 20–1.

Warner Barnes, *A Bibliography of Elizabeth Barrett Browning* (Austin, Tex., 1967).

Gladys W. Hudson, *An Elizabeth Barrett Browning Concordance*, 4 vols. (Detroit, 1973).

Biographical and Critical Studies

Dorothy Hewlett, *Elizabeth Barrett Browning* (London, 1953).

Gardner B. Taplin, *The Life of Elizabeth Barrett Browning* (New Haven, Conn., 1957).

Alethea Hayter, *Mrs Browning: A Poet's Work and its Setting* (London, 1962).

Virginia L. Radley, *Elizabeth Barrett Browning* (New York, 1972).

Daniel Karlin, *The Courtship of Robert Browning and Elizabeth Barrett* (Oxford, 1985).

Angela Leighton, *Elizabeth Barrett Browning* (Bloomington, Ind., 1986).

Helen Cooper, *Elizabeth Barrett Browning: Woman and Artist* (Chapel Hill, NC, 1988).

Margaret Forster, *Elizabeth Barrett Browning: A Biography* (London, 1988).

Dorothy Mermin, *Elizabeth Barrett Browning: The Origins of a New Poetry* (Chicago, 1989).

Critical Studies of Aurora Leigh

Virginia Woolf, '*Aurora Leigh*' (1931), in *Collected Essays* (London, 1966), i. 209–19.

Cora Kaplan, Introduction to her edition of *Aurora Leigh, with Other Poems* (London, 1978), 5–36.

Lorna Sage, 'The Heroine as Hero', *TLS* (14 Apr. 1978), 404.

James M. W. Borg, 'The Fashioning of Elizabeth Barrett Browning's *Aurora Leigh*' (Ph.D. diss. Northwestern, 1979).

Gardner B. Taplin, '*Aurora Leigh*: A Relearning', *Studies in Browning and his Circle*, 7 (1979), 7–23.

Barbara Charlesworth Gelpi, '*Aurora Leigh*: The Vocation of the Woman Poet', *Victorian Poetry*, 19 (1981), 35–48.

Virginia Steinmetz, 'Beyond the Sun: Patriarchal Images in *Aurora Leigh*', *Studies in Browning and his Circle*, 9 (1981), 18–41.

Dolores Rosenblum, 'Face to Face: Elizabeth Barrett. Browning's *Aurora Leigh* and Nineteenth-Century Poetry', *Victorian Studies*, 26 (1983), 321–38.

Virginia V. Steinmetz, 'Images of "Mother-Want" in Elizabeth Barrett Browning's *Aurora Leigh*', *Victorian Poetry*, 21 (1983), 351–67.

Sandra M. Gilbert, 'From *Patria* to *Matria*: Elizabeth Barrett Browning's Risorgimento', *PMLA* 99 (1984), 194–211.

George M. Ridenour, 'Robert Browning and *Aurora Leigh*', *Victorian Newsletter*, 67 (1985), 26–31.

Kathleen Blake, 'Elizabeth Barrett Browning and Wordsworth: The Romantic Poet as a Woman', *Victorian Poetry*, 24 (1986), 387–98.

Susan Stanford Friedman, 'Gender and Genre Anxiety: Elizabeth Barrett Browning and H.D. as Epic Poets', *Tulsa Studies in Women's Literature*, 5 (1986), 203–28.

Dorothy Mermin, 'Genre and Gender in *Aurora Leigh*', *Victorian Newsletter*, 69 (1986), 7–11.

Deirdre David, 'Elizabeth Barrett Browning: "Art's a Service"', in ead., *Intellectual Women and Victorian Patriarchy: Harriet Martineau, Elizabeth Barrett Browning, George Eliot* (Ithaca, NY, 1987), 97–158.

Marjorie Stone, 'Genre Subversion and Gender Inversion: *The Princess* and *Aurora Leigh*', *Victorian Poetry*, 25 (1987), 101–27.

Christine Sutphin, 'Revising Old Scripts: The Fusion of Independence and Intimacy in *Aurora Leigh*', *Browning Institute Studies*, 15 (1987), 43–54.

Ron Edmond, '"A printing woman who has lost her place": Elizabeth Barrett Browning's *Aurora Leigh*', in id., *Affairs of the Hearth: Victorian Poetry and Domestic Narrative* (London, 1988), 130–69.

Joyce Zonana, 'The Embodied Muse: Elizabeth Barrett Browning's *Aurora Leigh* and Feminist Poetics', *Tulsa Studies in Women's Literature*, 8 (1989), 241–62.

Alison Case, 'Gender and Narration in *Aurora Leigh*', *Victorian Poetry*, 29 (1991), 17–32.

A CHRONOLOGY OF
ELIZABETH BARRETT BROWNING

1806   (6 Mar.) Born in Coxhoe Hall, County Durham, the
         first of twelve children of Edward Barrett Moulton-
         Barrett, heir to a Jamaican plantation fortune, and Mary
         Graham-Clarke, daughter of a rich Newcastle-upon-Tyne
         merchant.

1809   Barrett family moves to Hope End, an estate of around
         500 acres near Ledbury in Herefordshire in sight of the
         Malvern Hills.

1817   Studies Greek and Latin with Daniel MacSwiney, tutor
         of her brother Edward (Bro), until the latter's departure
         for Charterhouse in 1820.

1820   *The Battle of Marathon*, an epic poem in 4 books in the
         manner of Pope's translation of Homer, privately printed
         by her father (50 copies).

1821   First serious illness, almost certainly a form of tuberculo-
         sis; (May) sent to the Spa Hotel, Gloucester, for medical
         treatment, which includes a spine-crib and opium (use of
         the latter continues throughout her life).

1826   *An Essay on Mind, with Other Poems* published
         anonymously.

1828   (May) Begins reading the Greek classics and Greek
         patristic writings with the blind scholar Hugh Stuart Boyd;
         (7 Oct.) death of mother.

1832   Difficulties with his Jamaican estates, including adverse
         legal decisions, a slave rebellion, and the continuing
         depression of sugar prices, force Elizabeth's father to sell
         Hope End; (Aug.) family moves to Sidmouth on the
         Devonshire coast.

1833   (May) *Prometheus Bound: Translated from the Greek of
         Aeschylus, and Miscellaneous Poems* published anonymously.

1835–8 Family moves to London, first to Gloucester Place and then (May 1838) to 50 Wimpole Street.

1838 (June) *The Seraphim, and Other Poems* published; (Aug.) sent to Torquay to recover from a serious illness, accompanied by Bro, her closest sibling.

1840 (11 July) Bro drowns in a sailing accident off Torquay; serious illness.

1841 (Jan.) Acquires Flush, a golden cocker spaniel; (Aug.) returns to Wimpole Street from Torquay, travelling prone in a specially designed carriage; for the next 5 years she rarely leaves her third-floor bedroom.

1842 'Some Account of the Greek Christian Poets' and 'The Book of the Poets' published in the *Athenaeum*.

1843 Health sufficiently improved to allow summer wheelchair outings with her maid.

1844 (Mar.) *A New Spirit of the Age* published, edited by R. H. Horne in collaboration with Barrett Browning, whose contributions include substantial parts of the articles on Carlyle, Leigh Hunt, Landor, Monckton Milnes, Tennyson, and Wordsworth; (Aug.) *Poems* (2 vols.) published; includes *A Drama of Exile*, 'The Cry of the Children', and 'Lady Geraldine's Courtship'; American edition published under the title *A Drama of Exile, and Other Poems*.

1845 (Jan.) Intensive correspondence with Robert Browning begins, continuing through the summer of the following year; (20 May) their first meeting.

1846 (12 Sept.) Marries Robert Browning in St Marylebone Church; a week later they leave secretly for Italy; from now until his death in 1857 her father refuses all communication with her.

1847 (Mar.) First miscarriage; (Apr.) moves with Robert Browning from Pisa to Florence.

1848 (May) Casa Guidi in Florence becomes their permanent home.

1849 (9 Mar.) Robert Wiedemann Barrett Browning (Pen) born.

1850   (July) Suffers fourth and most serious miscarriage; (Nov.) 2-volume edition of new and selected *Poems* published; includes *Sonnets from the Portuguese* (written 1845–6).

1851   (May) *Casa Guidi Windows: A Poem* published; contains impressions of, and reflections on, 'events in Tuscany of which she was a witness'; (July–Sept.) visit to London; (Sept.–July 1852) residence in Paris; witnesses Louis Napoleon's *coup d'état*; meets George Sand.

1852   (July–Oct.) Visit to London.

1853   Begins work on *Aurora Leigh*; winter in Rome.

1854   (June) Death of Flush.

1855   (Jan.) Serious illness; (July–Oct.) visit to London; (Oct.–June 1856) residence in Paris.

1856   (Spring) Finishes *Aurora Leigh*; (June–Oct.) fourth and last visit to London; (Oct.) returns to Florence; (Nov.) *Aurora Leigh* published in London and New York; death of John Kenyon, whose legacies make her and Robert Browning financially secure for the first time.

1857   (17 Apr.) Death of father.

1858   (July) Holiday in northern France; winter in Rome.

1859   (June) Revised fourth edition of *Aurora Leigh* published; serious illness; winter in Rome.

1860   (Mar.) *Poems before Congress* published; 7 of the 8 poems deal with current Italian political events; American edition published under the title *Napoleon III in Italy, and Other Poems*; (June) returns to Florence; (Nov.) death of sister Henrietta.

1861   Confined to her room during winter in Rome; (June) returns to Florence; (29 June) dies in the arms of Robert Browning; (1 July) buried in the Protestant Cemetery, Florence.

1862   (Mar.) *Last Poems* published; includes 'A Musical Instrument'.

Aurora Leigh

Dedication
to
John Kenyon,* Esq.

THE words 'cousin' and 'friend' are constantly recurring in this poem, the last pages of which have been finished under the hospitality of your roof, my own dearest cousin and friend—cousin and friend, in a sense of less equality and greater disinterestedness than Romney's.

Ending, therefore, and preparing once more to quit England, I venture to leave in your hands this book, the most mature of my works, and the one into which my highest convictions upon Life and Art have entered; that as, through my various efforts in literature and steps in life, you have believed in me, borne with me, and been generous to me, far beyond the common uses of mere relationship or sympathy of mind, so you may kindly accept, in sight of the public, this poor sign of esteem, gratitude, and affection from

Your unforgetting
E.B.B.

39 Devonshire Place
October 17, 1856

BOOK I

OF writing many books there is no end;*
And I who have written much in prose and verse
For others' uses, will write now for mine—
Will write my story for my better self
As when you paint your portrait for a friend,
Who keeps it in a drawer and looks at it
Long after he has ceased to love you, just
To hold together what he was and is.

I, writing thus, am still what men call young;
I have not so far left the coasts of life*   10
To travel inland, that I cannot hear
That murmur of the outer Infinite
Which unweaned babies smile at in their sleep
When wondered at for smiling; not so far,
But still I catch my mother at her post
Beside the nursery-door, with finger up,
'Hush, hush—here's too much noise!' while her sweet eyes
Leap forward, taking part against her word
In the child's riot. Still I sit and feel
My father's slow hand, when she had left us both, 20
Stroke out my childish curls across his knee,
And hear Assunta's daily jest (she knew
He liked it better than a better jest)
Inquire how many golden scudi went*
To make such ringlets. O my father's hand,
Stroke heavily, heavily the poor hair down,
Draw, press the child's head closer to thy knee!
I'm still too young, too young, to sit alone.

I write. My mother was a Florentine,
Whose rare blue eyes were shut from seeing me   30

When scarcely I was four years old, my life
A poor spark snatched up from a failing lamp
Which went out therefore. She was weak and frail;
She could not bear the joy of giving life,
The mother's rapture slew her. If her kiss
Had left a longer weight upon my lips
It might have steadied the uneasy breath,
And reconciled and fraternised my soul
With the new order. As it was, indeed,
I felt a mother-want about the world,   40
And still went seeking, like a bleating lamb
Left out at night in shutting up the fold—
As restless as a nest-deserted bird
Grown chill through something being away, though what
It knows not. I, Aurora Leigh, was born*
To make my father sadder, and myself
Not overjoyous, truly. Women know
The way to rear up children (to be just),
They know a simple, merry, tender knack
Of tying sashes, fitting baby-shoes,   50
And stringing pretty words that make no sense,
And kissing full sense into empty words,
Which things are corals to cut life upon,*
Although such trifles: children learn by such,
Love's holy earnest in a pretty play
And get not over-early solemnised,
But seeing, as in a rose-bush, Love's Divine*
Which burns and hurts not—not a single bloom,
Become aware and unafraid of Love.
Such good do mothers. Fathers love as well   60
—Mine did, I know—but still with heavier brains,
And wills more consciously responsible,
And not as wisely, since less foolishly;
So mothers have God's licence to be missed.

My father was an austere Englishman,
Who, after a dry life-time spent at home

In college-learning, law, and parish talk,
Was flooded with a passion unaware,
His whole provisioned and complacent past
Drowned out from him that moment. As he stood 70
In Florence, where he had come to spend a month
And note the secret of Da Vinci's drains,*
He musing somewhat absently perhaps
Some English question . . . whether men should pay*
The unpopular but necessary tax
With left or right hand—in the alien sun
In that great square of the Santissima
There drifted past him (scarcely marked enough
To move his comfortable island scorn)
A train of priestly banners, cross and psalm, 80
The white-veiled rose-crowned maidens holding up
Tall tapers, weighty for such wrists, aslant
To the blue luminous tremor of the air,
And letting drop the white wax as they went
To eat the bishop's wafer at the church;
From which long trail of chanting priests and girls,
A face flashed like a cymbal on his face
And shook with silent clangour brain and heart,
Transfiguring him to music. Thus, even thus,
He too received his sacramental gift 90
With eucharistic meanings; for he loved.

And thus beloved, she died. I've heard it said
That but to see him in the first surprise
Of widower and father, nursing me,
Unmothered little child of four years old,
His large man's hands afraid to touch my curls,
As if the gold would tarnish—his grave lips
Contriving such a miserable smile
As if he knew needs must, or I should die,
And yet 'twas hard—would almost make the stones 100
Cry out for pity. There's a verse he set
In Santa Croce to her memory—

'Weep for an infant too young to weep much
When death removed this mother'—stops the mirth
Today on women's faces when they walk
With rosy children hanging on their gowns,
Under the cloister to escape the sun
That scorches in the piazza. After which
He left our Florence and made haste to hide
Himself, his prattling child, and silent grief,   110
Among the mountains above Pelago;*
Because unmothered babes, he thought, had need
Of mother nature more than others use,
And Pan's white goats, with udders warm and full*
Of mystic contemplations, come to feed
Poor milkless lips of orphans like his own—
Such scholar-scraps he talked, I've heard from friends,
For even prosaic men who wear grief long
Will get to wear it as a hat aside
With a flower stuck in't. Father, then, and child,   120
We lived among the mountains many years,
God's silence on the outside of the house,
And we who did not speak too loud within,
And old Assunta to make up the fire,
Crossing herself whene'er a sudden flame
Which lightened from the firewood, made alive
That picture of my mother on the wall.

The painter drew it after she was dead,
And when the face was finished, throat and hands,
Her cameriera carried him, in hate*   130
Of the English-fashioned shroud, the last brocade
She dressed in at the Pitti; 'he should paint*
No sadder thing than that,' she swore, 'to wrong
Her poor signora.' Therefore very strange
The effect was. I, a little child, would crouch
For hours upon the floor with knees drawn up,
And gaze across them, half in terror, half
In adoration, at the picture there—

That swan-like supernatural white life
Just sailing upward from the red stiff silk   140
Which seemed to have no part in it nor power
To keep it from quite breaking out of bounds.
For hours I sat and stared. Assunta's awe
And my poor father's melancholy eyes
Still pointed that way. That way went my thoughts
When wandering beyond sight. And as I grew
In years, I mixed, confused, unconsciously,
Whatever I last read or heard or dreamed,
Abhorrent, admirable, beautiful,
Pathetical, or ghastly, or grotesque,   150
With still that face . . . which did not therefore change,
But kept the mystic level of all forms,
Hates, fears, and admirations, was by turns
Ghost, fiend, and angel, fairy, witch, and sprite,
A dauntless Muse who eyes a dreadful Fate,
A loving Psyche who loses sight of Love,*
A still Medusa with mild milky brows
All curdled and all clothed upon with snakes
Whose slime falls fast as sweat will; or anon
Our Lady of the Passion, stabbed with swords*   160
Where the Babe sucked; or Lamia in her first*
Moonlighted pallor, ere she shrunk and blinked
And shuddering wriggled down to the unclean;
Or my own mother, leaving her last smile
In her last kiss upon the baby-mouth
My father pushed down on the bed for that—
Or my dead mother, without smile or kiss,
Buried at Florence. All which images,
Concentred on the picture, glassed themselves
Before my meditative childhood, as   170
The incoherencies of change and death
Are represented fully, mixed and merged,
In the smooth fair mystery of perpetual Life.

And while I stared away my childish wits
Upon my mother's picture (ah, poor child!),

My father, who through love had suddenly
Thrown off the old conventions, broken loose
From chin-bands of the soul, like Lazarus,*
Yet had no time to learn to talk and walk
Or grow anew familiar with the sun—   180
Who had reached to freedom, not to action, lived,
But lived as one entranced, with thoughts, not aims—
Whom love had unmade from a common man
But not completed to an uncommon man—
My father taught me what he had learnt the best
Before he died and left me—grief and love.
And, seeing we had books among the hills,
Strong words of counselling souls confederate
With vocal pines and waters—out of books
He taught me all the ignorance of men,   190
And how God laughs in heaven when any man
Says 'Here I'm learned; this, I understand;
In that, I am never caught at fault or doubt.'
He sent the schools to school, demonstrating
A fool will pass for such through one mistake,
While a philosopher will pass for such,
Through said mistakes being ventured in the gross
And heaped up to a system.

                              I am like,
They tell me, my dear father. Broader brows
Howbeit, upon a slenderer undergrowth   200
Of delicate features—paler, near as grave;
But then my mother's smile breaks up the whole,
And makes it better sometimes than itself.

So, nine full years, our days were hid with God
Among his mountains: I was just thirteen,
Still growing like the plants from unseen roots
In tongue-tied Springs—and suddenly awoke
To full life and life's needs and agonies
With an intense, strong, struggling heart beside
A stone-dead father. Life, struck sharp on death,   210

Makes awful lightning. His last word was, 'Love—'
'Love, my child, love, love!' (then he had done with grief)
'Love, my child.' Ere I answered he was gone,
And none was left to love in all the world.

There, ended childhood. What succeeded next
I recollect as, after fevers, men
Thread back the passage of delirium,
Missing the turn still, baffled by the door;
Smooth endless days, notched here and there with knives;
A weary, wormy darkness, spurred i' the flank　　　220
With flame, that it should eat and end itself
Like some tormented scorpion. Then at last*
I do remember clearly, how there came
A stranger with authority, not right
(I thought not), who commanded, caught me up
From old Assunta's neck; how, with a shriek,
She let me go—while I, with ears too full
Of my father's silence to shriek back a word,
In all a child's astonishment at grief
Stared at the wharf-edge where she stood and moaned,　　230
My poor Assunta, where she stood and moaned!
The white walls, the blue hills, my Italy,
Drawn backward from the shuddering steamer-deck,
Like one in anger drawing back her skirts
Which suppliants catch at. Then the bitter sea
Inexorably pushed between us both,
And sweeping up the ship with my despair
Threw us out as a pasture to the stars.

Ten nights and days we voyaged on the deep;
Ten nights and days without the common face　　　240
Of any day or night; the moon and sun
Cut off from the green reconciling earth,
To starve into a blind ferocity
And glare unnatural; the very sky
(Dropping its bell-net down upon the sea

As if no human heart should 'scape alive)
Bedraggled with the desolating salt,
Until it seemed no more that holy heaven
To which my father went. All new and strange;
The universe turned stranger, for a child.   250

Then, land!—then, England! oh, the frosty cliffs
Looked cold upon me. Could I find a home
Among those mean red houses through the fog?
And when I heard my father's language first
From alien lips which had no kiss for mine
I wept aloud, then laughed, then wept, then wept,
And some one near me said the child was mad
Through much sea-sickness. The train swept us on.
Was this my father's England? the great isle?
The ground seemed cut up from the fellowship   260
Of verdure, field from field, as man from man;
The skies themselves looked low and positive,
As almost you could touch them with a hand,
And dared to do it they were so far off
From God's celestial crystals; all things blurred
And dull and vague. Did Shakespeare and his mates
Absorb the light here?—not a hill or stone
With heart to strike a radiant colour up
Or active outline on the indifferent air.

I think I see my father's sister stand   270
Upon the hall-step of her country-house
To give me welcome. She stood straight and calm,
Her somewhat narrow forehead braided tight
As if for taming accidental thoughts
From possible pulses; brown hair pricked with gray
By frigid use of life (she was not old
Although my father's elder by a year);
A nose drawn sharply, yet in delicate lines;
A close mild mouth, a little soured about
The ends, through speaking unrequited loves   280

Or peradventure niggardly half-truths;
Eyes of no colour—once they might have smiled,
But never, never have forgot themselves
In smiling; cheeks, in which was yet a rose
Of perished summers, like a rose in a book,
Kept more for ruth than pleasure—if past bloom,*
Past fading also.
                    She had lived, we'll say,
A harmless life, she called a virtuous life,
A quiet life, which was not life at all
(But that, she had not lived enough to know),   290
Between the vicar and the county squires,
The lord-lieutenant looking down sometimes
From the empyrean to assure their souls
Against chance vulgarisms, and, in the abyss
The apothecary, looked on once a year*
To prove their soundness of humility.
The poor-club exercised her Christian gifts
Of knitting stockings, stitching petticoats,
Because we are of one flesh after all
And need one flannel (with a proper sense   300
Of difference in the quality)—and still
The book-club, guarded from your modern trick
Of shaking dangerous questions from the crease,
Preserved her intellectual. She had lived
A sort of cage-bird life, born in a cage,*
Accounting that to leap from perch to perch
Was act and joy enough for any bird.
Dear heaven, how silly are the things that live
In thickets, and eat berries!
                                    I, alas,
A wild bird scarcely fledged, was brought to her cage,   310
And she was there to meet me. Very kind.
Bring the clean water, give out the fresh seed.

She stood upon the steps to welcome me,
Calm, in black garb. I clung about her neck—

Young babes, who catch at every shred of wool
To draw the new light closer, catch and cling
Less blindly. In my ears, my father's word
Hummed ignorantly, as the sea in shells,
'Love, love, my child.' She, black there with my grief,
Might feel my love—she was his sister once,   320
I clung to her. A moment she seemed moved,
Kissed me with cold lips, suffered me to cling,
And drew me feebly through the hall into
The room she sat in.
                              There, with some strange spasm
Of pain and passion, she wrung loose my hands
Imperiously, and held me at arm's length,
And with two gray-steel naked-bladed eyes
Searched through my face—ay, stabbed it through and
          through,
Through brows and cheeks and chin, as if to find
A wicked murderer in my innocent face,   330
If not here, there perhaps. Then, drawing breath,
She struggled for her ordinary calm
And missed it rather—told me not to shrink,
As if she had told me not to lie or swear—
'She loved my father and would love me too
As long as I deserved it.' Very kind.

I understood her meaning afterward;
She thought to find my mother in my face,
And questioned it for that. For she, my aunt,
Had loved my father truly, as she could,   340
And hated, with the gall of gentle souls,
My Tuscan mother who had fooled away*
A wise man from wise courses, a good man
From obvious duties, and, depriving her,
His sister, of the household precedence,
Had wronged his tenants, robbed his native land,
And made him mad, alike by life and death,
In love and sorrow. She had pored for years*

What sort of woman could be suitable
To her sort of hate, to entertain it with,   350
And so, her very curiosity
Became hate too, and all the idealism
She ever used in life, was used for hate,
Till hate, so nourished, did exceed at last
The love from which it grew, in strength and heat,
And wrinkled her smooth conscience with a sense
Of disputable virtue (say not, sin)
When Christian doctrine was enforced at church.

And thus my father's sister was to me
My mother's hater. From that day, she did   360
Her duty to me (I appreciate it
In her own word as spoken to herself),
Her duty, in large measure, well pressed out,
But measured always. She was generous, bland,
More courteous than was tender, gave me still
The first place—as if fearful that God's saints
Would look down suddenly and say, 'Herein
You missed a point, I think, through lack of love.'
Alas, a mother never is afraid
Of speaking angrily to any child,   370
Since love, she knows, is justified of love.

And I, I was a good child on the whole,
A meek and manageable child. Why not?
I did not live, to have the faults of life:
There seemed more true life in my father's grave
Than in all England. Since *that* threw me off
Who fain would cleave (his latest will, they say,
Consigned me to his land), I only thought
Of lying quiet there where I was thrown
Like seaweed on the rocks, and suffering her   380
To prick me to a pattern with her pin
Fibre from fibre, delicate leaf from leaf,
And dry out from my drowned anatomy

The last sea-salt left in me.
                  So it was.
I broke the copious curls upon my head
In braids, because she liked smooth-ordered hair.
I left off saying my sweet Tuscan words
Which still at any stirring of the heart
Came up to float across the English phrase
As lilies (*Bene* or *Che che*), because*   390
She liked my father's child to speak his tongue.
I learnt the collects and the catechism,
The creeds, from Athanasius back to Nice,
The Articles, the Tracts *against* the times*
(By no means Buonaventure's 'Prick of Love'),*
And various popular synopses of
Inhuman doctrines never taught by John,
Because she liked instructed piety.
I learnt my complement of classic French
(Kept pure of Balzac and neologism)*   400
And German also, since she liked a range
Of liberal education—tongues, not books.
I learnt a little algebra, a little
Of the mathematics—brushed with extreme flounce
The circle of the sciences, because
She misliked women who are frivolous.
I learnt the royal genealogies
Of Oviedo, the internal laws*
Of the Burmese empire—by how many feet
Mount Chimborazo outsoars Tenerife,*   410
What navigable river joins itself
To Lara, and what census of the year five
Was taken at Klagenfurt—because she liked
A general insight into useful facts.
I learnt much music—such as would have been
As quite impossible in Johnson's day*
As still it might be wished—fine sleights of hand
And unimagined fingering, shuffling off
The hearer's soul through hurricanes of notes

To a noisy Tophet; and I drew . . . costumes*   420
From French engravings, nereids neatly draped
(With smirks of simmering godship)—I washed in
Landscapes from nature (rather say, washed out).
I danced the polka and Cellarius,*
Spun glass, stuffed birds, and modelled flowers in wax,
Because she liked accomplishments in girls.
I read a score of books on womanhood*
To prove, if women do not think at all,
They may teach thinking (to a maiden-aunt
Or else the author)—books that boldly assert*   430
Their right of comprehending husband's talk
When not too deep, and even of answering
With pretty 'may it please you,' or 'so it is'—
Their rapid insight and fine aptitude,
Particular worth and general missionariness,
As long as they keep quiet by the fire
And never say 'no' when the world says 'ay,'
For that is fatal—their angelic reach
Of virtue, chiefly used to sit and darn,
And fatten household sinners—their, in brief,   440
Potential faculty in everything
Of abdicating power in it: she owned
She liked a woman to be womanly,
And English women, she thanked God and sighed
(Some people always sigh in thanking God),
Were models to the universe. And last
I learnt cross-stitch, because she did not like
To see me wear the night with empty hands
A-doing nothing. So, my shepherdess
Was something after all (the pastoral saints   450
Be praised for't), leaning lovelorn with pink eyes
To match her shoes, when I mistook the silks;
Her head uncrushed by that round weight of hat
So strangely similar to the tortoise-shell*
Which slew the tragic poet.
                                        By the way,

The works of women are symbolical.
We sew, sew, prick our fingers, dull our sight,
Producing what? A pair of slippers, sir,
To put on when you're weary—or a stool
To stumble over and vex you . . . 'curse that stool!'   460
Or else at best, a cushion, where you lean
And sleep, and dream of something we are not
But would be for your sake. Alas, alas!
This hurts most, this—that, after all, we are paid
The worth of our work, perhaps.

                              In looking down
Those years of education (to return)
I wonder if Brinvilliers suffered more*
In the water-torture . . . flood succeeding flood
To drench the incapable throat and split the veins . . .
Than I did. Certain of your feebler souls   470
Go out in such a process; many pine
To a sick, inodorous light; my own endured:
I had relations in the Unseen, and drew
The elemental nutriment and heat
From nature, as earth feels the sun at nights,
Or as a babe sucks surely in the dark.
I kept the life thrust on me, on the outside
Of the inner life with all its ample room
For heart and lungs, for will and intellect,
Inviolable by conventions. God,   480
I thank thee for that grace of thine!

                              At first
I felt no life which was not patience—did
The thing she bade me, without heed to a thing
Beyond it, sat in just the chair she placed,
With back against the window, to exclude
The sight of the great lime-tree on the lawn,
Which seemed to have come on purpose from the woods
To bring the house a message—ay, and walked
Demurely in her carpeted low rooms,
As if I should not, hearkening my own steps,   490

Misdoubt I was alive. I read her books,
Was civil to her cousin, Romney Leigh,
Gave ear to her vicar, tea to her visitors,
And heard them whisper, when I changed a cup
(I blushed for joy at that)—'The Italian child,
For all her blue eyes and her quiet ways,
Thrives ill in England: she is paler yet
Than when we came the last time; she will die.'

'Will die.' My cousin, Romney Leigh, blushed too,
With sudden anger, and approaching me   500
Said low between his teeth, 'You're wicked now?
You wish to die and leave the world a-dusk
For others, with your naughty light blown out?'
I looked into his face defyingly;
He might have known that, being what I was,
'Twas natural to like to get away
As far as dead folk can: and then indeed
Some people make no trouble when they die.
He turned and went abruptly, slammed the door
And shut his dog out.
                    Romney, Romney Leigh.   510
I have not named my cousin hitherto,
And yet I used him as a sort of friend;
My elder by few years, but cold and shy
And absent . . . tender, when he thought of it,
Which scarcely was imperative, grave betimes,
As well as early master of Leigh Hall,
Whereof the nightmare sat upon his youth
Repressing all its seasonable delights
And agonising with a ghastly sense
Of universal hideous want and wrong   520
To incriminate possession. When he came
From college to the country, very oft
He crossed the hill on visits to my aunt,
With gifts of blue grapes from the hothouses,
A book in one hand—mere statistics (if

I chanced to lift the cover), count of all
The goats whose beards grow sprouting down toward hell*
Against God's separative judgment-hour.
And she, she almost loved him—even allowed
That sometimes he should seem to sigh my way;   530
It made him easier to be pitiful,
And sighing was his gift. So, undisturbed
At whiles she let him shut my music up
And push my needles down, and lead me out
To see in that south angle of the house
The figs grow black as if by a Tuscan rock,
On some light pretext. She would turn her head
At other moments, go to fetch a thing,
And leave me breath enough to speak with him,
For his sake; it was simple.
                                   Sometimes too   540
He would have saved me utterly, it seemed,
He stood and looked so.
                           Once, he stood so near
He dropped a sudden hand upon my head
Bent down on woman's work, as soft as rain—
But then I rose and shook it off as fire,
The stranger's touch that took my father's place
Yet dared seem soft.
                           I used him for a friend
Before I ever knew him for a friend.
'Twas better, 'twas worse also, afterward:
We came so close, we saw our differences   550
Too intimately. Always Romney Leigh
Was looking for the worms, I for the gods.
A godlike nature his; the gods look down,
Incurious of themselves; and certainly
'Tis well I should remember, how, those days,
I was a worm too, and he looked on me.

A little by his act perhaps, yet more
By something in me, surely not my will,

I did not die. But slowly, as one in swoon,
To whom life creeps back in the form of death,   560
With a sense of separation, a blind pain
Of blank obstruction, and a roar i' the ears
Of visionary chariots which retreat
As earth grows clearer . . . slowly, by degrees,
I woke, rose up . . . where was I? in the world;
For uses therefore I must count worth while.

I had a little chamber in the house,
As green as any privet-hedge a bird
Might choose to build in, though the nest itself
Could show but dead-brown sticks and straws; the walls 570
Were green, the carpet was pure green, the straight
Small bed was curtained greenly, and the folds
Hung green about the window which let in
The outdoor world with all its greenery.
You could not push your head out and escape
A dash of dawn-dew from the honeysuckle,
But so you were baptised into the grace
And privilege of seeing . . .
                              First, the lime
(I had enough there, of the lime, be sure—
My morning-dream was often hummed away   580
By the bees in it); past the lime, the lawn,
Which, after sweeping broadly round the house,
Went trickling through the shrubberies in a stream
Of tender turf, and wore and lost itself
Among the acacias, over which you saw
The irregular line of elms by the deep lane
Which stopped the grounds and dammed the overflow
Of arbutus and laurel. Out of sight
The lane was; sunk so deep, no foreign tramp
Nor drover of wild ponies out of Wales   590
Could guess if lady's hall or tenant's lodge
Dispensed such odours—though his stick well-crooked
Might reach the lowest trail of blossoming briar

Which dipped upon the wall. Behind the elms,
And through their tops, you saw the folded hills
Striped up and down with hedges (burly oaks
Projecting from the line to show themselves),
Through which my cousin Romney's chimneys smoked
As still as when a silent mouth in frost
Breathes, showing where the woodlands hid Leigh Hall; 600
While, far above, a jut of table-land,
A promontory without water, stretched—
You could not catch it if the days were thick,
Or took it for a cloud; but, otherwise,
The vigorous sun would catch it up at eve
And use it for an anvil till he had filled
The shelves of heaven with burning thunderbolts,
Protesting against night and darkness: then,
When all his setting trouble was resolved
To a trance of passive glory, you might see   610
In apparition on the golden sky
(Alas, my Giotto's background!) the sheep run*
Along the fine clear outline, small as mice
That run along a witch's scarlet thread.

Not a grand nature. Not my chestnut-woods
Of Vallombrosa, cleaving by the spurs*
To the precipices. Not my headlong leaps
Of waters, that cry out for joy or fear
In leaping through the palpitating pines,
Like a white soul tossed out to eternity   620
With thrills of time upon it. Not indeed
My multitudinous mountains, sitting in
The magic circle, with the mutual touch
Electric, panting from their full deep hearts
Beneath the influent heavens, and waiting for
Communion and commission. Italy
Is one thing, England one.
                              On English ground
You understand the letter—ere the fall

How Adam lived in a garden. All the fields
Are tied up fast with hedges, nosegay-like;   630
The hills are crumpled plains, the plains parterres,
The trees, round, woolly, ready to be clipped,
And if you seek for any wilderness
You find, at best, a park. A nature tamed
And grown domestic like a barn-door fowl,
Which does not awe you with its claws and beak
Nor tempt you to an eyrie too high up,
But which, in cackling, sets you thinking of
Your eggs tomorrow at breakfast, in the pause
Of finer meditation.
                    Rather say,   640
A sweet familiar nature, stealing in
As a dog might, or child, to touch your hand
Or pluck your gown, and humbly mind you so
Of presence and affection, excellent
For inner uses, from the things without.

I could not be unthankful, I who was
Entreated thus and holpen. In the room*
I speak of, ere the house was well awake,
And also after it was well asleep,
I sat alone, and drew the blessing in   650
Of all that nature. With a gradual step,
A stir among the leaves, a breath, a ray,
It came in softly, while the angels made
A place for it beside me. The moon came,
And swept my chamber clean of foolish thoughts.
The sun came, saying, 'Shall I lift this light
Against the lime-tree, and you will not look?
I make the birds sing—listen! but, for you,
God never hears your voice, excepting when
You lie upon the bed at nights and weep.'   660

Then, something moved me. Then, I wakened up
More slowly than I verily write now,

But wholly, at last, I wakened, opened wide
The window and my soul, and let the airs
And outdoor sights sweep gradual gospels in,
Regenerating what I was. O Life,
How oft we throw it off and think—'Enough,
Enough of life in so much!—here's a cause
For rupture; herein we must break with Life,
Or be ourselves unworthy; here we are wronged,   670
Maimed, spoiled for aspiration: farewell Life!'
And so, as froward babes, we hide our eyes
And think all ended.—Then, Life calls to us
In some transformed, apocalyptic voice,
Above us, or below us, or around:
Perhaps we name it Nature's voice, or Love's,
Tricking ourselves, because we are more ashamed
To own our compensations than our griefs:
Still, Life's voice!—still, we make our peace with Life.

And I, so young then, was not sullen. Soon   680
I used to get up early, just to sit
And watch the morning quicken in the gray,
And hear the silence open like a flower
Leaf after leaf—and stroke with listless hand
The woodbine through the window, till at last
I came to do it with a sort of love,
At foolish unaware: whereat I smiled—
A melancholy smile, to catch myself
Smiling for joy.
                      Capacity for joy
Admits temptation. It seemed, next, worth while   690
To dodge the sharp sword set against my life;
To slip downstairs through all the sleepy house,
As mute as any dream there, and escape
As a soul from the body, out of doors,
Glide through the shrubberies, drop into the lane,
And wander on the hills an hour or two,
Then back again before the house should stir.

Or else I sat on in my chamber green,
And lived my life, and thought my thoughts, and prayed
My prayers without the vicar; read my books,   700
Without considering whether they were fit
To do me good. Mark, there. We get no good
By being ungenerous, even to a book,
And calculating profits—so much help
By so much reading. It is rather when
We gloriously forget ourselves and plunge
Soul-forward, headlong, into a book's profound,
Impassioned for its beauty and salt of truth—
'Tis then we get the right good from a book.

I read much. What my father taught before   710
From many a volume, Love re-emphasised
Upon the self-same pages: Theophrast*
Grew tender with the memory of his eyes,
And Aelian made mine wet. The trick of Greek*
And Latin, he had taught me, as he would
Have taught me wrestling or the game of fives*
If such he had known—most like a shipwrecked man
Who heaps his single platter with goats' cheese
And scarlet berries; or like any man
Who loves but one, and so gives all at once,   720
Because he has it, rather than because
He counts it worthy. Thus, my father gave;
And thus, as did the women formerly*
By young Achilles, when they pinned a veil
Across the boy's audacious front, and swept
With tuneful laughs the silver-fretted rocks,
He wrapped his little daughter in his large
Man's doublet, careless did it fit or no.

But, after I had read for memory,
I read for hope. The path my father's foot   730
Had trod me out (which suddenly broke off
What time he dropped the wallet of the flesh

And passed), alone I carried on, and set
My child-heart 'gainst the thorny underwood,
To reach the grassy shelter of the trees.
Ah babe i' the wood, without a brother-babe!*
My own self-pity, like the red-breast bird,
Flies back to cover all that past with leaves.

Sublimest danger, over which none weeps,
When any young wayfaring soul goes forth   740
Alone, unconscious of the perilous road,
The day-sun dazzling in his limpid eyes,
To thrust his own way, he an alien, through
The world of books! Ah, you!—you think it fine,
You clap hands—'A fair day!'—you cheer him on,
As if the worst, could happen, were to rest
Too long beside a fountain. Yet, behold,
Behold!—the world of books is still the world,
And worldlings in it are less merciful
And more puissant. For the wicked there   750
Are winged like angels; every knife that strikes
Is edged from elemental fire to assail
A spiritual life; the beautiful seems right
By force of beauty, and the feeble wrong
Because of weakness; power is justified
Though armed against Saint Michael; many a crown*
Covers bald foreheads. In the book-world, true,
There's no lack, neither, of God's saints and kings,
That shake the ashes of the grave aside
From their calm locks and undiscomfited   760
Look steadfast truths against Time's changing mask.
True, many a prophet teaches in the roads;
True, many a seer pulls down the flaming heavens
Upon his own head in strong martyrdom
In order to light men a moment's space.
But stay!—who judges?—who distinguishes*
'Twixt Saul and Nahash justly, at first sight,
And leaves King Saul precisely at the sin,

To serve King David? who discerns at once
The sound of the trumpets, when the trumpets blow   770
For Alaric as well as Charlemagne?
Who judges wizards, and can tell true seers*
From conjurors? the child, there? Would you leave
That child to wander in a battle-field
And push his innocent smile against the guns;
Or even in a catacomb—his torch
Grown ragged in the fluttering air, and all
The dark a-mutter round him? not a child.

I read books bad and good—some bad and good
At once (good aims not always make good books: 780
Well-tempered spades turn up ill-smelling soils
In digging vineyards even); books that prove
God's being so definitely, that man's doubt
Grows self-defined the other side the line,
Made atheist by suggestion; moral books,
Exasperating to license; genial books,
Discounting from the human dignity;*
And merry books, which set you weeping when
The sun shines—ay, and melancholy books,
Which make you laugh that any one should weep   790
In this disjointed life for one wrong more.

The world of books is still the world, I write,
And both worlds have God's providence, thank God,
To keep and hearten: with some struggle, indeed,
Among the breakers, some hard swimming through
The deeps—I lost breath in my soul sometimes
And cried, 'God save me if there's any God,'
But, even so, God saved me; and, being dashed
From error on to error, every turn
Still brought me nearer to the central truth.   800

I thought so. All this anguish in the thick
Of men's opinions . . . press and counter-press,

Now up, now down, now underfoot, and now
Emergent . . . all the best of it, perhaps,
But throws you back upon a noble trust
And use of your own instinct—merely proves
Pure reason stronger than bare inference*
At strongest. Try it—fix against heaven's wall
The scaling-ladders of school logic—mount
Step by step!—sight goes faster; that still ray   810
Which strikes out from you, how, you cannot tell,
And why, you know not (did you eliminate,
That such as you indeed should analyse?),
Goes straight and fast as light, and high as God.

The cygnet finds the water, but the man
Is born in ignorance of his element
And feels out blind at first, disorganised
By sin i' the blood—his spirit-insight dulled
And crossed by his sensations. Presently
He feels it quicken in the dark sometimes,   820
When, mark, be reverent, be obedient,
For such dumb motions of imperfect life
Are oracles of vital Deity
Attesting the Hereafter. Let who says
'The soul's a clean white paper,' rather say,*
A palimpsest, a prophet's holograph*
Defiled, erased and covered by a monk's—
The apocalypse, by a Longus! poring on**
Which obscene text, we may discern perhaps
Some fair, fine trace of what was written once,   830
Some upstroke of an alpha and omega
Expressing the old scripture.
                                    Books, books, books!
I had found the secret of a garret-room
Piled high with cases in my father's name,
Piled high, packed large—where, creeping in and out
Among the giant fossils of my past,
Like some small nimble mouse between the ribs

Of a mastodon, I nibbled here and there
At this or that box, pulling through the gap,
In heats of terror, haste, victorious joy, 840
The first book first. And how I felt it beat
Under my pillow, in the morning's dark,
An hour before the sun would let me read!
My books! At last because the time was ripe,
I chanced upon the poets.

      As the earth
Plunges in fury, when the internal fires
Have reached and pricked her heart, and, throwing flat
The marts and temples, the triumphal gates
And towers of observation, clears herself
To elemental freedom—thus, my soul, 850
At poetry's divine first finger-touch,
Let go conventions and sprang up surprised,
Convicted of the great eternities
Before two worlds.

     What's this, Aurora Leigh,
You write so of the poets, and not laugh?
Those virtuous liars, dreamers after dark,
Exaggerators of the sun and moon,
And soothsayers in a tea-cup?

        I write so
Of the only truth-tellers now left to God,
The only speakers of essential truth, 860
Opposed to relative, comparative,
And temporal truths; the only holders by
His sun-skirts, through conventional gray glooms;
The only teachers who instruct mankind
From just a shadow on a charnel-wall
To find man's veritable stature out
Erect, sublime—the measure of a man,
And that's the measure of an angel, says*
The apostle. Ay, and while your common men
Lay telegraphs, gauge railroads, reign, reap, dine,* 870
And dust the flaunty carpets of the world

A.L. - 4

For kings to walk on, or our president,*
The poet suddenly will catch them up
With his voice like a thunder—'This is soul,
This is life, this word is being said in heaven,
Here's God down on us! what are you about?'
How all those workers start amid their work,
Look round, look up, and feel, a moment's space,
That carpet-dusting, though a pretty trade,
Is not the imperative labour after all.   880

My own best poets, am I one with you,
That thus I love you—or but one through love?
Does all this smell of thyme about my feet
Conclude my visit to your holy hill
In personal presence, or but testify
The rustling of your vesture through my dreams
With influent odours? When my joy and pain,
My thought and aspiration, like the stops
Of pipe or flute, are absolutely dumb
Unless melodious, do you play on me   890
My pipers—and if, sooth, you did not blow,
Would no sound come? or is the music mine,
As a man's voice or breath is called his own,
Inbreathed by the Life-breather? There's a doubt
For cloudy seasons!
                    But the sun was high
When first I felt my pulses set themselves
For concord; when the rhythmic turbulence
Of blood and brain swept outward upon words,
As wind upon the alders, blanching them
By turning up their under-natures till   900
They trembled in dilation. O delight
And triumph of the poet, who would say
A man's mere 'yes,' a woman's common 'no,'
A little human hope of that or this,
And says the word so that it burns you through
With a special revelation, shakes the heart

Of all the men and women in the world,
As if one came back from the dead and spoke,
With eyes too happy, a familiar thing
Become divine i' the utterance! while for him   910
The poet, speaker, he expands with joy;
The palpitating angel in his flesh
Thrills inly with consenting fellowship
To those innumerous spirits who sun themselves
Outside of time.
    O life, O poetry
—Which means life in life! cognisant of life
Beyond this blood-beat, passionate for truth
Beyond these senses!—poetry, my life,
My eagle, with both grappling feet still hot*
From Zeus's thunder, who hast ravished me   920
Away from all the shepherds, sheep, and dogs,
And set me in the Olympian roar and round
Of luminous faces for a cup-bearer,
To keep the mouths of all the godheads moist
For everlasting laughters—I myself
Half drunk across the beaker with their eyes!
How those gods look!
    Enough so, Ganymede,
We shall not bear above a round or two.
We drop the golden cup at Heré's foot
And swoon back to the earth—and find ourselves   930
Face-down among the pine-cones, cold with dew,
While the dogs bark, and many a shepherd scoffs,
'What's come now to the youth?' Such ups and downs
Have poets.
    Am I such indeed? The name
Is royal, and to sign it like a queen,
Is what I dare not—though some royal blood
Would seem to tingle in me now and then,
With sense of power and ache—with imposthumes*
And manias usual to the race. Howbeit
I dare not: 'tis too easy to go mad   940

And ape a Bourbon in a crown of straws;*
The thing's too common.
                        Many fervent souls
Strike rhyme on rhyme, who would strike steel on steel
If steel had offered, in a restless heat
Of doing something. Many tender souls
Have strung their losses on a rhyming thread,
As children, cowslips: the more pains they take,
The work more withers. Young men, ay, and maids,
Too often sow their wild oats in tame verse,
Before they sit down under their own vine   950
And live for use. Alas, near all the birds
Will sing at dawn—and yet we do not take
The chaffering swallow for the holy lark.

In those days, though, I never analysed,
Not even myself. Analysis comes late.
You catch a sight of Nature, earliest,
In full front sun-face, and your eyelids wink
And drop before the wonder of't; you miss
The form, through seeing the light. I lived, those days,
And wrote because I lived—unlicensed else;   960
My heart beat in my brain. Life's violent flood
Abolished bounds—and, which my neighbour's field,
Which mine, what mattered? it is thus in youth!
We play at leap-frog over the god Term;*
The love within us and the love without
Are mixed, confounded; if we are loved or love,
We scarce distinguish: thus, with other power;
Being acted on and acting seem the same:
In that first onrush of life's chariot-wheels,
We know not if the forests move or we.   970

And so, like most young poets, in a flush
Of individual life I poured myself
Along the veins of others, and achieved
Mere lifeless imitations of live verse,

And made the living answer for the dead,
Profaning nature. 'Touch not, do not taste,
Nor handle'—we're too legal, who write young:
We beat the phorminx till we hurt our thumbs,*
As if still ignorant of counterpoint;
We call the Muse—'O Muse, benignant Muse'—   980
As if we had seen her purple-braided head,
With the eyes in it, start between the boughs
As often as a stag's. What make-believe,
With so much earnest! what effete results
From virile efforts! what cold wire-drawn odes,
From such white heats!—bucolics, where the cows
Would scare the writer if they splashed the mud
In lashing off the flies—didactics, driven
Against the heels of what the master said;*
And counterfeiting epics, shrill with trumps   990
A babe might blow between two straining cheeks
Of bubbled rose, to make his mother laugh;
And elegiac griefs, and songs of love,
Like cast-off nosegays picked up on the road,
The worse for being warm: all these things, writ
On happy mornings, with a morning heart,
That leaps for love, is active for resolve,
Weak for art only. Oft, the ancient forms
Will thrill, indeed, in carrying the young blood.
The wine-skins, now and then, a little warped,   1000
Will crack even, as the new wine gurgles in.
Spare the old bottles!—spill not the new wine.*

By Keats's soul, the man who never stepped*
In gradual progress like another man,
But, turning grandly on his central self,
Ensphered himself in twenty perfect years
And died, not young (the life of a long life
Distilled to a mere drop, falling like a tear
Upon the world's cold cheek to make it burn
For ever); by that strong excepted soul,   1010

I count it strange and hard to understand
That nearly all young poets should write old,
That Pope was sexagenary at sixteen,*
And beardless Byron academical,
And so with others. It may be perhaps
Such have not settled long and deep enough
In trance, to attain to clairvoyance—and still
The memory mixes with the vision, spoils,
And works it turbid.

          Or perhaps, again,
In order to discover the Muse-Sphinx,   1020
The melancholy desert must sweep round,
Behind you as before.—

             For me, I wrote
False poems, like the rest, and thought them true
Because myself was true in writing them.
I peradventure have writ true ones since
With less complacence.

             But I could not hide
My quickening inner life from those at watch.
They saw a light at a window now and then,
They had not set there: who had set it there?
My father's sister started when she caught   1030
My soul agaze in my eyes. She could not say
I had no business with a sort of soul,
But plainly she objected—and demurred
That souls were dangerous things to carry straight
Through all the spilt saltpetre of the world.*

She said sometimes, 'Aurora, have you done
Your task this morning? have you read that book?
And are you ready for the crochet here?'—
As if she said, 'I know there's something wrong;
I know I have not ground you down enough   1040
To flatten and bake you to a wholesome crust
For household uses and proprieties,
Before the rain has got into my barn

And set the grains a-sprouting. What, you're green
With outdoor impudence? you almost grow?'
To which I answered, 'Would she hear my task,
And verify my abstract of the book?
Or should I sit down to the crochet work?
Was such her pleasure?' Then I sat and teased
The patient needle till it spilt the thread,   1050
Which oozed off from it in meandering lace
From hour to hour. I was not, therefore, sad;
My soul was singing at a work apart
Behind the wall of sense, as safe from harm
As sings the lark when sucked up out of sight
In vortices of glory and blue air.

And so, through forced work and spontaneous work,
The inner life informed the outer life,
Reduced the irregular blood to a settled rhythm,
Made cool the forehead with fresh-sprinkling dreams,   1060
And, rounding to the spheric soul the thin,
Pined body, struck a colour up the cheeks
Though somewhat faint. I clenched my brows across
My blue eyes greatening in the looking-glass,
And said, 'We'll live, Aurora! we'll be strong.
The dogs are on us—but we will not die.'

Whoever lives true life, will love true love.
I learnt to love that England. Very oft,
Before the day was born, or otherwise
Through secret windings of the afternoons,   1070
I threw my hunters off and plunged myself
Among the deep hills, as a hunted stag
Will take the waters, shivering with the fear
And passion of the course. And when at last
Escaped, so many a green slope built on slope
Betwixt me and the enemy's house behind,
I dared to rest, or wander, in a rest
Made sweeter for the step upon the grass,

And view the ground's most gentle dimplement
(As if God's finger touched but did not press   1080
In making England), such an up and down
Of verdure—nothing too much up or down,
A ripple of land; such little hills, the sky
Can stoop to tenderly and the wheatfields climb;
Such nooks of valleys lined with orchises,
Fed full of noises by invisible streams;
And open pastures where you scarcely tell
White daisies from white dew—at intervals
The mythic oaks and elm-trees standing out
Self-poised upon their prodigy of shade—   1090
I thought my father's land was worthy too
Of being my Shakespeare's.
                                Very oft alone,
Unlicensed; not infrequently with leave
To walk the third with Romney and his friend
The rising painter, Vincent Carrington,
Whom men judge hardly as bee-bonneted,
Because he holds that, paint a body well,*
You paint a soul by implication, like
The grand first Master. Pleasant walks! for if
He said, 'When I was last in Italy,'   1100
It sounded as an instrument that's played
Too far off for the tune—and yet it's fine
To listen.
                Often we walked only two
If cousin Romney pleased to walk with me.
We read, or talked, or quarrelled, as it chanced.
We were not lovers, nor even friends well matched:
Say rather, scholars upon different tracks,
And thinkers disagreed, he, overfull
Of what is, and I, haply, overbold
For what might be.
                        But then the thrushes sang,   1110
And shook my pulses and the elms' new leaves;
At which I turned, and held my finger up,

And bade him mark that, howsoe'er the world
Went ill, as he related, certainly
The thrushes still sang in it. At the word
His brow would soften—and he bore with me
In melancholy patience, not unkind,
While breaking into voluble ecstasy
I flattered all the beauteous country round,
As poets use, the skies, the clouds, the fields,   1120
The happy violets hiding from the roads
The primroses run down to, carrying gold;
The tangled hedgerows, where the cows push out
Impatient horns and tolerant churning mouths
'Twixt dripping ash-boughs—hedgerows all alive
With birds and gnats and large white butterflies
Which look as if the May-flower had caught life
And palpitated forth upon the wind;
Hills, vales, woods, netted in a silver mist,
Farms, granges, doubled up among the hills;   1130
And cattle grazing in the watered vales,
And cottage-chimneys smoking from the woods,
And cottage-gardens smelling everywhere,
Confused with smells of orchards. 'See,' I said,
'And see! is God not with us on the earth?
And shall we put Him down by aught we do?
Who says there's nothing for the poor and vile
Save poverty and wickedness? behold!'
And ankle-deep in English grass I leaped
And clapped my hands, and called all very fair.   1140

In the beginning when God called all good,*
Even then was evil near us, it is writ;
But we indeed who call things good and fair,
The evil is upon us while we speak;
Deliver us from evil, let us pray.*

BOOK II

TIMES followed one another. Came a morn
I stood upon the brink of twenty years,
And looked before and after, as I stood
Woman and artist—either incomplete,
Both credulous of completion. There I held
The whole creation in my little cup,
And smiled with thirsty lips before I drank
'Good health to you and me, sweet neighbour mine,
And all these peoples.'

              I was glad, that day;
The June was in me, with its multitudes   10
Of nightingales all singing in the dark,
And rosebuds reddening where the calyx split.*
I felt so young, so strong, so sure of God!
So glad, I could not choose be very wise!
And, old at twenty, was inclined to pull
My childhood backward in a childish jest
To see the face of 't once more, and farewell!
In which fantastic mood I bounded forth
At early morning—would not wait so long
As even to snatch my bonnet by the strings,   20
But, brushing a green trail across the lawn
With my gown in the dew, took will and way
Among the acacias of the shrubberies,
To fly my fancies in the open air
And keep my birthday, till my aunt awoke
To stop good dreams. Meanwhile I murmured on
As honeyed bees keep humming to themselves,
'The worthiest poets have remained uncrowned
Till death has bleached their foreheads to the bone;
And so with me it must be unless I prove   30

Unworthy of the grand adversity,
And certainly I would not fail so much.
What, therefore, if I crown myself today
In sport, not pride, to learn the feel of it,
Before my brows be numbed as Dante's own
To all the tender pricking of such leaves?
Such leaves! what leaves?'

                         I pulled the branches down
To choose from.

               'Not the bay! I choose no bay*
(The fates deny us if we are overbold)
Nor myrtle—which means chiefly love; and love   40
Is something awful which one dares not touch
So early o' mornings. This verbena strains
The point of passionate fragrance; and hard by,
This guelder-rose, at far too slight a beck
Of the wind, will toss about her flower-apples.
Ah—there's my choice—that ivy on the wall,
That headlong ivy! not a leaf will grow
But thinking of a wreath. Large leaves, smooth leaves,
Serrated like my vines, and half as green.
I like such ivy, bold to leap a height   50
'Twas strong to climb; as good to grow on graves
As twist about a thyrsus; pretty too*
(And that's not ill), when twisted round a comb.'

Thus speaking to myself, half singing it,
Because some thoughts are fashioned like a bell
To ring with once being touched, I drew a wreath
Drenched, blinding me with dew, across my brow,
And fastening it behind so, turning faced
. . . My public!—cousin Romney—with a mouth
Twice graver than his eyes.

                    I stood there fixed—   60
My arms up, like the caryatid, sole*
Of some abolished temple, helplessly
Persistent in a gesture which derides

A former purpose. Yet my blush was flame,
As if from flax, not stone.

                   'Aurora Leigh,
The earliest of Auroras!'

                        Hand stretched out
I clasped, as shipwrecked men will clasp a hand,
Indifferent to the sort of palm. The tide
Had caught me at my pastime, writing down
My foolish name too near upon the sea   70
Which drowned me with a blush as foolish. 'You,
My cousin!'

            The smile died out in his eyes
And dropped upon his lips, a cold dead weight,
For just a moment, 'Here's a book I found!
No name writ on it—poems, by the form;
Some Greek upon the margin—lady's Greek*
Without the accents. Read it? Not a word.
I saw at once the thing had witchcraft in't,
Whereof the reading calls up dangerous spirits:
I rather bring it to the witch.'

                      'My book.   80
You found it' . . .

               'In the hollow by the stream
That beech leans down into—of which you said
The Oread in it has a Naiad's heart*
And pines for waters.'

                 'Thank you.'

                        'Thanks to *you*
My cousin! that I have seen you not too much
Witch, scholar, poet, dreamer, and the rest,
To be a woman also.'

                 With a glance
The smile rose in his eyes again and touched
The ivy on my forehead, light as air.
I answered gravely, 'Poets needs must be   90
Or men or women—more's the pity.'

                      'Ah,

But men, and still less women, happily,
Scarce need be poets. Keep to the green wreath,
Since even dreaming of the stone and bronze
Brings headaches, pretty cousin, and defiles
The clean white morning dresses.'

        'So you judge!
Because I love the beautiful I must
Love pleasure chiefly, and be overcharged
For ease and whiteness! well, you know the world,
And only miss your cousin, 'tis not much.   100
But learn this; I would rather take my part
With God's Dead, who afford to walk in white
Yet spread His glory, than keep quiet here
And gather up my feet from even a step
For fear to soil my gown in so much dust.
I choose to walk at all risks.—Here, if heads
That hold a rhythmic thought must ache perforce,
For my part I choose headaches—and today's
My birthday.'

     'Dear Aurora, choose instead
To cure them. You have balsams.'*

         'I perceive.   110
The headache is too noble for my sex.
You think the heartache would sound decenter,
Since that's the woman's special, proper ache,
And altogether tolerable, except
To a woman.'

     Saying which, I loosed my wreath,
And swinging it beside me as I walked,
Half petulant, half playful, as we walked,
I sent a sidelong look to find his thought—
As falcon set on falconer's finger may,
With sidelong head, and startled, braving eye, 120
Which means, 'You'll see—you'll see! I'll soon take flight,
You shall not hinder.' He, as shaking out
His hand and answering 'Fly then,' did not speak,
Except by such a gesture. Silently

We paced, until, just coming into sight
Of the house-windows, he abruptly caught
At one end of the swinging wreath, and said
'Aurora!' There I stopped short, breath and all.

'Aurora, let's be serious, and throw by
This game of head and heart. Life means, be sure,   130
Both heart and head—both active, both complete,
And both in earnest. Men and women make
The world, as head and heart make human life.
Work man, work woman, since there's work to do
In this beleaguered earth, for head and heart,
And thought can never do the work of love:
But work for ends, I mean for uses, not
For such sleek fringes (do you call them ends,
Still less God's glory?) as we sew ourselves
Upon the velvet of those baldaquins*   140
Held 'twixt us and the sun. That book of yours,
I have not read a page of; but I toss
A rose up—it falls calyx down, you see!
The chances are that, being a woman, young
And pure, with such a pair of large, calm eyes,
You write as well . . . and ill . . . upon the whole,
As other women. If as well, what then?
If even a little better . . . still, what then?
We want the Best in art now, or no art.
The time is done for facile settings up   150
Of minnow gods, nymphs here and tritons there;*
The polytheists have gone out in God,
That unity of Bests. No best, no God!
And so with art, we say. Give art's divine,
Direct, indubitable, real as grief,
Or leave us to the grief we grow ourselves
Divine by overcoming with mere hope
And most prosaic patience. You, you are young
As Eve with nature's daybreak on her face,
But this same world you are come to, dearest coz,   160

Has done with keeping birthdays, saves her wreaths
To hang upon her ruins—and forgets
To rhyme the cry with which she still beats back
Those savage, hungry dogs that hunt her down
To the empty grave of Christ. The world's hard pressed;
The sweat of labour in the early curse
Has (turning acrid in six thousand years)*
Become the sweat of torture. Who has time,
An hour's time . . . think!—to sit upon a bank
And hear the cymbal tinkle in white hands?   170
When Egypt's slain, I say, let Miriam sing!—*
Before—where's Moses?'
                            'Ah, exactly that.
Where's Moses?—is a Moses to be found?*
You'll seek him vainly in the bulrushes,
While I in vain touch cymbals. Yet concede,
Such sounding brass has done some actual good*
(The application in a woman's hand,
If that were credible, being scarcely spoilt)
In colonising beehives.'
                            'There it is!—
You play beside a death-bed like a child,   180
Yet measure to yourself a prophet's place
To teach the living. None of all these things,
Can women understand. You generalise
Oh, nothing—not even grief! Your quick-breathed hearts,
So sympathetic to the personal pang,
Close on each separate knife-stroke, yielding up
A whole life at each wound, incapable
Of deepening, widening a large lap of life
To hold the world-full woe. The human race
To you means, such a child, or such a man,   190
You saw one morning waiting in the cold,
Beside that gate, perhaps. You gather up
A few such cases, and when strong sometimes
Will write of factories and of slaves, as if
Your father were a negro, and your son

A spinner in the mills. All's yours and you,
All, coloured with your blood, or otherwise
Just nothing to you. Why, I call you hard
To general suffering. Here's the world half blind
With intellectual light, half brutalised   200
With civilisation, having caught the plague
In silks from Tarsus, shrieking east and west*
Along a thousand railroads, mad with pain
And sin too! . . . does one woman of you all
(You who weep easily) grow pale to see
This tiger shake his cage?—does one of you
Stand still from dancing, stop from stringing pearls
And pine and die because of the great sum
Of universal anguish?—Show me a tear*
Wet as Cordelia's, in eyes bright as yours,   210
Because the world is mad. You cannot count,
That you should weep for this account, not you!
You weep for what you know. A red-haired child
Sick in a fever, if you touch him once,
Though but so little as with a finger-tip,
Will set you weeping; but a million sick . . .
You could as soon weep for the rule of three
Or compound fractions. Therefore, this same world
Uncomprehended by you, must remain
Uninfluenced by you.—Women as you are,   220
Mere women, personal and passionate,
You give us doting mothers, and perfect wives,*
Sublime Madonnas, and enduring saints!
We get no Christ from you—and verily
We shall not get a poet, in my mind.'

'With which conclusion you conclude' . . .
                                                    'But this:
That you, Aurora, with the large live brow
And steady eyelids, cannot condescend
To play at art, as children play at swords,
To show a pretty spirit, chiefly admired   230

Because true action is impossible.
You never can be satisfied with praise
Which men give women when they judge a book
Not as mere work but as mere woman's work,
Expressing the comparative respect
Which means the absolute scorn. "Oh, excellent!
What grace, what facile turns, what fluent sweeps,
What delicate discernment . . . almost thought!
The book does honour to the sex, we hold.
Among our female authors we make room   240
For this fair writer, and congratulate
The country that produces in these times
Such women, competent to" . . . spell.'

                                   'Stop there,'
I answered, burning through his thread of talk
With a quick flame of emotion—'You have read
My soul, if not my book, and argue well
I would not condescend . . . we will not say
To such a kind of praise (a worthless end
Is praise of all kinds) but to such a use
Of holy art and golden life. I am young,   250
And peradventure weak—you tell me so—
Through being a woman. And, for all the rest,
Take thanks for justice. I would rather dance
At fairs on tight-rope, till the babies dropped
Their gingerbread for joy—than shift the types
For tolerable verse, intolerable
To men who act and suffer. Better far
Pursue a frivolous trade by serious means,
Than a sublime art frivolously.'

                                'You,
Choose nobler work than either, O moist eyes   260
And hurrying lips and heaving heart! We are young
Aurora, you and I. The world—look round—
The world, we're come to late, is swollen hard
With perished generations and their sins:
The civiliser's spade grinds horribly

On dead men's bones, and cannot turn up soil
That's otherwise than fetid. All success
Proves partial failure; all advance implies
What's left behind; all triumph, something crushed
At the chariot-wheels; all government, some wrong: 270
And rich men make the poor, who curse the rich,
Who agonise together, rich and poor,
Under and over, in the social spasm
And crisis of the ages. Here's an age
That makes its own vocation! here we have stepped
Across the bounds of time! here's nought to see,
But just the rich man and just Lazarus,*
And both in torments, with a mediate gulf,
Though not a hint of Abraham's bosom. Who
Being man, Aurora, can stand calmly by   280
And view these things, and never tease his soul
For some great cure? No physic for this grief,
In all the earth and heavens too?'

                    'You believe
In God, for your part?—ay? that He who makes,
Can make good things from ill things, best from worst,
As men plant tulips upon dunghills when
They wish them finest?'

                        'True. A death-heat is
The same as life-heat, to be accurate,
And in all nature is no death at all,
As men account of death, so long as God   290
Stands witnessing for life perpetually,
By being just God. That's abstract truth, I know,
Philosophy, or sympathy with God:
But I, I sympathise with man, not God
(I think I was a man for chiefly this),
And when I stand beside a dying bed,
'Tis death to me. Observe—it had not much
Consoled the race of mastodons to know,
Before they went to fossil, that anon
Their place would quicken with the elephant: 300

They were not elephants but mastodons;
And I, a man, as men are now and not
As men may be hereafter, feel with men
In the agonising present.'
                              'Is it so,'
I said, 'my cousin? is the world so bad,
While I hear nothing of it through the trees?
The world was always evil—but so bad?'

'So bad, Aurora. Dear, my soul is gray
With poring over the long sum of ill;
So much for vice, so much for discontent,   310
So much for the necessities of power,
So much for the connivances of fear,
Coherent in statistical despairs*
With such a total of distracted life . . .
To see it down in figures on a page,
Plain, silent, clear, as God sees through the earth
The sense of all the graves—that's terrible
For one who is not God, and cannot right
The wrong he looks on. May I choose indeed
But vow away my years, my means, my aims,   320
Among the helpers, if there's any help
In such a social strait? The common blood
That swings along my veins, is strong enough
To draw me to this duty.'*
                          Then I spoke.
'I have not stood long on the strand of life,
And these salt waters have had scarcely time
To creep so high up as to wet my feet:
I cannot judge these tides—I shall, perhaps.
A woman's always younger than a man
At equal years, because she is disallowed   330
Maturing by the outdoor sun and air,
And kept in long clothes past the age to walk.
Ah well, I know you men judge otherwise!
You think a woman ripens as a peach,

In the cheeks, chiefly. Pass it to me now;
I'm young in age, and younger still, I think,
As a woman. But a child may say amen
To a bishop's prayer and feel the way it goes,
And I, incapable to loose the knot
Of social questions, can approve, applaud　　　　340
August compassion, Christian thoughts that shoot
Beyond the vulgar white of personal aims.*
Accept my reverence.'
　　　　　　　　　There he glowed on me
With all his face and eyes. 'No other help?'
Said he—'no more than so?'
　　　　　　　　　　　　　'What help?' I asked.
'You'd scorn my help—as Nature's self, you say,
Has scorned to put her music in my mouth
Because a woman's. Do you now turn round
And ask for what a woman cannot give?'

'For what she only can, I turn and ask,'　　　　350
He answered, catching up my hands in his,
And dropping on me from his high-eaved brow
The full weight of his soul—'I ask for love,
And that, she can; for life in fellowship
Through bitter duties—that, I know she can;
For wifehood—will she?'
　　　　　　　　　　　'Now,' I said, 'may God
Be witness 'twixt us two!' and with the word,
Meseemed I floated into a sudden light
Above his stature—'am I proved too weak
To stand alone, yet strong enough to bear　　　　360
Such leaners on my shoulder? poor to think,
Yet rich enough to sympathise with thought?
Incompetent to sing, as blackbirds can,
Yet competent to love, like HIM?'
　　　　　　　　　　　　　I paused;
Perhaps I darkened, as the lighthouse will
That turns upon the sea. 'It's always so.

Anything does for a wife.'
                                        'Aurora, dear,
And dearly honoured'—he pressed in at once
With eager utterance—'you translate me ill.
I do not contradict my thought of you   370
Which is most reverent, with another thought
Found less so. If your sex is weak for art
(And I who said so, did but honour you
By using truth in courtship), it is strong
For life and duty. Place your fecund heart
In mine, and let us blossom for the world
That wants love's colour in the gray of time.
My talk, meanwhile, is arid to you, ay,
Since all my talk can only set you where
You look down coldly on the arena-heaps   380
Of headless bodies, shapeless, indistinct!
The Judgment-Angel scarce would find his way
Through such a heap of generalised distress
To the individual man with lips and eyes,
Much less Aurora. Ah my sweet, come down,
And hand in hand we'll go where yours shall touch
These victims, one by one! till, one by one,
The formless, nameless trunk of every man
Shall seem to wear a head with hair you know,
And every woman catch your mother's face   390
To melt you into passion.'
                                        'I am a girl,'
I answered slowly; 'you do well to name
My mother's face. Though far too early, alas,
God's hand did interpose 'twixt it and me,
I know so much of love as used to shine
In that face and another. Just so much;
No more indeed at all. I have not seen
So much love since, I pray you pardon me,
As answers even to make a marriage with
In this cold land of England. What you love,   400
Is not a woman, Romney, but a cause:

You want a helpmate, not a mistress, sir,
A wife to help your ends—in her no end!
Your cause is noble, your ends excellent,
But I, being most unworthy of these and that,
Do otherwise conceive of love. Farewell.'

'Farewell, Aurora? you reject me thus?'
He said.
            'Sir, you were married long ago.
You have a wife already whom you love,
Your social history. Bless you both, I say.   410
For my part, I am scarcely meek enough
To be the handmaid of a lawful spouse.
Do I look a Hagar, think you?'*
                                    'So you jest.'

'Nay, so, I speak in earnest,' I replied.
'You treat of marriage too much like, at least,
A chief apostle: you would bear with you
A wife . . . a sister . . . shall we speak it out?
A sister of charity.'
                        'Then, must it be
Indeed farewell? And was I so far wrong
In hope and in illusion, when I took   420
The woman to be nobler than the man,
Yourself the noblest woman, in the use
And comprehension of what love is—love,
That generates the likeness of itself
Through all heroic duties? so far wrong,
In saying bluntly, venturing truth on love,
"Come, human creature, love and work with me"—
Instead of, "Lady, thou art wondrous fair,
And, where the Graces walk before, the Muse
Will follow at the lightning of their eyes,   430
And where the Muse walks, lovers need to creep:
Turn round and love me, or I die of love."'

With quiet indignation I broke in.
'You misconceive the question like a man,
Who sees a woman as the complement
Of his sex merely. You forget too much
That every creature, female as the male,
Stands single in responsible act and thought
As also in birth and death. Whoever says
To a loyal woman, "Love and work with me,"   440
Will get fair answers if the work and love,
Being good themselves, are good for her—the best
She was born for. Women of a softer mood,
Surprised by men when scarcely awake to life,
Will sometimes only hear the first word, love,
And catch up with it any kind of work,
Indifferent, so that dear love go with it.
I do not blame such women, though, for love,
They pick much oakum; earth's fanatics make*
Too frequently heaven's saints. But *me* your work   450
Is not the best for—nor your love the best,
Nor able to commend the kind of work
For love's sake merely. Ah, you force me, sir,
To be overbold in speaking of myself:
I too have my vocation—work to do,
The heavens and earth have set me since I changed
My father's face for theirs, and, though your world
Were twice as wretched as you represent,
Most serious work, most necessary work
As any of the economists'. Reform,   460
Make trade a Christian possibility,
And individual right no general wrong;
Wipe out earth's furrows of the Thine and Mine,
And leave one green for men to play at bowls,
With innings for them all! . . . what then, indeed,
If mortals are not greater by the head
Than any of their prosperities? what then,
Unless the artist keep up open roads
Betwixt the seen and unseen—bursting through

The best of your conventions with his best,   470
The speakable, imaginable best
God bids him speak, to prove what lies beyond
Both speech and imagination? A starved man
Exceeds a fat beast: we'll not barter, sir,
The beautiful for barley.—And, even so,
I hold you will not compass your poor ends
Of barley-feeding and material ease,
Without a poet's individualism
To work your universal. It takes a soul,
To move a body: it takes a high-souled man,   480
To move the masses, even to a cleaner sty:
It takes the ideal, to blow a hair's-breadth off
The dust of the actual.—Ah, your Fouriers failed,*
Because not poets enough to understand
That life develops from within.—For me,
Perhaps I am not worthy, as you say,
Of work like this: perhaps a woman's soul
Aspires, and not creates: yet we aspire,
And yet I'll try out your perhapses, sir,
And if I fail . . . why, burn me up my straw   490
Like other false works—I'll not ask for grace;
Your scorn is better, cousin Romney. I
Who love my art, would never wish it lower
To suit my stature. I may love my art.
You'll grant that even a woman may love art,
Seeing that to waste true love on anything
Is womanly, past question.'

                  I retain
The very last word which I said that day,
As you the creaking of the door, years past,
Which let upon you such disabling news   500
You ever after have been graver. He,
His eyes, the motions in his silent mouth,
Were fiery points on which my words were caught,
Transfixed for ever in my memory
For his sake, not their own. And yet I know

I did not love him . . . nor he me . . . that's sure . . .
And what I said, is unrepented of,
As truth is always. Yet . . . a princely man!—
If hard to me, heroic for himself!
He bears down on me through the slanting years, 510
The stronger for the distance. If he had loved,
Ay, loved me, with that retributive face . . .
I might have been a common woman now
And happier, less known and less left alone,
Perhaps a better woman after all,
With chubby children hanging on my neck
To keep me low and wise. Ah me, the vines
That bear such fruit, are proud to stoop with it.
The palm stands upright in a realm of sand.

And I, who spoke the truth then, stand upright, 520
Still worthy of having spoken out the truth,
By being content I spoke it though it set
Him there, me here.—O woman's vile remorse,
To hanker after a mere name, a show,
A supposition, a potential love!
Does every man who names love in our lives,
Become a power for that? is love's true thing
So much best to us, that what personates love
Is next best? A potential love, forsooth!
I'm not so vile. No, no—he cleaves, I think, 530
This man, this image—chiefly for the wrong
And shock he gave my life, in finding me
Precisely where the devil of my youth*
Had set me, on those mountain-peaks of hope
All glittering with the dawn-dew, all erect
And famished for the noon—exclaiming, while
I looked for empire and much tribute, 'Come,
I have some worthy work for thee below.
Come, sweep my barns and keep my hospitals,
And I will pay thee with a current coin 540

Which men give women.'
                         As we spoke, the grass
Was trod in haste beside us, and my aunt,
With smile distorted by the sun—face, voice
As much at issue with the summer-day
As if you brought a candle out of doors,
Broke in with, 'Romney, here!—My child, entreat
Your cousin to the house, and have your talk,
If girls must talk upon their birthdays. Come.'

He answered for me calmly, with pale lips
That seemed to motion for a smile in vain.   550
'The talk is ended, madam, where we stand.
Your brother's daughter has dismissed me here;
And all my answer can be better said
Beneath the trees, than wrong by such a word
Your house's hospitalities. Farewell.'

With that he vanished. I could hear his heel
Ring bluntly in the lane, as down he leapt
The short way from us.—Then a measured speech
Withdrew me. 'What means this, Aurora Leigh?
My brother's daughter has dismissed my guests?'   560

The lion in me felt the keeper's voice
Through all its quivering dewlaps; I was quelled*
Before her—meekened to the child she knew:
I prayed her pardon, said, 'I had little thought
To give dismissal to a guest of hers,
In letting go a friend of mine who came
To take me into service as a wife—
No more than that, indeed.'
                              'No more, no more?
Pray Heaven,' she answered, 'that I was not mad.
I could not mean to tell her to her face   570
That Romney Leigh had asked me for a wife,

And I refused him?'
                              'Did he ask?' I said;
'I think he rather stooped to take me up
For certain uses which he found to do
For something called a wife. He never asked.'

'What stuff!' she answered; 'are they queens, these girls?
They must have mantles, stitched with twenty silks,
Spread out upon the ground, before they'll step
One footstep for the noblest lover born.'

'But I am born,' I said with firmness, 'I,   580
To walk another way than his, dear aunt.'

'You walk, you walk! A babe at thirteen months
Will walk as well as you,' she cried in haste,
'Without a steadying finger. Why, you child,
God help you, you are groping in the dark,
For all this sunlight. You suppose, perhaps,
That you, sole offspring of an opulent man,
Are rich and free to choose a way to walk?
You think, and it's a reasonable thought,
That I, beside, being well to do in life,   590
Will leave my handful in my niece's hand
When death shall paralyse these fingers? Pray,
Pray, child, albeit I know you love me not,
As if you loved me, that I may not die!
For when I die and leave you, out you go
(Unless I make room for you in my grave),
Unhoused, unfed, my dear, poor brother's lamb
(Ah heaven—that pains!)—without a right to crop
A single blade of grass beneath these trees,
Or cast a lamb's small shadow on the lawn,   600
Unfed, unfolded! Ah, my brother, here's
The fruit you planted in your foreign loves!—
Ay, there's the fruit he planted! never look
Astonished at me with your mother's eyes,

For it was they who set you where you are,
An undowered orphan. Child, your father's choice
Of that said mother, disinherited
His daughter, his and hers. Men do not think
Of sons and daughters, when they fall in love,
So much more than of sisters; otherwise   610
He would have paused to ponder what he did,
And shrunk before that clause in the entail
Excluding offspring by a foreign wife
(The clause set up a hundred years ago
By a Leigh who wedded a French dancing-girl
And had his heart danced over in return);
But this man shrank at nothing, never thought
Of you, Aurora, any more than me—
Your mother must have been a pretty thing,
For all the coarse Italian blacks and browns,   620
To make a good man, which my brother was,
Unchary of the duties to his house;*
But so it fell indeed. Our cousin Vane,
Vane Leigh, the father of this Romney, wrote
Directly on your birth, to Italy,
"I ask your baby daughter for my son
In whom the entail now merges by the law.
Betroth her to us out of love, instead
Of colder reasons, and she shall not lose
By love or law from henceforth"—so he wrote;   630
A generous cousin, was my cousin Vane.
Remember how he drew you to his knee
The year you came here, just before he died
And hollowed out his hands to hold your cheeks,
And wished them redder—you remember Vane?
And now his son who represents our house
And holds the fiefs and manors in his place,
To whom reverts my pittance when I die
(Except a few books and a pair of shawls),
The boy is generous like him, and prepared   620
To carry out his kindest word and thought

To you, Aurora. Yes, a fine young man
Is Romney Leigh; although the sun of youth
Has shone too straight upon his brain, I know,
And fevered him with dreams of doing good
To good-for-nothing people. But a wife
Will put all right, and stroke his temples cool
With healthy touches' . . .

                           I broke in at that.
I could not lift my heavy heart to breathe
Till then, but then I raised it, and it fell   650
In broken words like these—'No need to wait.
The dream of doing good to . . . me, at least,
Is ended, without waiting for a wife
To cool the fever for him. We've escaped
That danger—thank Heaven for it.'

                             'You,' she cried,
'Have got a fever. What, I talk and talk
An hour long to you—I instruct you how
You cannot eat or drink or stand or sit
Or even die, like any decent wretch
In all this unroofed and unfurnished world,   660
Without your cousin—and you still maintain
There's room 'twixt him and you, for flirting fans
And running knots in eyebrows? You must have
A pattern lover sighing on his knee?
You do not count enough, a noble heart
(Above book-patterns) which this very morn
Unclosed itself in two dear fathers' names
To embrace your orphaned life? fie, fie! But stay,
I write a word, and counteract this sin.'

She would have turned to leave me, but I clung.   670
'O sweet my father's sister, hear my word
Before you write yours. Cousin Vane did well,
And cousin Romney well—and I well too,
In casting back with all my strength and will
The good they meant me. O my God, my God!

God meant me good, too, when he hindered me
From saying "yes" this morning. If you write
A word, it shall be "no". I say no, no!
I tie up "no" upon His altar-horns,*
Quite out of reach of perjury! At least   680
My soul is not a pauper; I can live
At least my soul's life, without alms from men;
And if it must be in heaven instead of earth,
Let heaven look to it—I am not afraid.'

She seized my hands with both hers, strained them fast,
And drew her probing and unscrupulous eyes
Right through me, body and heart. 'Yet, foolish Sweet,
You love this man. I've watched you when he came,
And when he went, and when we've talked of him:
I am not old for nothing; I can tell   690
The weather-signs of love: you love this man.'

Girls blush sometimes because they are alive,
Half wishing they were dead to save the shame.
The sudden blush devours them, neck and brow;
They have drawn too near the fire of life, like gnats,
And flare up bodily, wings and all. What then?
Who's sorry for a gnat . . . or girl?
                              I blushed.
I feel the brand upon my forehead now
Strike hot, sear deep, as guiltless men may feel
The felon's iron, say, and scorn the mark   700
Of what they are not. Most illogical
Irrational nature of our womanhood,
That blushes one way, feels another way,
And prays, perhaps, another! After all,
We cannot be the equal of the male
Who rules his blood a little.
                              For although
I blushed indeed, as if I loved the man,
And her incisive smile, accrediting

That treason of false witness in my blush,
Did bow me downward like a swathe of grass   710
Below its level that struck me—I attest
The conscious skies and all their daily suns,
I think I loved him not—nor then, nor since,
Nor ever. Do we love the schoolmaster,
Being busy in the woods? much less, being poor,
The overseer of the parish? Do we keep
Our love to pay our debts with?

                White and cold
I grew next moment. As my blood recoiled
From that imputed ignominy, I made
My heart great with it. Then, at last, I spoke,   720
Spoke veritable words but passionate,
Too passionate perhaps . . . ground up with sobs
To shapeless endings. She let fall my hands
And took her smile off, in sedate disgust,
As peradventure she had touched a snake—
A dead snake, mind!—and turning round, replied,
'We'll leave Italian manners, if you please.
I think you had an English father, child,
And ought to find it possible to speak
A quiet "yes" or "no," like English girls,   730
Without convulsions. In another month
We'll take another answer—no, or yes.'
With that, she left me in the garden-walk.

I had a father! yes, but long ago—
How long it seemed that moment. Oh, how far,
How far and safe, God, dost thou keep thy saints
When once gone from us! We may call against
The lighted windows of thy fair June heaven
Where all the souls are happy—and not one,
Not even my father, look from work or play   740
To ask, 'Who is it that cries after us,
Below there, in the dusk?' Yet formerly
He turned his face upon me quick enough,

If I said 'father.' Now I might cry loud;
The little lark reached higher with his song
Than I with crying. Oh, alone, alone—
Not troubling any in heaven, nor any on earth,
I stood there in the garden, and looked up
The deaf blue sky that brings the roses out
On such June mornings.

               You who keep account   750
Of crisis and transition in this life,
Set down the first time Nature says plain 'no'
To some 'yes' in you, and walks over you
In gorgeous sweeps of scorn. We all begin
By singing with the birds, and running fast
With June days, hand in hand: but once, for all,
The birds must sing against us, and the sun
Strike down upon us like a friend's sword caught
By an enemy to slay us, while we read
The dear name on the blade which bites at us!—   760
That's bitter and convincing: after that,
We seldom doubt that something in the large
Smooth order of creation, though no more
Than haply a man's footstep, has gone wrong.

Some tears fell down my cheeks, and then I smiled,
As those smile who have no face in the world
To smile back to them. I had lost a friend
In Romney Leigh; the thing was sure—a friend,
Who had looked at me most gently now and then,
And spoken of my favourite books, 'our books,'   770
With such a voice! Well, voice and look were now
More utterly shut out from me I felt,
Than even my father's. Romney now was turned
To a benefactor, to a generous man,
Who had tied himself to marry . . . . me, instead
Of such a woman, with low timorous lids
He lifted with a sudden word one day,
And left, perhaps, for my sake.—Ah, self-tied

By a contract, male Iphigenia bound*
At a fatal Aulis for the winds to change   780
(But loose him, they'll not change), he well might seem
A little cold and dominant in love!
He had a right to be dogmatical,
This poor, good Romney. Love, to him, was made
A simple law-clause. If I married him,
I should not dare to call my soul my own
Which so he had bought and paid for: every thought
And every heart-beat down there in the bill;
Not one found honestly deductible
From any use that pleased him! He might cut   790
My body into coins to give away
Among his other paupers; change my sons,
While I stood dumb as Griseld, for black babes*
Or piteous foundlings; might unquestioned set
My right hand teaching in the Ragged Schools,*
My left hand washing in the Public Baths,*
What time my angel of the Ideal stretched
Both his to me in vain. I could not claim
The poor right of a mouse in a trap, to squeal,
And take so much as pity from myself.   800

Farewell, good Romney! if I loved you even,
I could but ill afford to let you be
So generous to me. Farewell, friend, since friend
Betwixt us two, forsooth, must be a word
So heavily overladen. And, since help
Must come to me from those who love me not,
Farewell, all helpers—I must help myself,
And am alone from henceforth.—Then I stooped
And lifted the soiled garland from the earth,
And set it on my head as bitterly   810
As when the Spanish monarch crowned the bones*
Of his dead love. So be it. I preserve
That crown still—in the drawer there! 'twas the first.
The rest are like it—those Olympian crowns,

We run for, till we lose sight of the sun
In the dust of the racing chariots!
                                        After that,
Before the evening fell, I had a note,
Which ran—'Aurora, sweet Chaldean, you read*
My meaning backward like your eastern books,
While I am from the west, dear. Read me now   820
A little plainer. Did you hate me quite
But yesterday? I loved you for my part;
I love you. If I spoke untenderly
This morning, my beloved, pardon it;
And comprehend me that I loved you so
I set you on the level of my soul,
And overwashed you with the bitter brine
Of some habitual thoughts. Henceforth, my flower,
Be planted out of reach of any such,
And lean the side you please, with all your leaves!   830
Write woman's verses and dream woman's dreams;
But let me feel your perfume in my home
To make my sabbath after working-days.
Bloom out your youth beside me—be my wife.'

I write in answer—'We Chaldeans discern
Still farther than we read. I know your heart,
And shut it like the holy book it is,
Reserved for mild-eyed saints to pore upon
Betwixt their prayers at vespers. Well, you're right,
I did not surely hate you yesterday;   840
And yet I do not love you enough today
To wed you, cousin Romney. Take this word,
And let it stop you as a generous man
From speaking farther. You may tease, indeed,
And blow about my feelings, or my leaves,
And here's my aunt will help you with east winds
And break a stalk, perhaps, tormenting me;
But certain flowers grow near as deep as trees,
And, cousin, you'll not move my root, not you,

With all your confluent storms. Then let me grow   850
Within my wayside hedge, and pass your way!
This flower has never as much to say to you
As the antique tomb which said to travellers, "Pause,"
"Siste, viator."' Ending thus, I signed.*

The next week passed in silence, so the next,
And several after: Romney did not come
Nor my aunt chide me. I lived on and on,
As if my heart were kept beneath a glass,
And everybody stood, all eyes and ears,
To see and hear it tick. I could not sit,   860
Nor walk, nor take a book, nor lay it down,
Nor sew on steadily, nor drop a stitch,
And a sigh with it, but I felt her looks
Still cleaving to me, like the sucking asp*
To Cleopatra's breast, persistently
Through the intermittent pantings. Being observed,
When observation is not sympathy,
Is just being tortured. If she said a word,
A 'thank you,' or an 'if it please you, dear,'
She meant a commination, or, at best,*   870
An exorcism against the devildom
Which plainly held me. So with all the house.
Susannah could not stand and twist my hair,
Without such glancing at the looking-glass
To see my face there, that she missed the plait.
And John—I never sent my plate for soup,
Or did not send it, but the foolish John
Resolved the problem, 'twixt his napkined thumbs,
Of what was signified by taking soup
Or choosing mackerel. Neighbours who dropped in   880
On morning visits, feeling a joint wrong,
Smiled admonition, sat uneasily,
And talked with measured, emphasised reserve,
Of parish news, like doctors to the sick,
When not called in—as if, with leave to speak,

They might say something. Nay, the very dog
Would watch me from his sun-patch on the floor,
In alternation with the large black fly
Not yet in reach of snapping. So I lived.

A Roman died so; smeared with honey, teased*   890
By insects, stared to torture by the noon:
And many patient souls 'neath English roofs
Have died like Romans. I, in looking back,
Wish only, now, I had borne the plague of all
With meeker spirits than were rife at Rome.

For, on the sixth week, the dead sea broke up,
Dashed suddenly through beneath the heel of Him
Who stands upon the sea and earth and swears*
Time shall be nevermore. The clock struck nine
That morning too—no lark was out of tune,   900
The hidden farms among the hills breathed straight
Their smoke toward heaven, the lime-tree scarcely stirred
Beneath the blue weight of the cloudless sky,
Though still the July air came floating through
The woodbine at my window, in and out,
With touches of the outdoor country news
For a bending forehead. There I sat, and wished
That morning-truce of God would last till eve,
Or longer. 'Sleep,' I thought, 'late sleepers—sleep,
And spare me yet the burden of your eyes.'   910

Then, suddenly, a single ghastly shriek
Tore upward from the bottom of the house.
Like one who wakens in a grave and shrieks,
The still house seemed to shriek itself alive,
And shudder through its passages and stairs
With slam of doors and clash of bells.—I sprang,
I stood up in the middle of the room,
And there confronted at my chamber-door,
A white face—shivering, ineffectual lips.

'Come, come,' they tried to utter, and I went: 920
As if a ghost had drawn me at the point
Of a fiery finger through the uneven dark,
I went with reeling footsteps down the stair,
Nor asked a question.
                        There she sat, my aunt—
Bolt upright in the chair beside her bed,
Whose pillow had no dint! she had used no bed
For that night's sleeping, yet slept well. My God,
The dumb derision of that gray, peaked face
Concluded something grave against the sun,
Which filled the chamber with its July burst 930
When Susan drew the curtains ignorant
Of who sat open-eyed behind her. There
She sat . . . it sat . . . we said 'she' yesterday . . .
And held a letter with unbroken seal
As Susan gave it to her hand last night:
All night she had held it. If its news referred
To duchies or to dunghills, not an inch
She'd budge, 'twas obvious, for such worthless odds:
Nor, though the stars were suns and overburned
Their spheric limitations, swallowing up 940
Like wax the azure spaces, could they force
Those open eyes to wink once. What last sight
Had left them blank and flat so—drawing out
The faculty of vision from the roots,
As nothing more, worth seeing, remained behind?

Were those the eyes that watched me, worried me?
That dogged me up and down the hours and days,
A beaten, breathless, miserable soul?
And did I pray, a half-hour back, but so,
To escape the burden of those eyes . . . those eyes? 950
'Sleep late' I said?—
                        Why now, indeed, they sleep.
God answers sharp and sudden on some prayers,
And thrusts the thing we have prayed for in our face,

A gauntlet with a gift in't. Every wish
Is like a prayer, with God.
                              I had my wish,
To read and meditate the thing I would,
To fashion all my life upon my thought,
And marry or not marry. Henceforth none
Could disapprove me, vex me, hamper me.
Full ground-room, in this desert newly made,   960
For Babylon or Balbec—when the breath,*
Now choked with sand, returns for building towns.

The heir came over on the funeral day,
And we two cousins met before the dead,
With two pale faces. Was it death or life
That moved us? When the will was read and done,
The official guests and witnesses withdrawn,
We rose up in a silence almost hard,
And looked at one another. Then I said,
'Farewell, my cousin.'
                              But he touched, just touched   970
My hat-strings tied for going (at the door
The carriage stood to take me), and said low,
His voice a little unsteady through his smile,
'Siste, viator.'
                  'Is there time,' I asked,
'In these last days of railroads, to stop short
Like Caesar's chariot (weighing half a ton)
On the Appian road for morals?'*
                                    'There is time,'
He answered grave, 'for necessary words,
Inclusive, trust me, of no epitaph
On man or act, my cousin. We have read   980
A will, which gives you all the personal goods
And funded monies of your aunt.'
                                    'I thank
Her memory for it. With three hundred pounds*
We buy in England even, clear standing-room

To stand and work in. Only two hours since,
I fancied I was poor.'
                    'And, cousin, still
You're richer than you fancy. The will says,
Three hundred pounds, and any other sum
*Of which the said testatrix dies possessed.**
I say she died possessed of other sums.'   990

'Dear Romney, need we chronicle the pence?
I'm richer than I thought—that's evident.
Enough so.'
                'Listen rather. You've to do
With business and a cousin,' he resumed,
'And both, I fear, need patience. Here's the fact.
The other sum (there *is* another sum,
Unspecified in any will which dates
After possession, yet bequeathed as much
And clearly as those said three hundred pounds)
Is thirty thousand. You will have it paid   1000
When? . . . where? My duty troubles you with words.'

He struck the iron when the bar was hot;
No wonder if my eyes sent out some sparks.
'Pause there! I thank you. You are delicate
In glosing gifts—but I, who share your blood,*
Am rather made for giving, like yourself,
Than taking, like your pensioners. Farewell.'

He stopped me with a gesture of calm pride.
'A Leigh,' he said, 'gives largesse and gives love,
But gloses never: if a Leigh could glose,   1010
He would not do it, moreover, to a Leigh,
With blood trained up along nine centuries
To hound and hate a lie from eyes like yours.
And now we'll make the rest as clear; your aunt
Possessed these monies.'
                        'You will make it clear,

My cousin, as the honour of us both,
Or one of us speaks vainly! that's not I.
My aunt possessed this sum—inherited
From whom, and when? bring documents, prove dates.'

'Why now indeed you throw your bonnet off   1020
As if you had time left for a logarithm!
The faith's the want. Dear cousin, give me faith,
And you shall walk this road with silken shoes,
As clean as any lady of our house
Supposed the proudest. Oh, I comprehend
The whole position from your point of sight.
I oust you from your father's halls and lands
And make you poor by getting rich—that's law;
Considering which, in common circumstance,
You would not scruple to accept from me   1030
Some compensation, some sufficiency
Of income—that were justice; but, alas,
I love you—there's mere nature; you reject
My love—there's nature also; and at once,
You cannot, from a suitor disallowed,
A hand thrown back as mine is, into yours
Receive a doit, a farthing—not for the world!*
That's woman's etiquette, and obviously
Exceeds the claim of nature, law, and right,
Unanswerable to all. I grant, you see,   1040
The case as you conceive it—leave you room
To sweep your ample skirts of womanhood,
While, standing humbly squeezed against the wall,
I own myself excluded from being just,
Restrained from paying indubitable debts,
Because denied from giving you my soul.
That's my misfortune!—I submit to it
As if, in some more reasonable age,
'Twould not be less inevitable. Enough.
You'll trust me, cousin, as a gentleman,   1050
To keep your honour, as you count it, pure,

Your scruples (just as if I thought them wise)
Safe and inviolate from gifts of mine.'

I answered mild but earnest. 'I believe
In no one's honour which another keeps,
Nor man's nor woman's. As I keep, myself,
My truth and my religion, I depute
No father, though I had one this side death,
Nor brother, though I had twenty, much less you,
Though twice my cousin, and once Romney Leigh,   1060
To keep my honour pure. You face, today,
A man who wants instruction, mark me, not
A woman who wants protection. As to a man,
Show manhood, speak out plainly, be precise
With facts and dates. My aunt inherited
This sum, you say—'
                'I said she died possessed
Of this, dear cousin.'
                  'Not by heritage.
Thank you: we're getting to the facts at last.
Perhaps she played at commerce with a ship
Which came in heavy with Australian gold?*   1070
Or touched a lottery with her finger-end,*
Which tumbled on a sudden into her lap
Some old Rhine tower or principality?
Perhaps she had to do with a marine
Sub-transatlantic railroad, which pre-pays
As well as pre-supposes? or perhaps
Some stale ancestral debt was after-paid
By a hundred years, and took her by surprise?—
You shake your head my cousin; I guess ill.'

'You need not guess, Aurora, nor deride;   1080
The truth is not afraid of hurting you.
You'll find no cause, in all your scruples, why
Your aunt should cavil at a deed of gift

'Twixt her and me.'

        'I thought so—ah! A gift.'

'You naturally thought so,' he resumed.
'A very natural gift.'

        'A gift, a gift!
Her individual life being stranded high
Above all want, approaching opulence,
Too haughty was she to accept a gift
Without some ultimate aim: ah, ah, I see—   1090
A gift intended plainly for her heirs,
And so accepted . . . if accepted . . . ah,
Indeed that might be; I am snared perhaps
Just so. But, cousin, shall I pardon you,
If thus you have caught me with a cruel springe?'

He answered gently, 'Need you tremble and pant
Like a netted lioness? is't my fault, mine,
That you're a grand wild creature of the woods
And hate the stall built for you? Anyway,
Though triply netted, need you glare at me?   1100
I do not hold the cords of such a net;
You're free from me, Aurora!'

        'Now may God
Deliver me from this strait! This gift of yours
Was tendered . . . when? accepted . . . when?' I asked.
'A month . . . a fortnight since? Six weeks ago
It was not tendered; by a word she dropped
I know it was not tendered nor received.
When was it? bring your dates.'

        'What matters when?
A half-hour ere she died, or a half-year,
Secured the gift, maintains the heritage   1110
Inviolable with law. As easy pluck
The golden stars from heaven's embroidered stole
To pin them on the gray side of this earth,

As make you poor again, thank God.'

                         'Not poor
Nor clean again from henceforth, you thank God?
Well, sir—I ask you—I insist at need—
Vouchsafe the special date, the special date.'

'The day before her death-day,' he replied,
'The gift was in her hands. We'll find that deed,
And certify that date to you.'

                     As one   1120
Who has climbed a mountain-height and carried up
His own heart climbing, panting in his throat
With the toil of the ascent, takes breath at last,
Looks back in triumph—so I stood and looked.
'Dear cousin Romney, we have reached the top
Of this steep question, and may rest, I think.
But first—I pray you pardon, that the shock
And surge of natural feeling and event
Has made me oblivious of acquainting you
That this, this letter (unread, mark, still sealed),   1130
Was found enfolded in the poor dead hand:
That spirit of hers had gone beyond the address,
Which could not find her though you wrote it clear—
I know your writing, Romney—recognise
The open-hearted *A*, the liberal sweep
Of the *G*. Now listen—let us understand:
You will not find that famous deed of gift,
Unless you find it in the letter here,
Which, not being mine, I give you back.—Refuse
To take the letter? well then—you and I,   1140
As writer and as heiress, open it
Together, by your leave.—Exactly so:
The words in which the noble offering's made,
Are nobler still, my cousin; and, I own,
The proudest and most delicate heart alive,
Distracted from the measure of the gift
By such a grace in giving, might accept

Your largesse without thinking any more
Of the burthen of it, than King Solomon*
Considered, when he wore his holy ring   1150
Charactered over with the ineffable spell,
How many carats of fine gold made up
Its money-value: so, Leigh gives to Leigh!
Or rather, might have given, observe—for that's
The point we come to. Here's a proof of gift,
But here's no proof, sir, of acceptancy,
But rather, disproof. Death's black dust, being blown,
Infiltrated through every secret fold
Of this sealed letter by a puff of fate,
Dried up for ever the fresh-written ink,   1160
Annulled the gift, disutilised the grace,
And left these fragments.'
                         As I spoke, I tore
The paper up and down, and down and up
And crosswise, till it fluttered from my hands,
As forest-leaves, stripped suddenly and rapt
By a whirlwind on Valdarno, drop again,*
Drop slow, and strew the melancholy ground
Before the amazèd hills . . . why, so, indeed,
I'm writing like a poet, somewhat large
In the type of the image, and exaggerate   1170
A small thing with a great thing, topping it—
But then I'm thinking how his eyes looked, his,
With what despondent and surprised reproach!
I think the tears were in them as he looked;
I think the manly mouth just trembled. Then
He broke the silence.
                         'I may ask, perhaps,
Although no stranger . . . only Romney Leigh,
Which means still less . . . than Vincent Carrington,
Your plans in going hence, and where you go.
This cannot be a secret.'
                         'All my life   1180
Is open to you, cousin. I go hence

To London, to the gathering-place of souls,
To live mine straight out, vocally, in books;
Harmoniously for others, if indeed
A woman's soul, like man's, be wide enough
To carry the whole octave (that's to prove)
Or, if I fail, still purely for myself.
Pray God be with me, Romney.'

       'Ah, poor child,
Who fight against the mother's 'tiring hand,*
And choose the headsman's! May God change his
  world   1190
For your sake, sweet, and make it mild as heaven,
And juster than I have found you.'

        But I paused.
'And you, my cousin?'—

      'I,' he said—'you ask?
You care to ask? Well, girls have curious minds
And fain would know the end of everything,
Of cousins therefore with the rest. For me,
Aurora, I've my work; you know my work;
And, having missed this year some personal hope,
I must beware the rather that I miss
No reasonable duty. While you sing   1200
Your happy pastorals of the meads and trees,
Bethink you that I go to impress and prove
On stifled brains and deafened ears, stunned deaf,
Crushed dull with grief, that nature sings itself,
And needs no mediate poet, lute or voice,
To make it vocal. While you ask of men
Your audience, I may get their leave perhaps
For hungry orphans to say audibly
"We're hungry, see"—for beaten and bullied wives
To hold their unweaned babies up in sight, 1210
Whom orphanage would better, and for all
To speak and claim their portion . . . by no means
Of the soil . . . but of the sweat in tilling it;
Since this is nowadays turned privilege,

To have only God's curse on us, and not man's.
Such work I have for doing, elbow-deep
In social problems—as you tie your rhymes,
To draw my uses to cohere with needs
And bring the uneven world back to its round,
Or, failing so much, fill up, bridge at least   1220
To smoother issues some abysmal cracks
And feuds of earth, intestine heats have made
To keep men separate—using sorry shifts
Of hospitals, almshouses, infant schools,
And other practical stuff of partial good
You lovers of the beautiful and whole
Despise by system.'
                    '*I* despise? The scorn
Is yours, my cousin. Poets become such
Through scorning nothing. You decry them for
The good of beauty sung and taught by them,   1230
While they respect your practical partial good
As being a part of beauty's self. Adieu!
When God helps all the workers for his world,
The singers shall have help of Him, not last.'

He smiled as men smile when they will not speak
Because of something bitter in the thought;
And still I feel his melancholy eyes
Look judgment on me. It is seven years since:
I know not if 'twas pity or 'twas scorn
Has made them so far-reaching: judge it ye   1240
Who have had to do with pity more than love
And scorn than hatred. I am used, since then,
To other ways, from equal men. But so,
Even so, we let go hands, my cousin and I,
And in between us rushed the torrent-world
To blanch our faces like divided rocks,
And bar for ever mutual sight and touch
Except through swirl of spray and all that roar.

BOOK III

'TODAY thou girdest up thy loins thyself
And goest where thou wouldest: presently*
Others shall gird thee,' said the Lord, 'to go
Where thou would'st not.' He spoke to Peter thus,
To signify the death which he should die
When crucified head downward.

                   If He spoke
To Peter then, He speaks to us the same;
The word suits many different martyrdoms,
And signifies a multiform of death,
Although we scarcely die apostles, we,   10
And have mislaid the keys of heaven and earth.*

For 'tis not in mere death that men die most,
And, after our first girding of the loins
In youth's fine linen and fair broidery
To run up hill and meet the rising sun,
We are apt to sit tired, patient as a fool,
While others gird us with the violent bands
Of social figments, feints, and formalisms,
Reversing our straight nature, lifting up
Our base needs, keeping down our lofty thoughts,   20
Head downward on the cross-sticks of the world.

Yet He can pluck us from that shameful cross.
God, set our feet low and our forehead high,
And show us how a man was made to walk!

Leave the lamp, Susan, and go up to bed.
The room does very well; I have to write
Beyond the stroke of midnight. Get away;

Your steps, for ever buzzing in the room,
Tease me like gnats. Ah, letters! throw them down
At once, as I must have them, to be sure,   30
Whether I bid you never bring me such
At such an hour, or bid you. No excuse;
You choose to bring them, as I choose perhaps
To throw them in the fire. Now get to bed,
And dream, if possible, I am not cross.

Why what a pettish, petty thing I grow—
A mere, mere woman, a mere flaccid nerve,
A kerchief left out all night in the rain,
Turned soft so—overtasked and overstrained
And overlived in this close London life!   40
And yet I should be stronger.
                                        Never burn
Your letters, poor Aurora! for they stare
With red seals from the table, saying each,
'Here's something that you know not.' Out alas,
'Tis scarcely that the world's more good and wise
Or even straighter and more consequent
Since yesterday at this time—yet, again,
If but one angel spoke from Ararat*
I should be very sorry not to hear:
So open all the letters! let me read.   50
Blanche Ord, the writer in the 'Lady's Fan,'
Requests my judgment on . . . that, afterwards.
Kate Ward desires the model of my cloak,
And signs, 'Elisha to you.' Pringle Sharpe*
Presents his work on 'Social Conduct,' craves
A little money for his pressing debts . . .
From me, who scarce have money for my needs;
Art's fiery chariot which we journey in
Being apt to singe our singing-robes to holes
Although you ask me for my cloak, Kate Ward!   60
Here's Rudgely knows it—editor and scribe;
He's 'forced to marry where his heart is not,

Because the purse lacks where he lost his heart.'
Ah—lost it because no one picked it up;
That's really loss—(and passable impudence).
My critic Hammond flatters prettily,
And wants another volume like the last.
My critic Belfair wants another book
Entirely different, which will sell (and live?),
A striking book, yet not a startling book,   70
The public blames originalities
(You must not pump spring-water unawares
Upon a gracious public full of nerves):
Good things, not subtle, new yet orthodox,
As easy reading as the dog-eared page
That's fingered by said public fifty years,
Since first taught spelling by its grandmother,
And yet a revelation in some sort:
That's hard, my critic Belfair. So—what next?
My critic Stokes objects to abstract thoughts;   80
'Call a man, John, a woman, Joan,' says he,
'And do not prate so of *humanities*':
Whereat I call my critic simply, Stokes.
My critic Jobson recommends more mirth
Because a cheerful genius suits the times,
And all true poets laugh unquenchably
Like Shakespeare and the gods. That's very hard.
The gods may laugh, and Shakespeare; Dante smiled
With such a needy heart on two pale lips
We cry, 'Weep rather, Dante.' Poems are   90
Men, if true poems: and who dares exclaim
At any man's door, 'Here, 'tis understood
The thunder fell last week and killed a wife
And scared a sickly husband—what of that?
Get up, be merry, shout and clap your hands,
Because a cheerful genius suits the times—'?
None says so to the man, and why indeed
Should any to the poem? A ninth seal;*
The apocalypse is drawing to a close.

Ha—this from Vincent Carrington—'Dear friend,   100
I want good counsel. Will you lend me wings
To raise me to the subject, in a sketch
I'll bring tomorrow—may I? at eleven?
A poet's only born to turn to use:
So save you! for the world . . . and Carrington.'
'(Writ after.) Have you heard of Romney Leigh,
Beyond what's said of him in newspapers,
His phalansteries there, his speeches here,*
His pamphlets, pleas, and statements, everywhere?
He dropped *me* long ago, but no one drops   110
A golden apple—though indeed one day
You hinted that, but jested. Well, at least
You know Lord Howe who sees him . . . whom he sees
And *you* see and I hate to see—for Howe
Stands high upon the brink of theories,
Observes the swimmers and cries "Very fine,"
But keeps dry linen equally—unlike
That gallant breaster, Romney. Strange it is,
Such sudden madness seizing a young man
To make earth over again—while I'm content   120
To make the pictures. Let me bring the sketch.
A tiptoe Danaë, overbold and hot,*
Both arms a-flame to meet her wishing Jove
Halfway, and burn him faster down; the face
And breasts upturned and straining, the loose locks
All glowing with the anticipated gold.
Or here's another on the self-same theme.
She lies here—flat upon her prison-floor,
The long hair swathed about her to the heel
Like wet seaweed. You dimly see her through   130
The glittering haze of that prodigious rain,
Half blotted out of nature by a love
As heavy as fate. I'll bring you either sketch.
I think, myself, the second indicates
More passion.'
                    Surely. Self is put away,

And calm with abdication. She is Jove,
And no more Danaë—greater thus. Perhaps
The painter symbolises unaware
Two states of the recipient artist-soul,
One, forward, personal, wanting reverence,   140
Because aspiring only. We'll be calm,
And know that, when indeed our Joves come down,
We all turn stiller than we have ever been.

Kind Vincent Carrington. I'll let him come.
He talks of Florence—and may say a word
Of something as it chanced seven years ago,
A hedgehog in the path, or a lame bird,
In those green country walks, in that good time
When certainly I was so miserable . . .
I seem to have missed a blessing ever since.   150

The music soars within the little lark,
And the lark soars. It is not thus with men.
We do not make our places with our strains—
Content, while they rise, to remain behind
Alone on earth instead of so in heaven.
No matter; I bear on my broken tale.

When Romney Leigh and I had parted thus,
I took a chamber up three flights of stairs
Not far from being as steep as some larks climb,
And there, in a certain house in Kensington,   160
Three years I lived and worked. Get leave to work
In this world—'tis the best you get at all;
For God, in cursing, gives us better gifts
Than men in benediction. God says, 'Sweat
For foreheads,' men say 'crowns,' and so we are crowned,
Ay, gashed by some tormenting circle of steel
Which snaps with a secret spring. Get work, get work;
Be sure 'tis better than what you work to get.

Serene and unafraid of solitude
I worked the short days out—and watched the sun   170
On lurid morns or monstrous afternoons
(Like some Druidic idol's fiery brass*
With fixed unflickering outline of dead heat,
From which the blood of wretches pent inside
Seems oozing forth to incarnadine the air)
Push out through fog with his dilated disk,
And startle the slant roofs and chimney-pots
With splashes of fierce colour. Or I saw
Fog only, the great tawny weltering fog,
Involve the passive city, strangle it   180
Alive, and draw it off into the void,
Spires, bridges, streets, and squares, as if a sponge
Had wiped out London—or as noon and night
Had clapped together and utterly struck out
The intermediate time, undoing themselves
In the act. Your city poets see such things
Not despicable. Mountains of the south,
When drunk and mad with elemental wines
They rend the seamless mist and stand up bare,
Make fewer singers, haply. No one sings*   190
Descending Sinai: on Parnassus mount
You take a mule to climb and not a muse
Except in fable and figure: forests chant
Their anthems to themselves, and leave you dumb.
But sit in London at the day's decline,
And view the city perish in the mist
Like Pharaoh's armaments in the deep Red Sea,*
The chariots, horsemen, footmen, all the host,
Sucked down and choked to silence—then, surprised
By a sudden sense of vision and of tune,   200
You feel as conquerors though you did not fight,
And you and Israel's other singing girls,
Ay, Miriam with them, sing the song you choose.

I worked with patience, which means almost power:
I did some excellent things indifferently,

Some bad things excellently. Both were praised,
The latter loudest. And by such a time
That I myself had set them down as sins
Scarce worth the price of sackcloth, week by week
Arrived some letter through the sedulous post,   210
Like these I've read, and yet dissimilar,
With pretty maiden seals—initials twined
Of lilies, or a heart marked *Emily*
(Convicting Emily of being all heart);
Or rarer tokens from young bachelors,
Who wrote from college, with the same goose-quill,
Suppose, they had just been plucked of, and a snatch
From Horace, 'Collegisse juvat,' set*
Upon the first page. Many a letter, signed
Or unsigned, showing the writers at eighteen   220
Had lived too long, although a muse should help
Their dawn by holding candles—compliments
To smile or sigh at. Such could pass with me
No more than coins from Moscow circulate
At Paris: would ten roubles buy a tag
Of ribbon on the boulevard, worth a sou?
I smiled that all this youth should love me—sighed
That such a love could scarcely raise them up
To love what was more worthy than myself;
Then sighed again, again, less generously,   230
To think the very love they lavished so,
Proved me inferior. The strong loved me not,
And he . . . my cousin Romney . . . did not write.
I felt the silent finger of his scorn
Prick every bubble of my frivolous fame
As my breath blew it, and resolve it back
To the air it came from. Oh, I justified
The measure he had taken of my height:
The thing was plain—he was not wrong a line;
I played at art, made thrusts with a toy-sword,   240
Amused the lads and maidens.
                                          Came a sigh

Deep, hoarse with resolution—I would work
To better ends, or play in earnest. 'Heavens,
I think I should be almost popular
If this went on!'—I ripped my verses up,
And found no blood upon the rapier's point;
The heart in them was just an embryo's heart
Which never yet had beat, that it should die;
Just gasps of make-believe galvanic life;*
Mere tones, inorganised to any tune.   250

And yet I felt it in me where it burnt,
Like those hot fire-seeds of creation held*
In Jove's clenched palm before the worlds were sown—
But I—I was not Juno even! my hand
Was shut in weak convulsion, woman's ill,
And when I yearned to loose a finger—lo,
The nerve revolted. 'Tis the same even now:
This hand may never, haply, open large,
Before the spark is quenched, or the palm charred,
To prove the power not else than by the pain.   260

It burns, it burnt—my whole life burnt with it,
And light, not sunlight and not torchlight, flashed
My steps out through the slow and difficult road.
I had grown distrustful of too forward Springs,
The season's books in drear significance
Of morals, dropping round me. Lively books?
The ash has livelier verdure than the yew;
And yet the yew's green longer, and alone
Found worthy of the holy Christmas time:
We'll plant more yews if possible, albeit   270
We plant the graveyards with them.
                                          Day and night
I worked my rhythmic thought, and furrowed up
Both watch and slumber with long lines of life
Which did not suit their season. The rose fell
From either cheek, my eyes globed luminous

Through orbits of blue shadow, and my pulse
Would shudder along the purple-veinèd wrist
Like a shot bird. Youth's stern, set face to face
With youth's ideal: and when people came
And said, 'You work too much, you are looking ill,'   280
I smiled for pity of them who pitied me,
And thought I should be better soon perhaps
For those ill looks. Observe—'I' means in youth
Just *I*, the conscious and eternal soul
With all its ends, and not the outside life,
The parcel-man, the doublet of the flesh,
The so much liver, lung, integument,
Which make the sum of 'I' hereafter when
World-talkers talk of doing well or ill.
I prosper if I gain a step, although   290
A nail then pierced my foot: although my brain
Embracing any truth froze paralysed,
I prosper: I but change my instrument;
I break the spade off, digging deep for gold,
And catch the mattock up.*

                              I worked on, on.
Through all the bristling fence of nights and days
Which hedges time in from the eternities,
I struggled—never stopped to note the stakes
Which hurt me in my course. The midnight oil
Would stink sometimes; there came some vulgar needs: 300
I had to live that therefore I might work,
And, being but poor, I was constrained, for life,
To work with one hand for the booksellers
While working with the other for myself
And art: you swim with feet as well as hands,
Or make small way. I apprehended this—
In England no one lives by verse that lives;
And, apprehending, I resolved by prose
To make a space to sphere my living verse.
I wrote for cyclopaedias, magazines,   310
And weekly papers, holding up my name

To keep it from the mud. I learnt the use
Of the editorial 'we' in a review
As courtly ladies the fine trick of trains,
And swept it grandly through the open doors
As if one could not pass through doors at all
Save so encumbered. I wrote tales beside,
Carved many an article on cherry-stones*
To suit light readers—something in the lines
Revealing, it was said, the mallet-hand,   320
But that, I'll never vouch for: what you do
For bread, will taste of common grain, not grapes,
Although you have a vineyard in Champagne;
Much less in Nephelococcygia*
As mine was, peradventure.
                                   Having bread
For just so many days, just breathing-room
For body and verse, I stood up straight and worked
My veritable work. And as the soul
Which grows within a child makes the child grow—
Or as the fiery sap, the touch from God,   330
Careering through a tree, dilates the bark
And roughs with scale and knob, before it strikes
The summer foliage out in a green flame—
So life, in deepening with me, deepened all
The course I took, the work I did. Indeed
The academic law convinced of sin;
The critics cried out on the falling off,
Regretting the first manner. But I felt
My heart's life throbbing in my verse to show
It lived, it also—certes incomplete,*   340
Disordered with all Adam in the blood,
But even its very tumours, warts and wens
Still organised by and implying life.

A lady called upon me on such a day.
She had the low voice of your English dames,
Unused, it seems, to need rise half a note

To catch attention—and their quiet mood,
As if they lived too high above the earth
For that to put them out in anything:
So gentle, because verily so proud;   350
So wary and afraid of hurting you,
By no means that you are not really vile,
But that they would not touch you with their foot
To push you to your place; so self-possessed
Yet gracious and conciliating, it takes
An effort in their presence to speak truth:
You know the sort of woman—brilliant stuff,
And out of nature. 'Lady Waldemar.'
She said her name quite simply, as if it meant
Not much indeed, but something—took my hands,   360
And smiled as if her smile could help my case,
And dropped her eyes on me and let them melt.
'Is this,' she said, 'the Muse?'
                                                      'No sybil even,'
I answered, 'since she fails to guess the cause
Which taxed you with this visit, madam.'
                                                                       'Good,'
She said, 'I value what's sincere at once.
Perhaps if I had found a literal Muse,
The visit might have taxed me. As it is,
You wear your blue so chiefly in your eyes,
My fair Aurora, in a frank good way,   370
It comforts me entirely for your fame,
As well as for the trouble of ascent
To this Olympus.'
                                     There, a silver laugh
Ran rippling through her quickened little breaths
The steep stair somewhat justified.
                                                          'But still
Your ladyship has left me curious why
You dared the risk of finding the said Muse?'

'Ah—keep me, notwithstanding, to the point,
Like any pedant? Is the blue in eyes*

As awful as in stockings after all,   380
I wonder, that you'd have my business out
Before I breathe—exact the epic plunge*
In spite of gasps? Well, naturally you think
I've come here, as the lion-hunters go
To deserts, to secure you with a trap
For exhibition in my drawing-rooms
On zoologic soirées? not in the least.
Roar softly at me; I am frivolous,
I dare say; I have played at wild-beast shows
Like other women of my class—but now   390
I meet my lion simply as Androcles*
Met his . . . when at his mercy.'
                              So, she bent
Her head, as queens may mock—then lifting up
Her eyelids with a real grave queenly look,
Which ruled and would not spare, not even herself—
'I think you have a cousin—Romney Leigh.'

'You bring a word from *him*?'—my eyes leapt up
To the very height of hers—'a word from *him*?'

'I bring a word about him, actually.
But first' (she pressed me with her urgent eyes),   400
'You do not love him—you?'
                              'You're frank at least
In putting questions, madam,' I replied;
'I love my cousin cousinly—no more.'

'I guessed as much. I'm ready to be frank
In answering also, if you'll question me,
Or even for something less. You stand outside,
You artist women, of the common sex;
You share not with us, and exceed us so
Perhaps by what you're mulcted in, your hearts*
Being starved to make your heads: so run the old   410
Traditions of you. I can therefore speak

Without the natural shame which creatures feel
When speaking on their level, to their like.
There's many a papist she, would rather die
Than own to her maid she put a ribbon on
To catch the indifferent eye of such a man,
Who yet would count adulteries on her beads
At holy Mary's shrine and never blush;
Because the saints are so far off, we lose
All modesty before them. Thus, today.   420
'Tis *I*, love Romney Leigh.'
                                                'Forbear,' I cried.
'If here's no Muse, still less is any saint;
Nor even a friend, that Lady Waldemar
Should make confessions' . . .
                                        'That's unkindly said.
If no friend, what forbids to make a friend
To join to our confession ere we have done?
I love your cousin. If it seems unwise
To say so, it's still foolisher (we're frank)
To feel so. My first husband left me young,
And pretty enough, so please you, and rich enough,   430
To keep my booth in Mayfair with the rest*
To happy issues. There are marquises
Would serve seven years to call me wife, I know,
And, after seven, I might consider it,
For there's some comfort in a marquisate
When all's said—yes, but after the seven years;
I, now, love Romney. You put up your lip,
So like a Leigh! so like him!—Pardon me,
I'm well aware I do not derogate*
In loving Romney Leigh. The name is good,   440
The means are excellent, but the man, the man—
Heaven help us both—I am near as mad as he,
In loving such an one.'
                            She slowly swung
Her heavy ringlets till they touched her smile,
As reasonably sorry for herself,

And thus continued.
                              'Of a truth, Miss Leigh,
I have not, without struggle, come to this.
I took a master in the German tongue,
I gamed a little, went to Paris twice;
But, after all, this love! . . . you eat of love,   450
And do as vile a thing as if you ate
Of garlic—which, whatever else you eat,
Tastes uniformly acrid, till your peach
Reminds you of your onion. Am I coarse?
Well, love's coarse, nature's coarse—ah, there's the rub!*
We fair fine ladies, who park out our lives
From common sheep-paths, cannot help the crows
From flying over—we're as natural still
As Blowsalinda. Drape as perfectly*
In Lyons' velvet—we are not, for that,*   460
Lay-figures, look you: we have hearts within,
Warm, live, improvident, indecent hearts,
As ready for outrageous ends and acts
As any distressed sempstress of them all
That Romney groans and toils for. We catch love
And other fevers in the vulgar way:
Love will not be outwitted by our wit,
Nor outrun by our equipages—mine
Persisted, spite of efforts. All my cards
Turned up but Romney Leigh; my German stopped   470
At germane Wertherism; my Paris rounds*
Returned me from the Champs Elysées just
A ghost, and sighing like Dido's. I came home*
Uncured—convicted rather to myself
Of being in love . . . in love! That's coarse you'll say.
I'm talking garlic.'
                              Coldly I replied.
'Apologise for atheism, not love!
For me, I do believe in love, and God.*
I know my cousin: Lady Waldemar
I know not: yet I say as much as this;   480

Whoever loves him, let her not excuse
But cleanse herself, that, loving such a man,
She may not do it with such unworthy love
He cannot stoop and take it.'
                          'That is said
Austerely, like a youthful prophetess,
Who knits her brows across her pretty eyes
To keep them back from following the gray flight
Of doves between the temple-columns. Dear,
Be kinder with me; let us two be friends.
I'm a mere woman—the more weak perhaps   490
Through being so proud; you're better; as for him,
He's best. Indeed he builds his goodness up
So high, it topples down to the other side
And makes a sort of badness; there's the worst
I have to say against your cousin's best!
And so be mild, Aurora, with my worst,
For his sake, if not mine.'
                          'I own myself
Incredulous of confidence like this
Availing him or you.'
                          'And I, myself,
Of being worthy of him with any love: 500
In your sense I am not so—let it pass.
And yet I save him if I marry him;
Let that pass too.'
                    'Pass, pass! we play police*
Upon my cousin's life, to indicate
What may or may not pass?' I cried. 'He knows
What's worthy of him; the choice remains with *him*;
And what he chooses, act or wife, I think
I shall not call unworthy, I, for one.'

''Tis somewhat rashly said,' she answered slow;
'Now let's talk reason, though we talk of love. 510
Your cousin Romney Leigh's a monster; there,
The word's out fairly, let me prove the fact.

We'll take, say, that most perfect of antiques*
They call the Genius of the Vatican
(Which seems too beauteous to endure itself
In this mixed world), and fasten it for once
Upon the torso of the Dancing Faun*
(Who might limp surely, if he did not dance),
Instead of Buonarroti's mask: what then?*
We show the sort of monster Romney is,   520
With godlike virtues and heroic aims
Subjoined to limping possibilities
Of mismade human nature. Grant the man
Twice godlike, twice heroic—still he limps,
And here's the point we come to.'

                            'Pardon me,
But, Lady Waldemar, the point's the thing
We never come to.'

                   'Caustic, insolent
At need! I like you'—(there, she took my hands)
'And now my lioness, help Androcles,
For all your roaring. Help me! for myself   530
I would not say so—but for him. He limps
So certainly, he'll fall into the pit
A week hence—so I lose him—so he is lost!
For when he's fairly married, he a Leigh,
To a girl of doubtful life, undoubtful birth,
Starved out in London till her coarse-grained hands
Are whiter than her morals—even you
May call his choice unworthy.'

                         'Married! lost!
He . . . Romney!'

                'Ah, you're moved at last,' she said.
'These monsters, set out in the open sun,   540
Of course throw monstrous shadows: those who think
Awry, will scarce act straightly. Who but he?
And who but you can wonder? He has been mad,
The whole world knows, since first, a nominal man,*

He soured the proctors, tried the gownsmen's wits,*
With equal scorn of triangles and wine,
And took no honours, yet was honourable.
They'll tell you he lost count of Homer's ships*
In Melbourne's poor-bills, Ashley's factory bills—*
Ignored the Aspasia we all dare to praise,*   550
For other women, dear, we could not name
Because we're decent. Well, he had some right
On his side probably; men always have,
Who go absurdly wrong. The living boor
Who brews your ale, exceeds in vital worth
Dead Caesar who "stops bungholes" in the cask;*
And also, to do good is excellent,
For persons of his income, even to boors:
I sympathise with all such things. But he
Went mad upon them . . . madder and more mad   560
From college times to these—as, going downhill,
The faster still, the farther. You must know
Your Leigh by heart: he has sown his black young curls
With bleaching cares of half a million men
Already. If you do not starve, or sin,
You're nothing to him: pay the income-tax
And break your heart upon't, he'll scarce be touched;
But come upon the parish, qualified
For the parish stocks, and Romney will be there
To call you brother, sister, or perhaps   570
A tenderer name still. Had I any chance
With Mister Leigh, who am Lady Waldemar
And never committed felony?'
                        'You speak
Too bitterly,' I said, 'for the literal truth.'

'The truth is bitter. Here's a man who looks
For ever on the ground! you must be low,
Or else a pictured ceiling overhead,
Good painting thrown away. For me, I've done

What women may, we're somewhat limited,
We modest women, but I've done my best.   580
—How men are perjured when they swear our eyes
Have meaning in them! they're just blue or brown,
They just can drop their lids a little. And yet
Mine did more, for I read half Fourier through,
Proudhon, Considérant, and Louis Blanc,*
With various others of his socialists,
And, if I had been a fathom less in love,
Had cured myself with gaping. As it was,
I quoted from them prettily enough
Perhaps, to make them sound half rational   590
To a saner man than he whene'er we talked
(For which I dodged occasion)—learnt by heart
His speeches in the Commons and elsewhere
Upon the social question; heaped reports
Of wicked women and penitentiaries
On all my tables (with a place for Sue),*
And gave my name to swell subscription-lists
Toward keeping up the sun at nights in heaven,
And other possible ends. All things I did,
Except the impossible . . . such as wearing gowns*   600
Provided by the Ten Hours' movement: there,
I stopped—we must stop somewhere. He, meanwhile,
Unmoved as the Indian tortoise 'neath the world,*
Let all that noise go on upon his back:
He would not disconcert or throw me out,
'Twas well to see a woman of my class
With such a dawn of conscience. For the heart,
Made firewood for his sake, and flaming up
To his face—he merely warmed his feet at it:
Just deigned to let my carriage stop him short   610
In park or street—he leaning on the door
With news of the committee which sat last
On pickpockets at suck.'

                              'You jest—you jest.'

'As martyrs jest, dear (if you read their lives),
Upon the axe which kills them. When all's done
By me ... for him—you'll ask him presently
The colour of my hair—he cannot tell,
Or answers "dark" at random; while, be sure,
He's absolute on the figure, five or ten,
Of my last subscription. Is it bearable,   620
And I a woman?'

              'Is it reparable,
Though *I* were a man?'

                   'I know not. That's to prove.
But first, this shameful marriage?'

                      'Ay?' I cried,
'Then really there's a marriage?'

                       'Yesterday
I held him fast upon it. "Mister Leigh,"
Said I, "shut up a thing, it makes more noise.
The boiling town keeps secrets ill; I've known
Yours since last week. Forgive my knowledge so:
You feel I'm not the woman of the world
The world thinks; you have borne with me before,   630
And used me in your noble work, our work,
And now you shall not cast me off because
You're at the difficult point, the *join*. 'Tis true
Even I can scarce admit the cogency
Of such a marriage ... where you do not love
(Except the class), yet marry and throw your name
Down to the gutter, for a fire-escape
To future generations! 'tis sublime,
A great example, a true Genesis
Of the opening social era. But take heed,   640
This virtuous act must have a patent weight,*
Or loses half its virtue. Make it tell,
Interpret it, and set it in the light,
And do not muffle it in a winter-cloak
As a vulgar bit of shame—as if, at best,
A Leigh had made a misalliance and blushed

A Howard should know it." Then, I pressed him more:
"He would not choose," I said, "that even his kin . . .
Aurora Leigh, even . . . should conceive his act
Less sacrifice, more fantasy." At which*   650
He grew so pale, dear . . . to the lips, I knew
I had touched him. "Do you know her," he inquired,
"My cousin Aurora?" "Yes," I said, and lied
(But truly we all know you by your books),
And so I offered to come straight to you,
Explain the subject, justify the cause,
And take you with me to Saint Margaret's Court
To see this miracle, this Marian Erle,
This drover's daughter (she's not pretty, he swears)
Upon whose finger, exquisitely pricked   660
By a hundred needles, we're to hang the tie
'Twixt class and class in England—thus indeed
By such a presence, yours and mine, to lift
The match up from the doubtful place. At once
He thanked me sighing, murmured to himself
"She'll do it perhaps, she's noble—thanked me twice,
And promised, as my guerdon, to put off*
His marriage for a month.'
                        I answered then.
'I understand your drift imperfectly.
You wish to lead me to my cousin's betrothed,   670
To touch her hand if worthy, and hold her hand
If feeble, thus to justify his match.
So be it then. But how this serves your ends,
And how the strange confession of your love
Serves this, I have to learn—I cannot see.'

She knit her restless forehead. 'Then, despite,
Aurora, that most radiant morning name,
You're dull as any London afternoon.
I wanted time, and gained it—wanted *you*,
And gain you! you will come and see the girl   680
In whose most prodigal eyes the lineal pearl

And pride of all your lofty race of Leighs
Is destined to solution. Authorised
By sight and knowledge, then, you'll speak your mind,
And prove to Romney, in your brilliant way,
He'll wrong the people and posterity
(Say such a thing is bad for me and you,
And you fail utterly) by concluding thus
An execrable marriage. Break it up,
Disroot it—peradventure presently   690
We'll plant a better fortune in its place.
Be good to me, Aurora, scorn me less
For saying the thing I should not. Well I know
I should not. I have kept, as others have,
The iron rule of womanly reserve
In lip and life, till now: I wept a week
Before I came here.'—Ending, she was pale;
The last words, haughtily said, were tremulous.
This palfrey pranced in harness, arched her neck,
And, only by the foam upon the bit,   700
You saw she champed against it.
                                        Then I rose.
'I love love: truth's no cleaner thing than love.
I comprehend a love so fiery hot
It burns its natural veil of august shame,
And stands sublimely in the nude, as chaste
As Medicean Venus. But I know,*
A love that burns through veils will burn through masks
And shrivel up treachery. What, love and lie!
Nay—go to the opera! your love's curable.

'I love and lie?' she said—'I lie, forsooth?'   710
And beat her taper foot upon the floor,
And smiled against the shoe—'You're hard, Miss Leigh.
Unversed in current phrases.—Bowling-greens
Of poets are fresher than the world's highways:
Forgive me that I rashly blew the dust
Which dims our hedges even, in your eyes,

And vexed you so much. You find, probably,
No evil in this marriage—rather good
Of innocence, to pastoralise in song:
You'll give the bond your signature, perhaps,   720
Beneath the lady's mark—indifferent
That Romney chose a wife could write her name,
In witnessing he loved her.'

                             'Loved!' I cried;
'Who tells you that he wants a wife to love?
He gets a horse to use, not love, I think:
There's work for wives as well—and after, straw,
When men are liberal. For myself, you err
Supposing power in me to break this match.
I could not do it, to save Romney's life,
And would not, to save mine.'

                            'You take it so,'   730
She said, 'farewell then. Write your books in peace,
As far as may be for some secret stir
Now obvious to me—for, most obviously,
In coming hither I mistook the way.'
Whereat she touched my hand and bent her head,
And floated from me like a silent cloud
That leaves the sense of thunder.

                              I drew breath,
Oppressed in my deliverance. After all*
This woman breaks her social system up
For love, so counted—the love possible   740
To such—and lilies are still lilies, pulled
By smutty hands, though spotted from their white;
And thus she is better haply, of her kind,
Than Romney Leigh, who lives by diagrams,
And crosses out the spontaneities
Of all his individual, personal life
With formal universals. As if man
Were set upon a high stool at a desk
To keep God's books for Him in red and black,
And feel by millions! What, if even God   750

Were chiefly God by living out Himself
To an individualism of the Infinite,
Eterne, intense, profuse—still throwing up
The golden spray of multitudinous worlds
In measure to the proclive weight and rush*
Of His inner nature—the spontaneous love
Still proof and outflow of spontaneous life?
Then live, Aurora.

        Two hours afterward,
Within Saint Margaret's Court I stood alone,
Close-veiled. A sick child, from an ague-fit,   760
Whose wasted right hand gambled 'gainst his left
With an old brass button in a blot of sun,
Jeered weakly at me as I passed across
The uneven pavement; while a woman, rouged
Upon the angular cheek-bones, kerchief torn,
Thin dangling locks, and flat lascivious mouth,
Cursed at a window both ways, in and out,
By turns some bed-rid creature and myself—
'Lie still there, mother! liker the dead dog
You'll be tomorrow. What, we pick our way,   770
Fine madam, with those damnable small feet!
We cover up our face from doing good,
As if it were our purse! What brings you here,
My lady? is't to find my gentleman
Who visits his tame pigeon in the eaves?
Our cholera catch you with its cramps and spasms,
And tumble up your good clothes, veil and all,
And turn your whiteness dead-blue.' I looked up;
I think I could have walked through hell that day,
And never flinched. 'The dear Christ comfort you,'   780
I said, 'you must have been most miserable,
To be so cruel'—and I emptied out
My purse upon the stones: when, as I had cast
The last charm in the cauldron, the whole court
Went boiling, bubbling up, from all its doors
And windows, with a hideous wail of laughs

And roar of oaths, and blows perhaps . . . I passed
Too quickly for distinguishing . . . and pushed
A little side-door hanging on a hinge,
And plunged into the dark, and groped and climbed   790
The long, steep, narrow stair 'twixt broken rail
And mildewed wall that let the plaster drop
To startle me in the blackness. Still, up, up!
So high lived Romney's bride. I paused at last
Before a low door in the roof, and knocked;
There came an answer like a hurried dove—
'So soon? can that be Mister Leigh? so soon?'
And, as I entered, an ineffable face
Met mine upon the threshold. 'Oh, not you,
Not you!'—the dropping of the voice implied,   800
'Then, if not you, for me not any one.'
I looked her in the eyes, and held her hands,
And said, 'I am his cousin—Romney Leigh's;
And here I come to see my cousin too.'
She touched me with her face and with her voice,
This daughter of the people. Such soft flowers,
From such rough roots? the people, under there,
Can sin so, curse so, look so, smell so . . . faugh!
Yet have such daughters?

                                    Nowise beautiful
Was Marian Erle. She was not white nor brown,   810
But could look either, like a mist that changed
According to being shone on more or less:
The hair, too, ran its opulence of curls
In doubt 'twixt dark and bright, nor left you clear
To name the colour. Too much hair perhaps
(I'll name a fault here) for so small a head,
Which seemed to droop on that side and on this,
As a full-blown rose uneasy with its weight
Though not a wind should trouble it. Again,
The dimple in the cheek had better gone   820
With redder, fuller rounds; and somewhat large
The mouth was, though the milky little teeth

Dissolved it to so infantine a smile.
For soon it smiled at me; the eyes smiled too,
But 'twas as if remembering they had wept,
And knowing they should, some day, weep again.

We talked. She told me all her story out,
Which I'll re-tell with fuller utterance,
As coloured and confirmed in aftertimes
By others and herself too. Marian Erle   830
Was born upon the ledge of Malvern Hill*
To eastward, in a hut built up at night
To evade the landlord's eye, of mud and turf,
Still liable, if once he looked that way,
To being straight levelled, scattered by his foot,
Like any other anthill. Born, I say;
God sent her to His world, commissioned right,
Her human testimonials fully signed,
Not scant in soul—complete in lineaments;
But others had to swindle her a place   840
To wail in when she had come. No place for her,
By man's law! born an outlaw, was this babe;
Her first cry in our strange and strangling air,
When cast in spasms out by the shuddering womb,
Was wrong against the social code—forced wrong:
What business had the baby to cry there?

I tell her story and grow passionate.
She, Marian, did not tell it so, but used
Meek words that made no wonder of herself
For being so sad a creature. 'Mister Leigh   850
Considered truly that such things should change.
They *will*, in heaven—but meantime, on the earth,
There's none can like a nettle as a pink,
Except himself. We're nettles, some of us,
And give offence by the act of springing up;
And, if we leave the damp side of the wall,
The hoes, of course, are on us.' So she said.

Her father earned his life by random jobs
Despised by steadier workmen—keeping swine
On commons, picking hops, or hurrying on   860
The harvest at wet seasons, or, at need,
Assisting the Welsh drovers, when a drove
Of startled horses plunged into the mist
Below the mountain-road, and sowed the wind
With wandering neighings. In between the gaps
Of such irregular work, he drank and slept,
And cursed his wife because, the pence being out,
She could not buy more drink. At which she turned
(The worm), and beat her baby in revenge
For her own broken heart. There's not a crime   870
But takes its proper change out still in crime
If once rung on the counter of this world:
Let sinners look to it.
                        Yet the outcast child,
For whom the very mother's face forwent
The mother's special patience, lived and grew;
Learnt early to cry low, and walk alone,
With that pathetic vacillating roll
Of the infant body on the uncertain feet
(The earth being felt unstable ground so soon),
At which most women's arms unclose at once   880
With irrepressive instinct. Thus, at three,
This poor weaned kid would run off from the fold,
This babe would steal off from the mother's chair,
And, creeping through the golden walls of gorse,
Would find some keyhole toward the secrecy
Of Heaven's high blue, and, nestling down, peer out—
Oh, not to catch the angels at their games,
She had never heard of angels—but to gaze
She knew not why, to see she knew not what,
A-hungering outward from the barren earth   890
For something like a joy. She liked, she said,
To dazzle black her sight against the sky,
For then, it seemed, some grand blind Love came down,

And groped her out, and clasped her with a kiss;
She learnt God that way, and was beat for it
Whenever she went home—yet came again,
As surely as the trapped hare, getting free,
Returns to his form. This grand blind Love, she said,
This skyey father and mother both in one,
Instructed her and civilised her more   900
Than even Sunday school did afterward,
To which a lady sent her to learn books
And sit upon a long bench in a row
With other children. Well, she laughed sometimes
To see them laugh and laugh and maul their texts;
But ofter she was sorrowful with noise
And wondered if their mothers beat them hard
That ever they should laugh so. There was one
She loved indeed—Rose Bell, a seven years' child
So pretty and clever, who read syllables   910
When Marian was at letters; *she* would laugh
At nothing—hold your finger up, she laughed,
Then shook her curls down over eyes and mouth
To hide her make-mirth from the schoolmaster:
And Rose's pelting glee, as frank as rain
On cherry-blossoms, brightened Marian too,
To see another merry whom she loved.
She whispered once (the children side by side,
With mutual arms entwined about their necks)
'Your mother lets you laugh so?' 'Ay,' said Rose,   920
'She lets me. She was dug into the ground
Six years since, I being but a yearling wean.
Such mothers let us play and lose our time,
And never scold nor beat us! don't you wish
You had one like that?' There, Marian breaking off
Looked suddenly in my face. 'Poor Rose,' said she,
'I heard her laugh last night in Oxford Street.
I'd pour out half my blood to stop that laugh.
Poor Rose, poor Rose!' said Marian.
                                        She resumed.

It tried her, when she had learnt at Sunday school   930
What God was, what he wanted from us all,
And how in choosing sin we vexed the Christ,
To go straight home and hear her father pull
The Name down on us from the thunder-shelf
Then drink away his soul into the dark
From seeing judgment. Father, mother, home,
Were God and heaven reversed to her: the more
She knew of Right, the more she guessed their wrong;
Her price paid down for knowledge, was to know
The vileness of her kindred: through her heart,   940
Her filial and tormented heart, henceforth,
They struck their blows at virtue. Oh, 'tis hard
To learn you have a father up in heaven
By a gathering certain sense of being, on earth,
Still worse than orphaned: 'tis too heavy a grief,
The having to thank God for such a joy!

And so passed Marian's life from year to year.
Her parents took her with them when they tramped,
Dodged lanes and heaths, frequented towns and fairs,
And once went farther and saw Manchester,   950
And once the sea, that blue end of the world,
That fair scroll-finis of a wicked book—*
And twice a prison—back at intervals,
Returning to the hills. Hills draw like heaven,
And stronger sometimes, holding out their hands
To pull you from the vile flats up to them.
And though perhaps these strollers still strolled back,
As sheep do, simply that they knew the way,
They certainly felt bettered unaware
Emerging from the social smut of towns   960
To wipe their feet clean on the mountain turf.
In which long wanderings, Marian lived and learned,
Endured and learned. The people on the roads
Would stop and ask her why her eyes outgrew
Her cheeks, and if she meant to lodge the birds

In all that hair; and then they lifted her,
The miller in his cart, a mile or twain,
The butcher's boy on horseback. Often too
The pedlar stopped, and tapped her on the head
With absolute forefinger, brown and ringed,   970
And asked if peradventure she could read,
And when she answered 'ay,' would toss her down
Some stray odd volume from his heavy pack,
A Thomson's Seasons, mulcted of the Spring,*
Or half a play of Shakespeare's, torn across
(She had to guess the bottom of a page
By just the top sometimes—as difficult,
As, sitting on the moon, to guess the earth!),
Or else a sheaf of leaves (for that small Ruth's*
Small gleanings) torn out from the heart of books,   980
From Churchyard Elegies and Edens Lost,*
From Burns, and Bunyan, Selkirk, and Tom Jones—*
'Twas somewhat hard to keep the things distinct,
And oft the jangling influence jarred the child
Like looking at a sunset full of grace
Through a pothouse window while the drunken oaths
Went on behind her. But she weeded out
Her book-leaves, threw away the leaves that hurt
(First tore them small, that none should find a word),
And made a nosegay of the sweet and good   990
To fold within her breast, and pore upon
At broken moments of the noontide glare,
When leave was given her to untie her cloak
And rest upon the dusty highway's bank
From the road's dust: or oft, the journey done,
Some city friend would lead her by the hand
To hear a lecture at an institute.
And thus she had grown, this Marian Erle of ours,
To no book-learning—she was ignorant
Of authors—not in earshot of the things   1000
Out-spoken o'er the heads of common men
By men who are uncommon—but within

The cadenced hum of such, and capable
Of catching from the fringes of the wind
Some fragmentary phrases, here and there,
Of that fine music—which, being carried in
To her soul, had reproduced itself afresh
In finer motions of the lips and lids.

She said, in speaking of it, 'If a flower
Were thrown you out of heaven at intervals,   1010
You'd soon attain to a trick of looking up—
And so with her.' She counted me her years,
Till *I* felt old; and then she counted me
Her sorrowful pleasures, till I felt ashamed.
She told me she was fortunate and calm
On such and such a season, sat and sewed,
With no one to break up her crystal thoughts,
While rhymes from lovely poems span around
Their ringing circles of ecstatic tune,*
Beneath the moistened finger of the Hour.   1020
Her parents called her a strange, sickly child,
Not good for much, and given to sulk and stare,
And smile into the hedges and the clouds,
And tremble if one shook her from her fit
By any blow, or word even. Outdoor jobs
Went ill with her, and household quiet work
She was not born to. Had they kept the north,
They might have had their pennyworth out of her
Like other parents, in the factories
(Your children work for you, not you for them,   1030
Or else they better had been choked with air
The first breath drawn); but, in this tramping life,
Was nothing to be done with such a child
But tramp and tramp. And yet she knitted hose
Not ill, and was not dull at needlework;
And all the country people gave her pence
For darning stockings past their natural age,

And patching petticoats from old to new,
And other light work done for thrifty wives.

One day, said Marian—the sun shone that day—   1040
Her mother had been badly beat, and felt
The bruises sore about her wretched soul
(That must have been): she came in suddenly,
And snatching in a sort of breathless rage
Her daughter's headgear comb, let down the hair
Upon her like a sudden waterfall,
Then drew her drenched and passive by the arm
Outside the hut they lived in. When the child
Could clear her blinded face from all that stream
Of tresses . . . there, a man stood, with beast's eyes   1050
That seemed as they would swallow her alive
Complete in body and spirit, hair and all—
And burning stertorous breath that hurt her cheek,*
He breathed so near. The mother held her tight,
Saying hard between her teeth—'Why wench, why wench,
The squire speaks to you now—the squire's too good;
He means to set you up, and comfort us.
Be mannerly at least.' The child turned round
And looked up piteous in the mother's face
(Be sure that mother's deathbed will not want   1060
Another devil to damn, than such a look),
'Oh, mother!' then, with desperate glance to heaven,
'God, free me from my mother,' she shrieked out,
'These mothers are too dreadful.' And, with force
As passionate as fear, she tore her hands
Like lilies from the rocks, from hers and his,
And sprang down, bounded headlong down the steep,
Away from both—away, if possible,
As far as God—away! They yelled at her,
As famished hounds at a hare. She heard them yell;   1070
She felt her name hiss after her from the hills,
Like shot from guns. On, on. And now she had cast
The voices off with the uplands. On. Mad fear

Was running in her feet and killing the ground;
The white roads curled as if she burnt them up,
The green fields melted, wayside trees fell back
To make room for her. Then her head grew vexed;
Trees, fields, turned on her and ran after her;
She heard the quick pants of the hills behind,
Their keen air pricked her neck: she had lost her feet,   1080
Could run no more, yet somehow went as fast,
The horizon red 'twixt steeples in the east
So sucked her forward, forward, while her heart
Kept swelling, swelling, till it swelled so big
It seemed to fill her body—when it burst
And overflowed the world and swamped the light;
'And now I am dead and safe,' thought Marian Erle—
She had dropped, she had fainted.

                                            As the sense returned,
The night had passed—not life's night. She was 'ware
Of heavy tumbling motions, creaking wheels,   1090
The driver shouting to the lazy team
That swung their rankling bells against her brain,
While, through the waggon's coverture and chinks,
The cruel yellow morning pecked at her
Alive or dead upon the straw inside—
At which her soul ached back into the dark
And prayed, 'no more of that.' A waggoner
Had found her in a ditch beneath the moon,
As white as moonshine save for the oozing blood.
At first he thought her dead; but when he had wiped   1100
The mouth and heard it sigh, he raised her up,
And laid her in his waggon in the straw,
And so conveyed her to the distant town
To which his business called himself, and left
That heap of misery at the hospital.

She stirred—the place seemed new and strange as death;
The white strait bed, with others strait and white,
Like graves dug side by side at measured lengths,

And quiet people walking in and out
With wonderful low voices and soft steps   1110
And apparitional equal care for each,
Astonished her with order, silence, law.
And when a gentle hand held out a cup,
She took it, as you do at sacrament,
Half awed, half melted—not being used, indeed,
To so much love as makes the form of love
And courtesy of manners. Delicate drinks
And rare white bread, to which some dying eyes
Were turned in observation. O my God,
How sick we must be, ere we make men just!   1120
I think it frets the saints in heaven to see
How many desolate creatures on the earth
Have learnt the simple dues of fellowship
And social comfort, in a hospital,
As Marian did. She lay there, stunned, half tranced,
And wished, at intervals of growing sense,
She might be sicker yet, if sickness made
The world so marvellous kind, the air so hushed,
And all her wake-time quiet as a sleep;
For now she understood (as such things were)   1130
How sickness ended very oft in heaven
Among the unspoken raptures—yet more sick,
And surelier happy. Then she dropped her lids,
And, folding up her hands as flowers at night,
Would lose no moment of the blessed time.

She lay and seethed in fever many weeks,
But youth was strong and overcame the test;
Revolted soul and flesh were reconciled
And fetched back to the necessary day
And daylight duties. She could creep about   1140
The long bare rooms, and stare out drearily
From any narrow window on the street,
Till someone who had nursed her as a friend
Said coldly to her, as an enemy,

'She had leave to go next week, being well enough'
(While only her heart ached). 'Go next week,' thought she,
'Next week! how would it be with her next week,
Let out into that terrible street alone
Among the pushing people . . . to go . . . where?'

One day, the last before the dreaded last,   1150
Among the convalescents, like herself
Prepared to go next morning, she sat dumb,
And heard half absently the women talk—
How one was famished for her baby's cheeks,
'The little wretch would know her! a year old
And lively, like his father!'—one was keen
To get to work, and fill some clamorous mouths;
And one was tender for her dear goodman
Who had missed her sorely—and one, querulous . . .
'Would pay backbiting neighbours who had dared*   1160
To talk about her as already dead'—
And one was proud . . . 'And if her sweetheart Luke
Had left her for a ruddier face than hers
(The gossip would be seen through at a glance),
Sweet riddance of such sweethearts—let him hang!
'Twere good to have been sick for such an end.'

And while they talked, and Marian felt the worse
For having missed the worst of all their wrongs,
A visitor was ushered through the wards
And paused among the talkers. 'When he looked   1170
It was as if he spoke, and when he spoke
He sang perhaps,' said Marian; 'could she tell?
She only knew' (so much she had chronicled,
As seraphs might the making of the sun)*
'That he who came and spake, was Romney Leigh,
And then and there she saw and heard him first.'

And when it was her turn to have the face
Upon her, all those buzzing pallid lips

Being satisfied with comfort—when he changed
To Marian, saying 'And *you?* you're going, where?'—   1180
She, moveless as a worm beneath a stone
Which someone's stumbling foot has spurned aside,
Writhed suddenly, astonished with the light,
And breaking into sobs cried, 'Where I go?
None asked me till this moment. Can I say
Where *I* go—when it has not seemed worth while
To God himself, who thinks of every one,
To think of me and fix where I shall go?'

'So young,' he gently asked her, 'you have lost
Your father and your mother?'

                   'Both,' she said,   1190
'Both lost! my father was burnt up with gin
Or ever I sucked milk, and so is lost.
My mother sold me to a man last month,
And so my mother's lost, 'tis manifest.
And I, who fled from her for miles and miles,
As if I had caught sight of the fire of hell
Through some wild gap (she was my mother, sir),
It seems I shall be lost too, presently,
And so we end, all three of us.'

                        'Poor child,'
He said—with such a pity in his voice,   1200
It soothed her more than her own tears—'poor child!
'Tis simple that betrayal by mother's love
Should bring despair of God's too. Yet be taught,
He's better to us than many mothers are,
And children cannot wander beyond reach
Of the sweep of His white raiment. Touch and hold!
And if you weep still, weep where John was laid*
While Jesus loved him.'

                   'She could say the words,'
She told me, 'exactly as he uttered them
A year back, since in any doubt or dark   1210
They came out like the stars, and shone on her

With just their comfort. Common words, perhaps;
The ministers in church might say the same;
But *he*, he made the church with what he spoke—
The difference was the miracle,' said she.

Then catching up her smile to ravishment,
She added quickly, 'I repeat his words,
But not his tones: can any one repeat
The music of an organ, out of church?
And when he said "poor child," I shut my eyes   1220
To feel how tenderly his voice broke through,
As the ointment-box broke on the Holy feet*
To let out the rich medicative nard.'

She told me how he had raised and rescued her
With reverent pity, as, in touching grief,
He touched the wounds of Christ—and made her feel
More self-respecting. Hope he called belief
In God—work, worship—therefore let us pray!
And thus, to snatch her soul from atheism,
And keep it stainless from her mother's face,   1230
He sent her to a famous sempstress-house*
Far off in London, there to work and hope.

With that, they parted. She kept sight of Heaven,
But not of Romney. He had good to do
To others: through the days and through the nights
She sewed and sewed and sewed. She drooped sometimes,
And wondered, while along the tawny light
She struck the new thread into her needle's eye,
How people without mothers on the hills
Could choose the town to live in!—then she drew   1240
The stitch, and mused how Romney's face would look,
And if 'twere likely he'd remember hers
When they two had their meeting after death.

BOOK IV

THEY met still sooner. 'Twas a year from thence
That Lucy Gresham, the sick sempstress girl,
Who sewed by Marian's chair so still and quick,
And leant her head upon its back to cough
More freely, when, the mistress turning round,
The others took occasion to laugh out,
Gave up at last. Among the workers, spoke
A bold girl with black eyebrows and red lips;
'You know the news? Who's dying, do you think?
Our Lucy Gresham. I expected it   10
As little as Nell Hart's wedding. Blush not, Nell,
Thy curls be red enough without thy cheeks,
And, some day, there'll be found a man to dote
On red curls.—Lucy Gresham swooned last night,
Dropped sudden in the street while going home;
And now the baker says, who took her up
And laid her by her grandmother in bed,
He'll give her a week to die in. Pass the silk.
Let's hope he gave her a loaf too, within reach,
For otherwise they'll starve before they die,   20
That funny pair of bedfellows! Miss Bell,
I'll thank you for the scissors. The old crone
Is paralytic—that's the reason why
Our Lucy's thread went faster than her breath,
Which went too quick, we all know. Marian Erle!
Why, Marian Erle, you're not the fool to cry?
Your tears spoil Lady Waldemar's new dress,
You piece of pity!'
                        Marian rose up straight,
And, breaking through the talk and through the work,
Went outward, in the face of their surprise,   30

To Lucy's home, to nurse her back to life
Or down to death. She knew, by such an act,
All place and grace were forfeit in the house,
Whose mistress would supply the missing hand
With necessary, not inhuman haste,
And take no blame. But pity, too, had dues:
She could not leave a solitary soul
To founder in the dark, while she sat still
And lavished stitches on a lady's hem
As if no other work were paramount.   40
'Why, God,' thought Marian, 'has a missing hand
This moment; Lucy wants a drink, perhaps.
Let others miss me! never miss me, God!'

So Marian sat by Lucy's bed, content
With duty, and was strong, for recompense,
To hold the lamp of human love arm-high
To catch the death-strained eyes and comfort them,
Until the angels, on the luminous side
Of death, had got theirs ready. And she said,
If Lucy thanked her sometimes, called her kind,   50
It touched her strangely. 'Marian Erle, called kind!
What, Marian, beaten and sold, who could not die!
'Tis verily good fortune to be kind.
Ah you,' she said, 'who are born to such a grace,
Be sorry for the unlicensed class, the poor,*
Reduced to think the best good fortune means
That others, simply, should be kind to them.'

From sleep to sleep when Lucy had slid away
So gently, like the light upon a hill,
Of which none names the moment that it goes   60
Though all see when 'tis gone—a man came in
And stood beside the bed. The old idiot wretch
Screamed feebly, like a baby overlain,
'Sir, sir, you won't mistake me for the corpse?
Don't look at *me*, sir! never bury *me*!

Although I lie here I'm alive as you,
Except my legs and arms—I eat and drink
And understand (that you're the gentleman
Who fits the funerals up, Heaven speed you, sir),
And certainly I should be livelier still   70
If Lucy here . . . sir, Lucy is the corpse . . .
Had worked more properly to buy me wine;
But Lucy, sir, was always slow at work,
I shan't lose much by Lucy. Marian Erle,
Speak up and show the gentleman the corpse.'

And then a voice said, 'Marian Erle.' She rose;
It was the hour for angels—there, stood hers!
She scarcely marvelled to see Romney Leigh.
As light November snows to empty nests,
As grass to graves, as moss to mildewed stones,   80
As July suns to ruins, through the rents,
As ministering spirits to mourners, through a loss,
As Heaven itself to men, through pangs of death,
He came uncalled wherever grief had come.
'And so,' said Marian Erle, 'we met anew,'
And added softly, 'so, we shall not part.'

He was not angry that she had left the house
Wherein he placed her. Well—she had feared it might
Have vexed him. Also, when he found her set
On keeping, though the dead was out of sight,   90
That half-dead, half-live body left behind
With cankerous heart and flesh, which took your best
And cursed you for the little good it did
(Could any leave the bed-rid wretch alone,
So joyless she was thankless even to God,
Much more to you?), he did not say 'twas well,
Yet Marian thought he did not take it ill—
Since day by day he came, and every day
She felt within his utterance and his eyes

A closer, tenderer presence of the soul,
Until at last he said, 'We shall not part.'

On that same day, was Marian's work complete:
She had smoothed the empty bed, and swept the floor
Of coffin sawdust, set the chairs anew
The dead had ended gossip in, and stood
In that poor room so cold and orderly,
The door-key in her hand, prepared to go
As *they* had, howbeit not their way. He spoke.

'Dear Marian, of one clay God made us all,
And though men push and poke and paddle in't   110
(As children play at fashioning dirt-pies)
And call their fancies by the name of facts,
Assuming difference, lordship, privilege,
When all's plain dirt—they come back to it at last,
The first grave-digger proves it with a spade,
And pats all even. Need we wait for this,
You, Marian, and I, Romney?'
                                   She, at that,
Looked blindly in his face, as when one looks
Through driving autumn-rains to find the sky.
He went on speaking.
                          'Marian, I being born   120
What men call noble, and you, issued from
The noble people—though the tyrannous sword
Which pierced Christ's heart, has cleft the world in twain
'Twixt class and class, opposing rich to poor,
Shall *we* keep parted? Not so. Let us lean
And strain together rather, each to each,
Compress the red lips of this gaping wound
As far as two souls can—ay, lean and league,
I from my superabundance—from your want
You—joining in a protest 'gainst the wrong   130
On both sides.'
                     All the rest, he held her hand

In speaking, which confused the sense of much.
Her heart against his words beat out so thick,
They might as well be written on the dust
Where some poor bird, escaping from hawk's beak,
Has dropped and beats its shuddering wings—the lines
Are rubbed so—yet 'twas something like to this
—'That they two, standing at the two extremes
Of social classes, had received one seal,
Been dedicate and drawn beyond themselves   140
To mercy and ministration—he, indeed,
Through what he knew, and she, through what she felt,
He, by man's conscience, she, by woman's heart,
Relinquishing their several 'vantage posts
Of wealthy ease and honourable toil,
To work with God at love. And since God willed
That putting out his hand to touch this ark*
He found a woman's hand there, he'd accept
The sign too, hold the tender fingers fast,
And say, "My fellow-worker, be my wife!"'   150

She told the tale with simple, rustic turns—
Strong leaps of meaning in her sudden eyes
That took the gaps of any imperfect phrase
Of the unschooled speaker: I have rather writ
The thing I understood so, than the thing
I heard so. And I cannot render right
Her quick gesticulation, wild yet soft,
Self-startled from the habitual mood she used,
Half sad, half languid—like dumb creatures (now
A rustling bird, and now a wandering deer,   160
Or squirrel 'gainst the oak-gloom flashing up
His sidelong burnished head, in just her way
Of savage spontaneity) that stir
Abruptly the green silence of the woods,
And make it stranger, holier, more profound;
As Nature's general heart confessed itself
Of life, and then fell backward on repose.

I kissed the lips that ended.—'So indeed
He loves you, Marian?'

               'Loves me!' She looked up
With a child's wonder when you ask him first   170
Who made the sun—a puzzled blush, that grew,
Then broke off in a rapid radiant smile
Of sure solution. 'Loves me! he loves all—
And me, of course. He had not asked me else
To work with him for ever and be his wife.'

Her words reproved me. This perhaps was love—
To have its hand too full of gifts to give,
For putting out a hand to take a gift;
To love so much, the perfect round of love
Includes, in strict conclusion, being loved;   180
As Eden-dew went up and fell again,
Enough for watering Eden. Obviously
She had not thought about his love at all:
The cataracts of her soul had poured themselves,
And risen self-crowned in rainbow: would she ask
Who crowned her?—it sufficed that she was crowned.
With women of my class 'tis otherwise:
We haggle for the small change of our gold,
And so much love accord for so much love,
Rialto-prices. Are we therefore wrong?*   190
If marriage be a contract, look to it then,
Contracting parties should be equal, just,
But if, a simple fealty on one side,
A mere religion—right to give, is all,
And certain brides of Europe duly ask
To mount the pile as Indian widows do,*
The spices of their tender youth heaped up,
The jewels of their gracious virtues worn,
More gems, more glory—to consume entire
For a living husband: as the man's alive,   200
Not dead, the woman's duty's by so much
Advanced in England beyond Hindustan.

I sat there musing, till she touched my hand
With hers, as softly as a strange white bird
She feared to startle in touching. 'You are kind.
But are you, peradventure, vexed at heart
Because your cousin takes me for a wife?
I know I am not worthy—nay, in truth,
I'm glad on't, since, for that, he chooses me.
He likes the poor things of the world the best;   210
I would not therefore, if I could, be rich.
It pleasures him to stoop for buttercups;
I would not be a rose upon the wall
A queen might stop at, near the palace-door,
To say to a courtier, "Pluck that rose for me,
It's prettier than the rest." O Romney Leigh!
I'd rather far be trodden by his foot,
Than lie in a great queen's bosom.'
                                          Out of breath
She paused.
              'Sweet Marian, do you disavow
The roses with that face?'
                              She dropped her head   220
As if the wind had caught that flower of her
And bent it in the garden—then looked up
With grave assurance. 'Well, you think me bold!
But so we all are, when we're praying God.
And if I'm bold—yet, lady, credit me,
That, since I know myself for what I am,
Much fitter for his handmaid than his wife,
I'll prove the handmaid and the wife at once,
Serve tenderly, and love obediently,
And be a worthier mate, perhaps, than some   230
Who are wooed in silk among their learned books;
While I shall set myself to read his eyes,
Till such grow plainer to me than the French
To wisest ladies. Do you think I'll miss
A letter, in the spelling of his mind?
No more than they do when they sit and write

Their flying words with flickering wild-fowl tails,
Nor ever pause to ask how many *t*'s,
Should that be *y* or *i*, they know't so well:
I've seen them writing, when I brought a dress   240
And waited—floating out their soft white hands
On shining paper. But they're hard sometimes,
For all those hands!—we've used out many nights,
And worn the yellow daylight into shreds
Which flapped and shivered down our aching eyes
Till night appeared more tolerable, just
That pretty ladies might look beautiful,
Who said at last . . . "You're lazy in that house!
You're slow in sending home the work—I count
I've waited near an hour for't." Pardon me,   250
I do not blame them, madam, nor misprize;
They are fair and gracious; ay, but not like you,
Since none but you has Mister Leigh's own blood
Both noble and gentle—and, without it . . . well,
They are fair, I said; so fair, it scarce seems strange
That, flashing out in any looking-glass
The wonder of their glorious brows and breasts,
They're charmed so, they forget to look behind
And mark how pale we've grown, we pitiful
Remainders of the world. And so perhaps   260
If Mister Leigh had chosen a wife from these,
She might, although he's better than her best
And dearly she would know it, steal a thought
Which should be all his, an eye-glance from his face,
To plunge into the mirror opposite
In search of her own beauty's pearl; while *I* . . .
Ah, dearest lady, serge will outweigh silk
For winter-wear when bodies feel a-cold,
And I'll be a true wife to your cousin Leigh.'

Before I answered he was there himself.   270
I think he had been standing in the room
And listened probably to half her talk,

Arrested, turned to stone—as white as stone.
Will tender sayings make men look so white?
He loves her then profoundly.

                              'You are here,
Aurora? Here I meet you!'—We clasped hands.

'Even so, dear Romney. Lady Waldemar
Has sent me in haste to find a cousin of mine
Who shall be.'

                  'Lady Waldemar is good.'

'Here's one, at least, who is good,' I sighed, and touched 280
Poor Marian's happy head, as doglike she
Most passionately patient, waited on,
A-tremble for her turn of greeting words;
'I've sat a full hour with your Marian Erle,
And learnt the thing by heart—and from my heart
Am therefore competent to give you thanks
For such a cousin.'

                  'You accept at last
A gift from me, Aurora, without scorn?
At last I please you?'—How his voice was changed.

'You cannot please a woman against her will, 290
And once you vexed me. Shall we speak of that?
We'll say, then, you were noble in it all
And I not ignorant—let it pass. And now
You please me, Romney, when you please yourself;
So, please you, be fanatical in love,
And I'm well pleased. Ah, cousin! at the old hall,
Among the gallery portraits of our Leighs,
We shall not find a sweeter signory*
Than this pure forehead's.'

                          Not a word he said.
How arrogant men are!—Even philanthropists, 300
Who try to take a wife up in the way

They put down a subscription-cheque—if once
She turns and says, 'I will not tax you so,
Most charitable sir'—feel ill at ease
As though she had wronged them somehow. I suppose
We women should remember what we are,
And not throw back an obolus inscribed*
With Caesar's image, lightly. I resumed.

'It strikes me, some of those sublime Vandykes*
Were not too proud to make good saints in heaven;   310
And if so, then they're not too proud today,
To bow down (now the ruffs are off their necks)
And own this good, true, noble Marian, yours,
And mine, I'll say!—For poets (bear the word),
Half poets even, are still whole democrats—
Oh, not that we're disloyal to the high,
But loyal to the low, and cognisant
Of the less scrutable majesties. For me,
I comprehend your choice, I justify
Your right in choosing.'
                        'No, no, no,' he sighed,   320
With a sort of melancholy impatient scorn,
As some grown man who never had a child
Puts by some child who plays at being a man,
'You did not, do not, cannot comprehend
My choice, my ends, my motives, nor myself:
No matter now; we'll let it pass, you say.
I thank you for your generous cousinship
Which helps this present; I accept for her
Your favourable thoughts. We're fallen on days,
We two who are not poets, when to wed   330
Requires less mutual love than common love
For two together to bear out at once
Upon the loveless many. Work in pairs,
In galley-couplings or in marriage-rings,
The difference lies in the honour, not the work—
And such we're bound to, I and she. But love

(You poets are benighted in this age,
The hour's too late for catching even moths,
You've gnats instead), love!—love's fool-paradise
Is out of date, like Adam's. Set a swan 340
To swim the Trenton, rather than true love*
To float its fabulous plumage safely down
The cataracts of this loud transition-time—
Whose roar for ever henceforth in my ears
Must keep me deaf to music.'
                                    There, I turned
And kissed poor Marian, out of discontent.
The man had baffled, chafed me, till I flung
For refuge to the woman—as, sometimes,
Impatient for some crowded room's close smell,
You throw a window open and lean out 350
To breathe a long breath in the dewy night
And cool your angry forehead. She, at least,
Was not built up as walls are, brick by brick,
Each fancy squared, each feeling ranged by line,
The very heat of burning youth applied
To indurate form and system! excellent bricks,*
A well-built wall—which stops you on the road,
And into which you cannot see an inch
Although you beat your head against it—pshaw!

'Adieu,' I said, 'for this time, cousins both, 360
And, cousin Romney, pardon me the word,
Be happy!—oh, in some esoteric sense
Of course!—I mean no harm in wishing well.
Adieu, my Marian:—may she come to me,
Dear Romney, and be married from my house?
It is not part of your philosophy
To keep your bird upon the blackthorn?'
                                        'Ay,'
He answered, 'but it is. I take my wife
Directly from the people—and she comes,
As Austria's daughter to imperial France,* 370

Betwixt her eagles, blinking not her race,
From Margaret's Court at garret-height, to meet
And wed me at Saint James's, nor put off*
Her gown of serge for that. The things we do,
We do: we'll wear no mask, as if we blushed.'

'Dear Romney, you're the poet,' I replied,
But felt my smile too mournful for my word,
And turned and went. Ay, masks, I thought—beware
Of tragic masks we tie before the glass,
Uplifted on the cothurn half a yard*   380
Above the natural stature! we would play
Heroic parts to ourselves—and end, perhaps,
As impotently as Athenian wives*
Who shrieked in fits at the Eumenides.

His foot pursued me down the stair. 'At least
You'll suffer me to walk with you beyond
These hideous streets, these graves, where men alive
Packed close with earthworms, burr unconsciously*
About the plague that slew them; let me go.
The very women pelt their souls in mud   390
At any woman who walks here alone.
How came you here alone?—you are ignorant.'

We had a strange and melancholy walk:
The night came drizzling downward in dark rain,
And, as we walked, the colour of the time,
The act, the presence, my hand upon his arm,
His voice in my ear, and mine to my own sense,
Appeared unnatural. We talked modern books
And daily papers, Spanish marriage-schemes*
And English climate—was't so cold last year?   400
And will the wind change by tomorrow morn?
Can Guizot stand? is London full? is trade*
Competitive? has Dickens turned his hinge*
A-pinch upon the fingers of the great?

And are potatoes to grow mythical*
Like moly? will the applie die out too?*
Which way is the wind tonight? south-east? due east?
We talked on fast, while every common word
Seemed tangled with the thunder at one end,
And ready to pull down upon our heads   410
A terror out of sight. And yet to pause
Were surelier mortal: we tore greedily up
All silence, all the innocent breathing-points,
As if, like pale conspirators in haste,
We tore up papers where our signatures
Imperilled us to an ugly shame or death.

I cannot tell you why it was. 'Tis plain
We had not loved nor hated: wherefore dread
To spill gunpowder on ground safe from fire?
Perhaps we have lived too closely, to diverge   420
So absolutely: leave two clocks, they say,
Wound up to different hours, upon one shelf,
And slowly, through the interior wheels of each,
The blind mechanic motion sets itself
A-throb to feel out for the mutual time.
It was not so with us, indeed: while he
Struck midnight, I kept striking six at dawn,
While he marked judgment, I, redemption day;
And such exception to a general law
Imperious upon inert matter even,   430
Might make us, each to either, insecure,
A beckoning mystery or a troubling fear.

I mind me, when we parted at the door,
How strange his good-night sounded—like good-night
Beside a deathbed, where the morrow's sun
Is sure to come too late for more good-days:
And all that night I thought . . . ' "Good-night," said he.'

And so, a month passed. Let me set it down
At once—I have been wrong, I have been wrong.

We are wrong always when we think too much   440
Of what we think or are: albeit our thoughts
Be verily bitter as self-sacrifice,
We're no less selfish. If we sleep on rocks
Or roses, sleeping past the hour of noon
We're lazy. This I write against myself.
I had done a duty in the visit paid
To Marian, and was ready otherwise
To give the witness of my presence and name
Whenever she should marry.—Which, I thought,
Sufficed. I even had cast into the scale   450
An overweight of justice toward the match;
The Lady Waldemar had missed her tool,
Had broken it in the lock as being too straight
For a crooked purpose, while poor Marian Erle
Missed nothing in my accents or my acts:
I had not been ungenerous on the whole,
Nor yet untender; so, enough. I felt
Tired, overworked: this marriage somewhat jarred;
Or, if it did not, all the bridal noise,
The pricking of the map of life with pins,   460
In schemes of . . . 'Here we'll go,' and 'There we'll stay,'
And 'Everywhere we'll prosper in our love,'
Was scarce my business: let them order it;
Who else should care? I threw myself aside,
As one who had done her work and shuts her eyes
To rest the better.
                    I, who should have known,
Forereckoned mischief! Where we disavow
Being keeper to our brother we're his Cain.*

I might have held that poor child to my heart
A little longer! 'twould have hurt me much   470
To have hastened by its beats the marriage-day,
And kept her safe meantime from tampering hands
Or, peradventure, traps. What drew me back
From telling Romney plainly the designs

Of Lady Waldemar, as spoken out
To me . . . me? had I any right, ay, right,
With womanly compassion and reserve
To break the fall of woman's impudence?—
To stand by calmly, knowing what I knew,
And hear him call her *good*?
                     Distrust that word.   480
'There is none good save God,' said Jesus Christ.*
If He once, in the first creation-week,
Called creatures good—for ever, afterward,*
The Devil only has done it, and his heirs,
The knaves who win so, and the fools who lose;
The word's grown dangerous. In the middle age,
I think they called malignant fays and imps
Good people. A good neighbour, even in this,
Is fatal sometimes—cuts your morning up
To mincemeat of the very smallest talk,   490
Then helps to sugar her bohea at night*
With your reputation. I have known good wives,
As chaste, or nearly so, as Potiphar's;*
And good, good mothers, who would use a child
To better an intrigue; good friends, beside
(Very good), who hung succinctly round your neck
And sucked your breath, as cats are fabled to do
By sleeping infants. And we all have known
Good critics who have stamped out poets' hopes,
Good statesmen who pulled ruin on the state,   500
Good patriots who for a theory risked a cause,
Good kings who disembowelled for a tax,
Good popes who brought all good to jeopardy,
Good Christians who sat still in easy chairs
And damned the general world for standing up.—
Now may the good God pardon all good men!

How bitterly I speak—how certainly
The innocent white milk in us is turned,
By much persistent shining of the sun!—

Shake up the sweetest in us long enough   510
With men, it drops to foolish curd, too sour
To feed the most untender of Christ's lambs.

I should have thought—a woman of the world
Like her I'm meaning, centre to herself,
Who has wheeled on her own pivot half a life
In isolated self-love and self-will,
As a windmill seen at distance radiating
Its delicate white vans against the sky,*
So soft and soundless, simply beautiful,
Seen nearer—what a roar and tear it makes,   520
How it grinds and bruises!—if she loves at last,
Her love's a readjustment of self-love,
No more—a need felt of another's use
To her one advantage, as the mill wants grain,
The fire wants fuel, the very wolf wants prey,
And none of these is more unscrupulous
Than such a charming woman when she loves.
She'll not be thwarted by an obstacle
So trifling as . . . her soul is . . . much less yours!—
Is God a consideration?—she loves you,   530
Not God; she will not flinch for Him indeed:
She did not for the Marchioness of Perth,
When wanting tickets for the fancy ball.
She loves you, sir, with passion, to lunacy,
She loves you like her diamonds . . . almost.

                                                  Well,
A month passed so, and then the notice came,
On such a day the marriage at the church.
I was not backward.

                    Half Saint Giles in frieze**
Was bidden to meet Saint James in cloth of gold,
And, after contract at the altar, pass   540
To eat a marriage-feast on Hampstead Heath.
Of course the people came in uncompelled,
Lame, blind, and worse—sick, sorrowful, and worse,

The humours of the peccant social wound
All pressed out, poured down upon Pimlico,
Exasperating the unaccustomed air
With a hideous interfusion. You'd suppose
A finished generation, dead of plague,
Swept outward from their graves into the sun,
The moil of death upon them. What a sight!*   550
A holiday of miserable men
Is sadder than a burial-day of kings.

They clogged the streets, they oozed into the church
In a dark slow stream, like blood. To see that sight,
The noble ladies stood up in their pews,
Some pale for fear, a few as red for hate,
Some simply curious, some just insolent,
And some in wondering scorn—'What next? what next?'
These crushed their delicate rose-lips from the smile
That misbecame them in a holy place,   560
With broidered hems of perfumed handkerchiefs;
Those passed the salts, with confidence of eyes
And simultaneous shiver of moiré silk:*
While all the aisles, alive and black with heads,
Crawled slowly toward the altar from the street,
As bruised snakes crawl and hiss out of a hole
With shuddering involution, swaying slow
From right to left, and then from left to right,
In pants and pauses. What an ugly crest
Of faces rose upon you everywhere   570
From that crammed mass! you did not usually
See faces like them in the open day:
They hide in cellars, not to make you mad
As Romney Leigh is.—Faces!—O my God,
We call those, faces? men's and women's . . . ay,
And children's—babies, hanging like a rag
Forgotten on their mother's neck—poor mouths,
Wiped clean of mother's milk by mother's blow
Before they are taught her cursing. Faces? . . . phew,

We'll call them vices, festering to despairs,   580
Or sorrows, petrifying to vices: not
A finger-touch of God left whole on them,
All ruined, lost—the countenance worn out
As the garment, the will dissolute as the act,
The passions loose and draggling in the dirt
To trip a foot up at the first free step!
Those, faces? 'twas as if you had stirred up hell
To heave its lowest dreg-fiends uppermost
In fiery swirls of slime—such strangled fronts,
Such obdurate jaws were thrown up constantly   590
To twit you with your race, corrupt your blood,
And grind to devilish colours all your dreams
Henceforth—though, haply, you should drop asleep
By clink of silver waters, in a muse
On Raffael's mild Madonna of the Bird.*

I've waked and slept through many nights and days
Since then—but still that day will catch my breath
Like a nightmare. There are fatal days, indeed,
In which the fibrous years have taken root
So deeply, that they quiver to their tops   600
Whene'er you stir the dust of such a day.

My cousin met me with his eyes and hand,
And then, with just a word . . . that 'Marian Erle
Was coming with her bridesmaids presently,'
Made haste to place me by the altar-stair
Where he and other noble gentlemen
And high-born ladies, waited for the bride.

We waited. It was early: there was time
For greeting and the morning's compliment,
And gradually a ripple of women's talk   610
Arose and fell and tossed about a spray
Of English *s*'s, soft as a silent hush,

And, notwithstanding, quite as audible
As louder phrases thrown out by the men.
—'Yes, really, if we need to wait in church
We need to talk there.'—'She? 'tis Lady Ayr,
In blue—not purple! that's the dowager.'
—'She looks as young'—'She flirts as young, you mean.
Why if you had seen her upon Thursday night,
You'd call Miss Norris modest.'—'*You* again!   620
I waltzed with you three hours back. Up at six,
Up still at ten; scarce time to change one's shoes:
I feel as white and sulky as a ghost,
So pray don't speak to me, Lord Belcher.'—'No,
I'll look at you instead, and it's enough
While you have that face.' 'In church, my lord! fie, fie!'
—'Adair, you stayed for the Division?'—'Lost*
By one.' 'The devil it is! I'm sorry for't.
And if I had not promised Mistress Grove' . . .
'You might have kept your word to Liverpool.'*   630
—'Constituents must remember, after all,
We're mortal.'—'We remind them of it.'—'Hark,
The bride comes! here she comes, in a stream of milk!'
—'There? Dear, you are asleep still; don't you know
The five Miss Granvilles? always dressed in white
To show they're ready to be married.'—'Lower!
The aunt is at your elbow.'—'Lady Maud,
Did Lady Waldemar tell you she had seen
This girl of Leigh's?' 'No—wait! 'twas Mistress Brookes,
Who told me Lady Waldemar told her—   640
No, 'twasn't Mistress Brookes.'—'She's pretty?'—'Who?
Mistress Brookes? Lady Waldemar?'—'How hot!
Pray is't the law today we're not to breathe?
You're treading on my shawl—I thank you, sir.'
—'They say the bride's a mere child, who can't read,
But knows the things she shouldn't, with wide-awake
Great eyes. I'd go through fire to look at her.'
—'You do, I think.'—'And Lady Waldemar
(You see her; sitting close to Romney Leigh.

How beautiful she looks, a little flushed!)   650
Has taken up the girl, and methodised*
Leigh's folly. Should I have come here, you suppose,
Except she'd asked me?'—'She'd have served him more
By marrying him herself.'

      'Ah—there she comes,
The bride, at last!'

       'Indeed, no. Past eleven.
She puts off her patched petticoat today
And puts on Mayfair manners, so begins
By setting us to wait.'—'Yes, yes, this Leigh
Was always odd; it's in the blood, I think;
His father's uncle's cousin's second son   660
Was, was . . . you understand me; and for him,
He's stark—has turned quite lunatic upon
This modern question of the poor—the poor.
An excellent subject when you're moderate;
You've seen Prince Albert's model lodging-house?*
Does honour to his Royal Highness. Good!
But would he stop his carriage in Cheapside
To shake a common fellow by the fist
Whose name was . . . Shakespeare? no. We draw a line,
And if we stand not by our order, we   670
In England, we fall headlong. Here's a sight—
A hideous sight, a most indecent sight!
My wife would come, sir, or I had kept her back.
By heaven, sir, when poor Damiens' trunk and limbs*
Were torn by horses, women of the court
Stood by and stared, exactly as today
On this dismembering of society,
With pretty, troubled faces.'

       'Now, at last.
She comes now.'

     'Where? who sees? you push me, sir,
Beyond the point of what is mannerly.   680
You're standing, madam, on my second flounce

I do beseech you . . .'

              'No—it's not the bride.
Half-past eleven. How late. The bridegroom, mark,
Gets anxious and goes out.'

                       'And as I said
These Leighs! our best blood running in the rut!
It's something awful. We had pardoned him
A simple misalliance got up aside
For a pair of sky-blue eyes; the House of Lords
Has winked at such things, and we've all been young.
But here's an intermarriage reasoned out,   690
A contract (carried boldly to the light
To challenge observation, pioneer
Good acts by a great example) 'twixt the extremes
Of martyrised society—on the left
The well-born, on the right the merest mob,
To treat as equals!—'tis anarchical;
It means more than it says; 'tis damnable.
Why, sir, we can't have even our coffee good,
Unless we strain it.'

              'Here, Miss Leigh!'

                            'Lord Howe,
You're Romney's friend. What's all this waiting for?'   700

'I cannot tell. The bride has lost her head
(And way, perhaps!) to prove her sympathy
With the bridegroom.'

                 'What—you also, disapprove!'

'Oh, *I* approve of nothing in the world,'
He answered, 'not of you, still less of me,
Nor even of Romney, though he's worth us both.
We're all gone wrong. The tune in us is lost;
And whistling down back alleys to the moon
Will never catch it.'

              Let me draw Lord Howe.
A born aristocrat, bred radical,   710

And educated socialist, who still
Goes floating, on traditions of his kind,
Across the theoretic flood from France,
Though, like a drenched Noah on a rotten deck,
Scarce safer for his place there. He, at least,
Will never land on Ararat, he knows,
To recommence the world on the new plan:
Indeed, he thinks, said world had better end,
He sympathises rather with the fish
Outside, than with the drowned paired beasts within   720
Who cannot couple again or multiply—
And that's the sort of Noah he is, Lord Howe.
He never could be anything complete,
Except a loyal, upright gentleman,
A liberal landlord, graceful diner-out,
And entertainer more than hospitable,
Whom authors dine with and forget the hock.
Whatever he believes, and it is much,
But nowise certain, now here and now there,
He still has sympathies beyond his creed   730
Diverting him from action. In the House,
No party counts upon him, while for all
His speeches have a noticeable weight.
Men like his books too (he has written books),
Which, safe to lie beside a bishop's chair,
At times outreach themselves with jets of fire
At which the foremost of the progressists
May warm audacious hands in passing by.
Of stature over-tall, lounging for ease;
Light hair, that seems to carry a wind in it,   740
And eyes that, when they look on you, will lean
Their whole weight, half in indolence and half
In wishing you unmitigated good,
Until you know not if to flinch from him
Or thank him.—'Tis Lord Howe.

                            'We're all gone wrong,'
Said he, 'and Romney, that dear friend of ours,

Is nowise right. There's one true thing on earth,
That's love! he takes it up, and dresses it,
And acts a play with it, as Hamlet did,*
To show what cruel uncles we have been,   750
And how we should be uneasy in our minds
While he, Prince Hamlet, weds a pretty maid
(Who keeps us too long waiting, we'll confess)
By symbol, to instruct us formally
To fill the ditches up 'twixt class and class,
And live together in phalansteries.
What then?—he's mad, our Hamlet! clap his play,
And bind him.'

             'Ah Lord Howe, this spectacle
Pulls stronger at us than the Dane's. See there!
The crammed aisles heave and strain and steam with life. 760
Dear Heaven, what life!'

             'Why, yes—a poet sees;
Which makes him different from a common man.
I, too, see somewhat, though I cannot sing;
I should have been a poet, only that
My mother took fright at the ugly world,
And bore me tongue-tied. If you'll grant me now
That Romney gives us a fine actor-piece
To make us merry on his marriage-morn,
The fable's worse than Hamlet's I'll concede.
The terrible people, old and poor and blind,   770
Their eyes eat out with plague and poverty
From seeing beautiful and cheerful sights,
We'll liken to a brutalised King Lear,*
Led out—by no means to clear scores with wrongs—
His wrongs are so far back, he has forgot
(All's past like youth); but just to witness here
A simple contract—he, upon his side,
And Regan with her sister Goneril
And all the dappled courtiers and court-fools
On their side. Not that any of these would say   780
They're sorry, neither. What is done, is done,

And violence is now turned privilege,
As cream turns cheese, if buried long enough.
What could such lovely ladies have to do
With the old man there, in those ill-odorous rags,
Except to keep the wind-side of him? Lear
Is flat and quiet, as a decent grave;
He does not curse his daughters in the least:
Be these his daughters? Lear is thinking of
His porridge chiefly . . . is it getting cold   790
At Hampstead? will the ale be served in pots?
Poor Lear, poor daughters! Bravo, Romney's play!'

A murmur and a movement drew around,
A naked whisper touched us. Something wrong.
What's wrong? The black crowd, as an overstrained
Cord, quivered in vibration, and I saw . . .
Was that *his* face I saw? . . . his . . . Romney Leigh's . . .
Which tossed a sudden horror like a sponge
Into all eyes—while himself stood white upon
The topmost altar-stair and tried to speak,   800
And failed, and lifted higher above his head
A letter . . . as a man who drowns and gasps.

'My brothers, bear with me! I am very weak.
I meant but only good. Perhaps I meant
Too proudly, and God snatched the circumstance
And changed it therefore. There's no marriage—none.
She leaves me—she departs—she disappears,
I lose her. Yet I never forced her "ay,"
To have her "no" so cast into my teeth
In manner of an accusation, thus.   810
My friends, you are dismissed. Go, eat and drink
According to the programme—and farewell!'

He ended. There was silence in the church.
We heard a baby sucking in its sleep
At the farthest end of the aisle. Then spoke a man,

'Now, look to it, coves, that all the beef and drink
Be not filched from us like the other fun,
For beer's spilt easier than a woman's lost!
This gentry is not honest with the poor;
They bring us up, to trick us.'—'Go it, Jim,'   820
A woman screamed back—'I'm a tender soul,
I never banged a child at two years old
And drew blood from him, but I sobbed for it
Next moment—and I've had a plague of seven.
I'm tender; I've no stomach even for beef,
Until I know about the girl that's lost,
That's killed, mayhap. I did misdoubt, at first,
The fine lord meant no good by her or us.
He, maybe, got the upper hand of her
By holding up a wedding-ring, and then . . .   830
A choking finger on her throat last night,
And just a clever tale to keep us still,
As she is, poor lost innocent. "Disappear!"
Who ever disappears except a ghost?
And who believes a story of a ghost?
I ask you—would a girl go off, instead
Of staying to be married? a fine tale!
A wicked man, I say, a wicked man!
For my part I would rather starve on gin
Than make my dinner on his beef and beer.'—   840
At which a cry rose up—'We'll have our rights.
We'll have the girl, the girl! Your ladies there
Are married safely and smoothly every day,
And *she* shall not drop through into a trap
Because she's poor and of the people: shame!
We'll have no tricks played off by gentlefolks;
We'll see her righted.'
                    Through the rage and roar
I heard the broken words which Romney flung
Among the turbulent masses, from the ground
He held still with his masterful pale face—   850
As huntsmen throw the ration to the pack,

Who, falling on it headlong, dog on dog
In heaps of fury, rend it, swallow it up
With yelling hound-jaws—his indignant words,
His suppliant words, his most pathetic words,
Whereof I caught the meaning here and there
By his gesture . . . torn in morsels, yelled across,
And so devoured. From end to end, the church
Rocked round us like the sea in storm, and then
Broke up like the earth in earthquake. Men cried out   860
'Police'—and women stood and shrieked for God,
Or dropped and swooned; or, like a herd of deer
(For whom the black woods suddenly grow alive,
Unleashing their wild shadows down the wind
To hunt the creatures into corners, back
And forward), madly fled, or blindly fell,
Trod screeching underneath the feet of those
Who fled and screeched.
              The last sight left to me
Was Romney's terrible calm face above
The tumult!—the last sound was 'Pull him down!   870
Strike—kill him!' Stretching my unreasoning arms,
As men in dreams, who vainly interpose
'Twixt gods and their undoing, with a cry
I struggled to precipitate myself
Head-foremost to the rescue of my soul
In that white face . . . till someone caught me back,
And so the world went out—I felt no more.

What followed was told after by Lord Howe,
Who bore me senseless from the strangling crowd
In church and street, and then returned alone   880
To see the tumult quelled. The men of law
Had fallen as thunder on a roaring fire,
And made all silent—while the people's smoke
Passed eddying slowly from the emptied aisles.

Here's Marian's letter, which a ragged child
Brought running, just as Romney at the porch
Looked out expectant of the bride. He sent
The letter to me by his friend Lord Howe
Some two hours after, folded in a sheet
On which his well-known hand had left a word.   890
Here's Marian's letter.

                    'Noble friend, dear saint,
Be patient with me. Never think me vile,
Who might tomorrow morning be your wife
But that I loved you more than such a name.
Farewell, my Romney. Let me write it once—
My Romney.

              ''Tis so pretty a coupled word,
I have no heart to pluck it with a blot.
We say "my God" sometimes, upon our knees,
Who is not therefore vexed: so bear with it . . .
And me. I know I'm foolish, weak, and vain;   900
Yet most of all I'm angry with myself
For losing your last footstep on the stair
That last time of your coming—yesterday!
The very first time I lost step of yours
(Its sweetness comes the next to what you speak),
But yesterday sobs took me by the throat
And cut me off from music.

                            'Mister Leigh,
You'll set me down as wrong in many things.
You've praised me, sir, for truth—and now you'll learn
I had not courage to be rightly true.   910
I once began to tell you how she came,
The woman . . . and you stared upon the floor
In one of your fixed thoughts . . . which put me out
For that day. After, someone spoke of me,
So wisely, and of you, so tenderly,
Persuading me to silence for your sake . . .
Well, well! it seems this moment I was wrong
In keeping back from telling you the truth:

There might be truth betwixt us two, at least,
If nothing else. And yet 'twas dangerous.   920
Suppose a real angel came from heaven
To live with men and women! he'd go mad,
If no considerate hand should tie a blind
Across his piercing eyes. 'Tis thus with you:
You see us too much in your heavenly light;
I always thought so, angel—and indeed
There's danger that you beat yourself to death
Against the edges of this alien world,
In some divine and fluttering pity.

                                   'Yes,
It would be dreadful for a friend of yours,   930
To see all England thrust you out of doors
And mock you from the windows. You might say,
Or think (that's worse), "There's someone in the house
I miss and love still." Dreadful!

                              'Very kind,
I pray you mark, was Lady Waldemar.
She came to see me nine times, rather ten—
So beautiful, she hurts one like the day
Let suddenly on sick eyes.

                         'Most kind of all,
Your cousin!—ah, most like you! Ere you came
She kissed me mouth to mouth: I felt her soul   940
Dip through her serious lips in holy fire.
God help me, but it made me arrogant;
I almost told her that you would not lose
By taking me to wife: though ever since
I've pondered much a certain thing she asked . . .
"He loves you, Marian?" . . . in a sort of mild
Derisive sadness . . . as a mother asks
Her babe, "You'll touch that star, you think?"

                                       'Farewell!
I know I never touched it.

                         'This is worst:
Babes grow and lose the hope of things above;   950

A silver threepence sets them leaping high—
But no more stars! mark that.
                'I've writ all night
Yet told you nothing. God, if I could die,
And let this letter break off innocent
Just here! But no—for your sake . . .
                  'Here's the last:
I never could be happy as your wife,
I never could be harmless as your friend,
I never will look more into your face
Till God says, "Look!" I charge you, seek me not,
Nor vex yourself with lamentable thoughts   960
That peradventure I have come to grief;
Be sure I'm well, I'm merry, I'm at ease,
But such a long way, long way, long way off,
I think you'll find me sooner in my grave,
And that's my choice, observe. For what remains,
An overgenerous friend will care for me
And keep me happy . . . happier . . .
                  'There's a blot!
This ink runs thick . . . we light girls lightly weep . . .
And keep me happier . . . was the thing to say,
Than as your wife I could be.—O my star,   970
My saint, my soul! for surely you're my soul!
Through whom God touched me! I am not so lost
I cannot thank you for the good you did,
The tears you stopped, which fell down bitterly,
Like these—the times you made me weep for joy
At hoping I should learn to write your notes
And save the tiring of your eyes, at night;
And most for that sweet thrice you kissed my lips
Saying "Dear Marian."
              ''Twould be hard to read,
This letter, for a reader half as learn'd;   980
But you'll be sure to master it in spite
Of ups and downs. My hand shakes, I am blind;
I'm poor at writing at the best—and yet

I tried to <u>make my *g*'s</u> the way you showed.
Farewell. Christ love you.—Say "poor Marian" now.'

Poor Marian!—wanton Marian!—was it so,
Or so? For days, her touching, <u>foolish lines</u>
We mused on with conjectural fantasy,
As if some riddle of a summer-cloud
On which one tries unlike similitudes   990
Of now a spotted Hydra-skin cast off,*
And now a screen of carven ivory
That shuts the heavens' conventual secrets up
From mortals overbold. We sought the sense:
She loved him so perhaps (such words mean love),
That, worked on by some shrewd perfidious tongue
(And then I thought of Lady Waldemar),
She left him, not to hurt him; or perhaps
She loved one in her class—or did not love,
But mused upon her wild bad tramping life   1000
Until the free blood fluttered at her heart,
And black bread eaten by the roadside hedge
Seemed sweeter than being put to Romney's school
Of philanthropical self-sacrifice
Irrevocably.—Girls are girls, beside,
Thought I, and like a wedding by one rule.
You seldom catch these birds except with chaff:
They feel it almost an immoral thing
To go out and be married in broad day,
Unless some winning special flattery should   1010
Excuse them to themselves for't . . . 'No one parts
Her hair with such a silver line as you,
One moonbeam from the forehead to the crown!'
Or else . . . 'You bite your lip in such a way,
It spoils me for the smiling of the rest,'
And so on. Then a worthless gaud or two
To keep for love—a ribbon for the neck,
Or some glass pin—they have their weight with girls.

And Romney sought her many days and weeks:
He sifted all the refuse of the town, 1020
Explored the trains, inquired among the ships,
And felt the country through from end to end;
No Marian!—Though I hinted what I knew—
A friend of his had reasons of her own
For throwing back the match—he would not hear:
The lady had been ailing ever since,
The shock had harmed her. Something in his tone
Repressed me; something in me shamed my doubt
To a sigh repressed too. He went on to say
That, putting questions where his Marian lodged, 1030
He found she had received for visitors,
Besides himself and Lady Waldemar
And, that once, me—a dubious woman dressed
Beyond us both: the rings upon her hands
Had dazed the children when she threw them pence;
'She wore her bonnet as the queen might hers,
To show the crown,' they said—'a scarlet crown
Of roses that had never been in bud.'

When Romney told me that—for now and then
He came to tell me how the search advanced, 1040
His voice dropped: I bent forward for the rest:
The woman had been with her, it appeared,
At first from week to week, then day by day,
And last, 'twas sure . . .

                     I looked upon the ground
To escape the anguish of his eyes, and asked
As low as when you speak to mourners new
Of those they cannot bear yet to call dead,
'If Marian had as much as named to him
A certain Rose, an early friend of hers,
A ruined creature.'

                     'Never.'—Starting up 1050
He strode from side to side about the room,
Most like some prisoned lion sprung awake,

A.L. - 9

Who has felt the desert sting him through his dreams.
'What was I to her, that she should tell me aught?
A friend! was *I* a friend? I see all clear.
Such devils would pull angels out of heaven,
Provided they could reach them; 'tis their pride;
And that's the odds 'twixt soul and body plague!
The veriest slave who drops in Cairo's street,
Cries, "Stand off from me," to the passengers;   1060
While these blotched souls are eager to infect,
And blow their bad breath in a sister's face
As if they got some ease by it.'
                                        I broke through.
'Some natures catch no plagues. I've read of babes
Found whole and sleeping by the spotted breast
Of one a full day dead. I hold it true,*
As I'm a woman and know womanhood,
That Marian Erle, however lured from place,
Deceived in way, keeps pure in aim and heart
As snow that's drifted from the garden-bank   1070
To the open road.'
                              'Twas hard to hear him laugh.
'The figure's happy. Well—a dozen carts
And trampers will secure you presently
A fine white snow-drift. Leave it there, your snow!
'Twill pass for soot ere sunset. Pure in aim?
She's pure in aim, I grant you—like myself,
Who thought to take the world upon my back
To carry it o'er a chasm of social ill,
And end by letting slip through impotence
A single soul, a child's weight in a soul,   1080
Straight down the pit of hell! yes, I and she
Have reason to be proud of our pure aims.'
Then softly, as the last repenting drops
Of a thunder-shower, he added, 'The poor child,
Poor Marian! 'twas a luckless day for her,
When first she chanced on my philanthropy.'

He drew a chair beside me, and sat down;
And I, instinctively, as women use
Before a sweet friend's grief—when, in his ear,
They hum the tune of comfort though themselves   1090
Most ignorant of the special words of such,
And quiet so and fortify his brain
And give it time and strength for feeling out
To reach the availing sense beyond that sound—
Went murmuring to him what, if written here,
Would seem not much, yet fetched him better help
Than peradventure if it had been more.

I've known the pregnant thinkers of our time,
And stood by breathless, hanging on their lips,
When some chromatic sequence of fine thought*   1100
In learned modulation phrased itself
To an unconjectured harmony of truth:
And yet I've been more moved, more raised, I say,
By a simple word . . . a broken easy thing
A three-years infant might at need repeat,
A look, a sigh, a touch upon the palm,
Which meant less than 'I love you,' than by all
The full-voiced rhetoric of those master-mouths.

'Ah dear Aurora,' he began at last,
His pale lips fumbling for a sort of smile,   1110
'Your printer's devils have not spoilt your heart:
That's well. And who knows but, long years ago
When you and I talked, you were somewhat right
In being so peevish with me? You, at least,
Have ruined no one through your dreams. Instead,
You've helped the facile youth to live youth's day
With innocent distraction, still perhaps
Suggestive of things better than your rhymes.
The little shepherd-maiden, eight years old,
I've seen upon the mountains of Vaucluse,*   1120
Asleep i' the sun, her head upon her knees,
The flocks all scattered—is more laudable

Than any sheep-dog trained imperfectly,
Who bites the kids through too much zeal.'

                                   'I look
As if I had slept, then?'
                        He was touched at once
By something in my face. Indeed 'twas sure
That he and I—despite a year or two
Of younger life on my side, and on his
The heaping of the years' work on the days,
The three-hour speeches from the member's seat,   1130
The hot committees in and out of doors,
The pamphlets, 'Arguments,' 'Collective Views,'
Tossed out as straw before sick houses, just*
To show one's sick and so be trod to dirt
And no more use—through this world's underground,
The burrowing, groping effort, whence the arm
And heart come torn—'twas sure that he and I*
Were, after all, unequally fatigued;
That he, in his developed manhood, stood
A little sunburnt by the glare of life,   1140
While I . . . it seemed no sun had shone on me,
So many seasons I had missed my Springs.
My cheeks had pined and perished from their orbs,
And all the youth-blood in them had grown white
As dew on autumn cyclamens: alone
My eyes and forehead answered for my face.

He said, 'Aurora, you are changed—are ill!'

'Not so, my cousin—only not asleep,'
I answered, smiling gently. 'Let it be.
You scarcely found the poet of Vaucluse*   1150
As drowsy as the shepherds. What is art
But life upon the larger scale, the higher,
When, graduating up in a spiral line
Of still expanding and ascending gyres,
It pushes toward the intense significance

Of all things, hungry for the Infinite?
Art's life—and where we live, we suffer and toil.'

He seemed to sift me with his painful eyes.
'You take it gravely, cousin; you refuse
Your dreamland's right of common and green rest.   1160
You break the mythic turf where danced the nymphs,
With crooked ploughs of actual life—let in
The axes to the legendary woods,
To pay the poll-tax. You are fallen indeed*
On evil days, you poets, if yourselves
Can praise that art of yours no otherwise;
And, if you cannot . . . better take a trade
And be of use: 'twere cheaper for your youth.'

'Of use!' I softly echoed, 'there's the point
We sweep about for ever in argument,   1170
Like swallows which the exasperate, dying year
Sets spinning in black circles, round and round,
Preparing for far flights o'er unknown seas.
And we, where tend we?'
                                    'Where?' he said, and sighed.
'The whole creation, from the hour we are born,
Perplexes us with questions. Not a stone*
But cries behind us, every weary step,
"Where, where?" I leave stones to reply to stones.
Enough for me and for my fleshly heart
To hearken the invocations of my kind,   1180
When men catch hold upon my shuddering nerves
And shriek, "What help? what hope? what bread i' the
      house,
What fire i' the frost?" There must be some response,
Though mine fail utterly. This social Sphinx
Who sits between the sepulchres and stews,*
Makes mock and mow against the crystal heavens,*
And bullies God—exacts a word at least
From each man standing on the side of God,

However paying a sphinx-price for it.
We pay it also if we hold our peace,   1190
In pangs and pity. Let me speak and die.
Alas, you'll say I speak and kill instead.'

I pressed in there. 'The best men, doing their best,
Know peradventure least of what they do:
Men usefullest i' the world are simply used;
The nail that holds the wood must pierce it first,
And He alone who wields the hammer sees
The work advanced by the earliest blow. Take heart.'

'Ah, if I could have taken yours!' he said,
'But that's past now.' Then rising—'I will take   1200
At least your kindness and encouragement.
I thank you. Dear, be happy. Sing your songs,
If that's your way! but sometimes slumber too,
Nor tire too much with following, out of breath,
The rhymes upon your mountains of Delight.
Reflect, if Art be in truth the higher life,
You need the lower life to stand upon
In order to reach up unto that higher;
And none can stand a-tiptoe in the place
He cannot stand in with two stable feet.   1210
Remember then!—for Art's sake, hold your life.'

We parted so. I held him in respect.
I comprehended what he was in heart
And sacrificial greatness. Ay, but he
Supposed me a thing too small to deign to know:
He blew me, plainly, from the crucible
As some intruding, interrupting fly,
Not worth the pains of his analysis
Absorbed on nobler subjects. Hurt a fly!
He would not for the world: he's pitiful   1220
To flies even. 'Sing,' says he, 'and tease me still,
If that's your way, poor insect.' That's your way!

BOOK V

AURORA LEIGH, be humble. Shall I hope
To speak my poems in mysterious tune
With man and nature?—with the lava-lymph*
That trickles from successive galaxies
Still drop by drop a-down the finger of God
In still new worlds?—with summer-days in this
That scarce dare breathe they are so beautiful?
With Spring's delicious trouble in the ground,
Tormented by the quickened blood of roots,
And softly pricked by golden crocus-sheaves   10
In token of the harvest-time of flowers?
With winters and with autumns—and beyond
With the human heart's large seasons, when it hopes
And fears, joys, grieves, and loves?—with all that strain
Of sexual passion, which devours the flesh
In a sacrament of souls? with mother's breasts
Which, round the new-made creatures hanging there,
Throb luminous and harmonious like pure spheres?—
With multitudinous life, and finally
With the great escapings of ecstatic souls,   20
Who, in a rush of too long prisoned flame,
Their radiant faces upward, burn away
This dark of the body, issuing on a world
Beyond our mortal?—can I speak my verse
So plainly in tune to these things and the rest,
That men shall feel it catch them on the quick,
As having the same warrant over them
To hold and move them if they will or no,
Alike imperious as the primal rhythm
Of that theurgic nature?—I must fail,*   30
Who fail at the beginning to hold and move

One man—and he my cousin, and he my friend,
And he born tender, made intelligent,
Inclined to ponder the precipitous sides
Of difficult questions; yet, obtuse to *me*,
Of *me*, incurious! likes me very well,
And wishes me a paradise of good,
Good looks, good means, and good digestion—ay,
But otherwise evades me, puts me off
With kindness, with a tolerant gentleness—   40
Too light a book for a grave man's reading! Go,
Aurora Leigh: be humble.

                    There it is,
We women are too apt to look to one,
Which proves a certain impotence in art.
We strain our natures at doing something great,
Far less because it's something great to do,
Than haply that we, so, commend ourselves
As being not small, and more appreciable
To some one friend. We must have mediators
Betwixt our highest conscience and the judge;   50
Some sweet saint's blood must quicken in our palms,
Or all the life in heaven seems slow and cold:
Good only being perceived as the end of good,
And God alone pleased—that's too poor, we think,
And not enough for us by any means.
Ay—Romney, I remember, told me once
We miss the abstract when we comprehend.
We miss it most when we aspire—and fail.

Yet, so, I will not.—This vile woman's way
Of trailing garments, shall not trip me up: 60
I'll have no traffic with the personal thought
In art's pure temple. Must I work in vain,
Without the approbation of a man?
It cannot be; it shall not. Fame itself,
That approbation of the general race,
Presents a poor end (though the arrow speed,

Shot straight with vigorous finger to the white),
And the highest fame was never reached except
By what was aimed above it. Art for art,
And good for God Himself, the essential Good!　　70
We'll keep our aims sublime, our eyes erect,
Although our woman-hands should shake and fail;
And if we fail . . . But must we?—

　　　　　　　　　　　　　Shall I fail?
The Greeks said grandly in their tragic phrase,
'Let no one be called happy till his death.'*
To which I add—Let no one till his death
Be called unhappy. Measure not the work
Until the day's out and the labour done,
Then bring your gauges. If the day's work's scant,
Why, call it scant; affect no compromise;　　80
And, in that we have nobly striven at least,
Deal with us nobly, women though we be,
And honour us with truth if not with praise.*

My ballads prospered; but the ballad's race
Is rapid for a poet who bears weights
Of thought and golden image. He can stand
Like Atlas, in the sonnet—and support*
His own heavens pregnant with dynastic stars;
But then he must stand still, nor take a step.

In that descriptive poem called 'The Hills,'　　90
The prospects were too far and indistinct.
'Tis true my critics said, 'A fine view, that!'
The public scarcely cared to climb my book
For even the finest, and the public's right;
A tree's mere firewood, unless humanised—
Which well the Greeks knew when they stirred its bark
With close-pressed bosoms of subsiding nymphs,
And made the forest-rivers garrulous
With babble of gods. For us, we are called to mark
A still more intimate humanity　　100

In this inferior nature, or ourselves
Must fall like dead leaves trodden underfoot
By veritable artists. Earth (shut up
By Adam, like a fakir in a box*
Left too long buried) remained stiff and dry,
A mere dumb corpse, till Christ the Lord came down,
Unlocked the doors, forced open the blank eyes,
And used His kingly chrism to straighten out
The leathery tongue turned back into the throat;
Since when, she lives, remembers, palpitates   110
In every limb, aspires in every breath,
Embraces infinite relations. Now
We want no half-gods, Panomphaean Joves,*
Fauns, Naiads, Tritons, Oreads and the rest,
To take possession of a senseless world
To unnatural vampire-uses. See the earth,*
The body of our body, the green earth,
Indubitably human like this flesh
And these articulated veins through which
Our heart drives blood. There's not a flower of spring   120
That dies ere June, but vaunts itself allied*
By issue and symbol, by significance
And correspondence, to that spirit-world
Outside the limits of our space and time,
Whereto we are bound. Let poets give it voice
With human meanings—else they miss the thought,
And henceforth step down lower, stand confessed
Instructed poorly for interpreters,
Thrown out by an easy cowslip in the text.*

Even so my pastoral failed: it was a book   130
Of surface-pictures—pretty, cold, and false
With literal transcript—the worse done, I think,
For being not ill-done: let me set my mark
Against such doings, and do otherwise.
This strikes me.—If the public whom we know
Could catch me at such admissions, I should pass

For being right modest. Yet how proud we are,
In daring to look down upon ourselves!

The critics say that epics have died out
With Agamemnon and the goat-nursed gods;   140
I'll not believe it. I could never deem
As Payne Knight did (the mythic mountaineer*
Who travelled higher than he was born to live,
And showed sometimes the goitre in his throat
Discoursing of an image seen through fog),
That Homer's heroes measured twelve feet high.*
They were but men—his Helen's hair turned gray
Like any plain Miss Smith's who wears a front;*
And Hector's infant whimpered at a plume*
As yours last Friday at a turkey-cock.   150
All actual heroes are essential men,*
And all men possible heroes: every age,*
Heroic in proportions, double-faced,
Looks backward and before, expects a morn
And claims an epos.*
                            Ay, but every age
Appears to souls who live in't (ask Carlyle)*
Most unheroic. Ours, for instance, ours:
The thinkers scout it, and the poets abound*
Who scorn to touch it with a finger-tip:
A pewter age—mixed metal, silver-washed;   160
An age of scum, spooned off the richer past,
An age of patches for old gaberdines,
An age of mere transition, meaning nought
Except that what succeeds must shame it quite
If God please. That's wrong thinking, to my mind,
And wrong thoughts make poor poems.
                                    Every age,
Through being beheld too close, is ill-discerned
By those who have not lived past it. We'll suppose
Mount Athos carved, as Alexander schemed,*
To some colossal statue of a man.   170

The peasants, gathering brushwood in his ear,
Had guessed as little as the browsing goats
Of form or feature of humanity
Up there—in fact, had travelled five miles off
Or ere the giant image broke on them,
Full human profile, nose and chin distinct,
Mouth, muttering rhythms of silence up the sky
And fed at evening with the blood of suns;
Grand torso—hand, that flung perpetually
The largesse of a silver river down   180
To all the country pastures. 'Tis even thus
With times we live in—evermore too great
To be apprehended near.
                          But poets should
Exert a double vision; should have eyes
To see near things as comprehensively
As if afar they took their point of sight,
And distant things as intimately deep
As if they touched them. Let us strive for this.
I do distrust the poet who discerns
No character or glory in his times,   190
And trundles back his soul five hundred years,
Past moat and drawbridge, into a castle-court,
To sing—oh, not of lizard or of toad
Alive i' the ditch there—'twere excusable,
But of some black chief, half knight, half sheep-lifter,
Some beauteous dame, half chattel and half queen,
As dead as must be, for the greater part,
The poems made on their chivalric bones;
And that's no wonder: death inherits death.

Nay, if there's room for poets in this world   200
A little overgrown (I think there is),
Their sole work is to represent the age,
Their age, not Charlemagne's—this live, throbbing age,
That brawls, cheats, maddens, calculates, aspires,
And spends more passion, more heroic heat,

Betwixt the mirrors of its drawing-rooms,
Than Roland with his knights at Roncesvalles.*
To flinch from modern varnish, coat or flounce,
Cry out for togas and the picturesque,
Is fatal—foolish too. King Arthur's self   210
Was commonplace to Lady Guinevere;
And Camelot to minstrels seemed as flat
As Fleet Street to our poets.*
                                    Never flinch,
But still, unscrupulously epic, catch
Upon the burning lava of a song
The full-veined, heaving, double-breasted Age:*
That, when the next shall come, the men of that
May touch the impress with reverent hand, and say
'Behold—behold the paps we all have sucked!
This bosom seems to beat still, or at least   220
It sets ours beating: this is living art,
Which thus presents and thus records true life.'

What form is best for poems? Let me think
Of forms less, and the external. Trust the spirit,
As sovran nature does, to make the form;
For otherwise we only imprison spirit
And not embody. Inward evermore
To outward—so in life, and so in art
Which still is life.
                        Five acts to make a play.
And why not fifteen? why not ten? or seven?   230
What matter for the number of the leaves,
Supposing the tree lives and grows? exact
The literal unities of time and place,
When 'tis the essence of passion to ignore
Both time and place? Absurd. Keep up the fire,
And leave the generous flames to shape themselves.

'Tis true the stage requires obsequiousness
To this or that convention; 'exit' here
And 'enter' there; the points for clapping, fixed,

Like Jacob's white-peeled rods before the rams,*   240
And all the close-curled imagery clipped
In manner of their fleece at shearing-time.
Forget to prick the galleries to the heart
Precisely at the fourth act—culminate
Our five pyramidal acts with one act more—
We're lost so: Shakespeare's ghost could scarcely plead*
Against our just damnation. Stand aside;
We'll muse for comfort that, last century,
On this same tragic stage on which we have failed,
A wigless Hamlet would have failed the same.*   250

And whosoever writes good poetry,
Looks just to art. He does not write for you
Or me—for London or for Edinburgh;
He will not suffer the best critic known
To step into his sunshine of free thought
And self-absorbed conception and exact
An inch-long swerving of the holy lines.
If virtue done for popularity
Defiles like vice, can art, for praise or hire,
Still keep its splendour and remain pure art?   260
Eschew such serfdom. What the poet writes,
He writes: mankind accepts it if it suits,
And that's success: if not, the poem's passed
From hand to hand, and yet from hand to hand,
Until the unborn snatch it, crying out
In pity on their fathers being so dull,
And that's success too.
                              I will write no plays;
Because the drama, less sublime in this,
Makes lower appeals, submits more menially,
Adopts the standard of the public taste   270
To chalk its height on, wears a dog-chain round
Its regal neck, and learns to carry and fetch
The fashions of the day to please the day,
Fawns close on pit and boxes, who clap hands

Commending chiefly its docility
And humour in stage-tricks—or else indeed
Gets hissed at, howled at, stamped at like a dog,
Or worse, we'll say. For dogs, unjustly kicked,
Yell, bite at need; but if your dramatist
(Being wronged by some five hundred nobodies   280
Because their grosser brains most naturally
Misjudge the fineness of his subtle wit)
Shows teeth an almond's breadth, protests the length
Of a modest phrase—'My gentle countrymen,
There's something in it haply of your fault'—
Why then, besides five hundred nobodies,
He'll have five thousand and five thousand more
Against him—the whole public—all the hoofs
Of King Saul's father's asses, in full drove,*
And obviously deserve it. He appealed   290
To these—and why say more if they condemn,
Than if they praise him?—Weep, my Aeschylus,
But low and far, upon Sicilian shores!*
For since 'twas Athens (so I read the myth)
Who gave commission to that fatal weight
The tortoise, cold and hard, to drop on thee
And crush thee—better cover thy bald head;
She'll hear the softest hum of Hyblan bee*
Before thy loudest protestation!
                          Then
The risk's still worse upon the modern stage: 300
I could not, for so little, accept success,
Nor would I risk so much, in ease and calm,
For manifester gains: let those who prize,
Pursue them: I stand off. And yet, forbid,
That any irreverent fancy or conceit
Should litter in the Drama's throne-room where
The rulers of our art, in whose full veins
Dynastic glories mingle, sit in strength
And do their kingly work—conceive, command,
And, from the imagination's crucial heat,*   310

Catch up their men and women all a-flame
For action, all alive and forced to prove
Their life by living out heart, brain, and nerve,
Until mankind makes witness, 'These be men
As we are', and vouchsafes the greeting due*
To Imogen and Juliet—sweetest kin*
On art's side.

        'Tis that, honouring to its worth
The drama, I would fear to keep it down
To the level of the footlights. Dies no more
The sacrificial goat, for Bacchus slain,*   320
His filmed eyes fluttered by the whirling white
Of choral vestures—troubled in his blood,
While tragic voices that clanged keen as swords,
Leapt high together with the altar-flame
And made the blue air wink. The waxen mask,
Which set the grand still front of Themis' son*
Upon the puckered visage of a player—
The buskin, which he rose upon and moved,
As some tall ship first conscious of the wind
Sweeps slowly past the piers—the mouthpiece, where   330
The mere man's voice with all its breaths and breaks
Went sheathed in brass, and clashed on even heights
Its phrasèd thunders—these things are no more,
Which once were. And concluding, which is clear,
The growing drama has outgrown such toys
Of simulated stature, face, and speech,
It also peradventure may outgrow
The simulation of the painted scene,
Boards, actors, prompters, gaslight, and costume,
And take for a worthier stage the soul itself,   340
Its shifting fancies and celestial lights,
With all its grand orchestral silences
To keep the pauses of its rhythmic sounds.

Alas, I still see something to be done,
And what I do, falls short of what I see,

Though I waste myself on doing. Long green days,
Worn bare of grass and sunshine—long calm nights,
From which the silken sleeps were fretted out,
Be witness for me, with no amateur's
Irreverent haste and busy idleness   350
I set myself to art! What then? what's done?
What's done, at last?

                Behold, at last, a book.
If life-blood's necessary, which it is—
(By that blue vein a-throb on Mahomet's brow,*
Each prophet-poet's book must show man's blood!)
If life-blood's fertilising, I wrung mine
On every leaf of this—unless the drops
Slid heavily on one side and left it dry.
That chances often: many a fervid man
Writes books as cold and flat as graveyard stones   360
From which the lichen's scraped; and if Saint Preux*
Had written his own letters, as he might,
We had never wept to think of the little mole
'Neath Julie's drooping eyelid. Passion is
But something suffered, after all.

                      While Art
Sets action on the top of suffering:
The artist's part is both to be and do,
Transfixing with a special, central power
The flat experience of the common man,
And turning outward, with a sudden wrench,   370
Half agony, half ecstasy, the thing
He feels the inmost—never felt the less
Because he sings it. Does a torch less burn
For burning next reflectors of blue steel,
That *he* should be the colder for his place
'Twixt two incessant fires—his personal life's,
And that intense refraction which burns back
Perpetually against him from the round
Of crystal conscience he was born into
If artist-born? O sorrowful great gift   380

Conferred on poets, of a twofold life,
When one life has been found enough for pain!
We, staggering 'neath our burden as mere men,
Being called to stand up straight as demi-gods,
Support the intolerable strain and stress
Of the universal, and send clearly up
With voices broken by the human sob,
Our poems to find rhymes among the stars!

But soft—a 'poet' is a word soon said,
A book's a thing soon written. Nay, indeed,   390
The more the poet shall be questionable,
The more unquestionably comes his book.
And this of mine—well, granting to myself
Some passion in it—furrowing up the flats,
Mere passion will not prove a volume worth
Its gall and rags even. Bubbles round a keel
Mean nought, excepting that the vessel moves.
There's more than passion goes to make a man
Or book, which is a man too.
                        I am sad.
I wonder if Pygmalion had these doubts*   400
And, feeling the hard marble first relent,
Grow supple to the straining of his arms,
And tingle through its cold to his burning lip,
Supposed his senses mocked, supposed the toil
Of stretching past the known and seen to reach
The archetypal Beauty out of sight,
Had made his heart beat fast enough for two,
And with his own life dazed and blinded him!
Not so; Pygmalion loved—and whoso loves
Believes the impossible.
                        But I am sad: 410
I cannot thoroughly love a work of mine,
Since none seems worthy of my thought and hope
More highly mated. He has shot them down,
My Phoebus Apollo, soul within my soul,*

Who judges, by the attempted, what's attained,
And with the silver arrow from his height
Has struck down all my works before my face
While I said nothing. Is there aught to say?
I called the artist but a greatened man.
He may be childless also, like a man.   420

I laboured on alone. The wind and dust
And sun of the world beat blistering in my face;
And hope, now for me, now against me, dragged
My spirits onward, as some fallen balloon,
Which, whether caught by blossoming tree or bare,
Is torn alike. I sometimes touched my aim,
Or seemed—and generous souls cried out, 'Be strong,
Take courage; now you're on our level—now!
The next step saves you!' I was flushed with praise,
But, pausing just a moment to draw breath,   430
I could not choose but murmur to myself
'Is this all? all that's done? and all that's gained?
If this then be success, 'tis dismaller
Than any failure.'
                        O my God, my God,
O supreme Artist, who as sole return
For all the cosmic wonder of thy work,
Demandest of us just a word . . . a name,
'My Father!' thou hast knowledge, only thou,
How dreary 'tis for women to sit still
On winter nights by solitary fires   440
And hear the nations praising them far off,
Too far! ay, praising our quick sense of love,
Our very heart of passionate womanhood,
Which could not beat so in the verse without
Being present also in the unkissed lips
And eyes undried because there's none to ask
The reason they grew moist.
                                    To sit alone
And think for comfort how, that very night,

Affianced lovers, leaning face to face
With sweet half-listenings for each other's breath,   450
Are reading haply from a page of ours,
To pause with a thrill (as if their cheeks had touched)
When such a stanza, level to their mood,
Seems floating their own thought out—'So I feel
For thee'—'And I, for thee: this poet knows
What everlasting love is!'—how, that night,
Some father, issuing from the misty roads
Upon the luminous round of lamp and hearth
And happy children, having caught up first
The youngest there until it shrink and shriek   460
To feel the cold chin prick its dimples through
With winter from the hills, may throw i' the lap
Of the eldest (who has learnt to drop her lids
To hide some sweetness newer than last year's)
Our book and cry . . . 'Ah you, you care for rhymes;
So here be rhymes to pore on under trees,
When April comes to let you! I've been told
They are not idle as so many are,
But set hearts beating pure as well as fast.
'Tis yours, the book; I'll write your name in it,   470
That so you may not lose, however lost
In poet's lore and charming reverie,
The thought of how your father thought of *you*
In riding from the town.'
                                  To have our books
Appraised by love, associated with love,
While *we* sit loveless! is it hard, you think?
At least 'tis mournful. Fame, indeed, 'twas said,
Means simply love. It was a man said that:*
And then, there's love and love: the love of all
(To risk in turn a woman's paradox)   480
Is but a small thing to the love of one.
You bid a hungry child be satisfied
With a heritage of many corn-fields: nay,
He says he's hungry—he would rather have

That little barley-cake you keep from him
While reckoning up his harvests. So with us
(Here, Romney, too, we fail to generalise!);
We're hungry.

     Hungry! but it's pitiful
To wail like unweaned babes and suck our thumbs
Because we're hungry. Who, in all the world   490
(Wherein we are haply set to pray and fast,
And learn what good is by its opposite),
Has never hungered? Woe to him who has found
The meal enough! if Ugolino's full,*
His teeth have crunched some foul unnatural thing:
For here satiety proves penury
More utterly irremediable. And since
We needs must hunger—better, for man's love,
Than God's truth! better, for companions sweet,
Than great convictions! let us bear our weights, 500
Preferring dreary hearths to desert souls.
Well, well! they say we're envious, we who rhyme;
But I, because I am a woman perhaps
And so rhyme ill, am ill at envying.
I never envied Graham his breadth of style,
Which gives you, with a random smutch or two*
(Near-sighted critics analyse to smutch),
Such delicate perspectives of full life:
Nor Belmore, for the unity of aim
To which he cuts his cedarn poems, fine   510
As sketchers do their pencils: nor Mark Gage,
For that caressing colour and trancing tone
Whereby you're swept away and melted in
The sensual element, which with a back wave
Restores you to the level of pure souls
And leaves you with Plotinus. None of these,*
For native gifts or popular applause,
I've envied; but for this—that when by chance
Says someone—'There goes Belmore, a great man!
He leaves clean work behind him, and requires 520

No sweeper up of the chips' . . . a girl I know,
Who answers nothing, save with her brown eyes,
Smiles unaware as if a guardian saint
Smiled in her—for this, too—that Gage comes home
And lays his last book's prodigal review
Upon his mother's knee, where, years ago,
He laid his childish spelling-book and learned
To chirp and peck the letters from her mouth,
As young birds must. 'Well done,' she murmured then;
She will not say it now more wonderingly: 530
And yet the last 'Well done' will touch him more,
As catching up today and yesterday
In a perfect chord of love: and so, Mark Gage,
I envy you your mother!—and you, Graham,
Because you have a wife who loves you so,
She half forgets, at moments, to be proud
Of being Graham's wife, until a friend observes,
'The boy here, has his father's massive brow,
Done small in wax . . . if we push back the curls.'

Who loves me? Dearest father—mother sweet—   540
I speak the names out sometimes by myself,
And make the silence shiver. They sound strange,
As Hindustani to an Ind-born man
Accustomed many years to English speech;
Or lovely poet-words grown obsolete,
Which will not leave off singing. Up in heaven
I have my father—with my mother's face
Beside him in a blotch of heavenly light;
No more for earth's familiar, household use,
No more. The best verse written by this hand,   550
Can never reach them where they sit, to seem
Well done to *them*. Death quite unfellows us,
Sets a dreadful odds betwixt the live and dead,
And makes us part as those at Babel did*
Through sudden ignorance of a common tongue.

A living Caesar would not dare to play
At bowls with such as my dead father is.

And yet this may be less so than appears,
This change and separation. Sparrows five*
For just two farthings, and God cares for each.   560
If God is not too great for little cares,
Is any creature, because gone to God?
I've seen some men, veracious, nowise mad,*
Who have thought or dreamed, declared and testified,
They heard the Dead a-ticking like a clock
Which strikes the hours of the eternities,
Beside them, with their natural ears—and known
That human spirits feel the human way
And hate the unreasoning awe which waves them off
From possible communion. It may be.   570

At least, earth separates as well as Heaven.
For instance, I have not seen Romney Leigh
Full eighteen months . . . add six, you get two years.
They say he's very busy with good works—
Has parted Leigh Hall into almshouses.
He made one day an almshouse of his heart,
Which ever since is loose upon the latch
For those who pull the string.—I never did.

It always makes me sad to go abroad,
And now I'm sadder that I went tonight   580
Among the lights and talkers at Lord Howe's.
His wife is gracious, with her glossy braids,
And even voice, and gorgeous eyeballs, calm
As her other jewels. If she's somewhat cold,
Who wonders, when her blood has stood so long
In the ducal reservoir she calls her line
By no means arrogantly? she's not proud;
Not prouder than the swan is of the lake
He has always swum in—'tis her element;

And so she takes it with a natural grace,   590
Ignoring tadpoles. She just knows perhaps
There *are* who travel without outriders,*
Which isn't her fault. Ah, to watch her face,
When good Lord Howe expounds his theories
Of social justice and equality!
'Tis curious, what a tender, tolerant bend
Her neck takes: for she loves him, likes his talk,
'Such clever talk—that dear, odd Algernon!'
She listens on, exactly as if he talked
Some Scandinavian myth of Lemures,*   600
Too pretty to dispute, and too absurd.

She's gracious to me as her husband's friend,
And would be gracious, were I not a Leigh,
Being used to smile just so, without her eyes,
On Joseph Strangways, the Leeds mesmerist,*
And Delia Dobbs, the lecturer from 'the States'
Upon the 'Woman's question.' Then, for him,*
I like him; he's my friend. And all the rooms
Were full of crinkling silks that swept about
The fine dust of most subtle courtesies.   610
What then?—why then, we come home to be sad.

How lovely, one I love not looked tonight!
She's very pretty, Lady Waldemar.
Her maid must use both hands to twist that coil
Of tresses, then be careful lest the rich
Bronze rounds should slip—she missed, though, a gray hair,
A single one—I saw it; otherwise
The woman looked immortal. How they told,
Those alabaster shoulders and bare breasts,
On which the pearls, drowned out of sight in milk,   620
Were lost, excepting for the ruby-clasp!
They split the amaranth velvet bodice down
To the waist or nearly, with the audacious press
Of full-breathed beauty. If the heart within

Were half as white!—but, if it were, perhaps
The breast were closer covered and the sight
Less aspectable, by half, too.*

          I heard
The young man with the German student's look—
A sharp face, like a knife in a cleft stick,
Which shot up straight against the parting-line   630
So equally dividing the long hair—
Say softly to his neighbour (thirty-five
And medieval), 'Look that way, Sir Blaise.
She's Lady Waldemar—to the left—in red—
Whom Romney Leigh, our ablest man just now,
Is soon about to marry.'

              Then replied
Sir Blaise Delorme, with quiet, priestlike voice,
Too used to syllable damnations round
To make a natural emphasis worth while:
'Is Leigh your ablest man? the same, I think,   640
Once jilted by a recreant pretty maid
Adopted from the people? Now, in change,
He seems to have plucked a flower from the other side
Of the social hedge.'

           'A flower, a flower,' exclaimed
My German student—his own eyes full-blown
Bent on her. He was twenty, certainly.

Sir Blaise resumed with gentle arrogance,
As if he had dropped his alms into a hat
And gained the right to counsel—'My young friend,
I doubt your ablest man's ability   650
To get the least good or help meet for him,
For pagan phalanstery or Christian home,
From such a flowery creature.'

                'Beautiful!'
My student murmured rapt—'Mark how she stirs!
Just waves her head, as if a flower indeed,
Touched far off by the vain breath of our talk.'

At which that bilious Grimwald (he who writes
For the Renovator), who had seemed absorbed
Upon the table-book of autographs
(I dare say mentally he crunched the bones   660
Of all those writers, wishing them alive
To feel his tooth in earnest), turned short round
With low carnivorous laugh—'A flower, of course!*
She neither sews nor spins—and takes no thought
Of her garments . . . falling off.'
                            The student flinched;
Sir Blaise, the same; then both, drawing back their chairs
As if they spied black beetles on the floor,
Pursued their talk, without a word being thrown
To the critic.
                    Good Sir Blaise's brow is high
And noticeably narrow: a strong wind,   670
You fancy, might unroof him suddenly,
And blow that great top attic off his head
So piled with feudal relics. You admire
His nose in profile, though you miss his chin;
But, though you miss his chin, you seldom miss
His ebon cross worn innermostly (carved
For penance by a saintly Styrian monk*
Whose flesh was too much with him), slipping through
Some unaware unbuttoned casualty
Of the under-waistcoat. With an absent air   680
Sir Blaise sat fingering it and speaking low,
While I, upon the sofa, heard it all.

'My dear young friend, if we could bear our eyes,
Like blessedest Saint Lucy, on a plate,*
They would not trick us into choosing wives,
As doublets, by the colour. Otherwise
Our fathers chose—and therefore, when they had hung
Their household keys about a lady's waist,
The sense of duty gave her dignity;
She kept her bosom holy to her babes,   690

And, if a moralist reproved her dress,
'Twas, "Too much starch!"—and not, "Too little lawn!"'

'Now, pshaw!' returned the other in a heat,
A little fretted by being called 'young friend,'
Or so I took it—'for Saint Lucy's sake,
If she's the saint to swear by, let us leave*
Our fathers—plagued enough about our sons!'
(He stroked his beardless chin) 'yes, plagued, sir, plagued:
The future generations lie on us
As heavy as the nightmare of a seer;   700
Our meat and drink grow painful prophecy:
I ask you—have we leisure, if we liked,
To hollow out our weary hands to keep
Your intermittent rushlight of the past*
From draughts in lobbies? Prejudice of sex
And marriage-law . . . the socket drops them through
While we two speak—however may protest
Some over-delicate nostrils like your own,
'Gainst odours thence arising.'

                      'You are young,'
Sir Blaise objected.

               'If I am,' he said   710
With fire—'though somewhat less so than I seem,
The young run on before, and see the thing
That's coming. Reverence for the young, I cry.
In that new church for which the world's near ripe,
You'll have the younger in the Elder's chair,
Presiding with his ivory front of hope
O'er foreheads clawed by cruel carrion-birds
Of life's experience.'

                  'Pray your blessing, sir,'
Sir Blaise replied good-humouredly—'I plucked
A silver hair this morning from my beard,   720
Which left me your inferior. Would I were
Eighteen and worthy to admonish you!
If young men of your order run before

To see such sights as sexual prejudice
And marriage-law dissolved—in plainer words,
A general concubinage expressed
In a universal pruriency—the thing
Is scarce worth running fast for, and you'd gain
By loitering with your elders.'

                'Ah,' he said,
'Who, getting to the top of Pisgah-hill,*   730
Can talk with one at bottom of the view,
To make it comprehensible? Why, Leigh
Himself, although our ablest man, I said,
Is scarce advanced to see as far as this,
Which some are: he takes up imperfectly
The social question—by one handle—leaves
The rest to trail. A Christian socialist*
Is Romney Leigh, you understand.'

                         'Not I.
I disbelieve in Christian-pagans, much
As you in women-fishes. If we mix*   740
Two colours, we lose both, and make a third
Distinct from either. Mark you! to mistake
A colour is the sign of a sick brain,
And mine, I thank the saints, is clear and cool:
A neutral tint is here impossible.
The church—and by the church, I mean of course
The catholic, apostolic, mother-church—*
Draws lines as plain and straight as her own wall;
Inside of which are Christians, obviously,
And outside . . . dogs.'

                   'We thank you. Well I know   750
The ancient mother-church would fain still bite,
For all her toothless gums—as Leigh himself
Would fain be a Christian still, for all his wit.
Pass that; you two may settle it, for me.
You're slow in England. In a month I learnt
At Göttingen enough philosophy*
To stock your English schools for fifty years;

Pass that, too. Here alone, I stop you short
—Supposing a true man like Leigh could stand
Unequal in the stature of his life   760
To the height of his opinions. Choose a wife
Because of a smooth skin?—not he, not he!
He'd rail at Venus' self for creaking shoes,
Unless she walked his way of righteousness:
And if he takes a Venus Meretrix*
(No imputation on the lady there),
Be sure that, by some sleight of Christian art,
He has metamorphosed and converted her
To be a Blessed Virgin.'

          'Soft!' Sir Blaise drew breath
As if it hurt him—'Soft! no blasphemy,   770
I pray you!'

       'The first Christians did the thing:
Why not the last?' asked he of Göttingen,
With just that shade of sneering on the lip,
Compensates for the lagging of the beard—
'And so the case is. If that fairest fair
Is talked of as the future wife of Leigh,
She's talked of too, at least as certainly,
As Leigh's disciple. You may find her name
On all his missions and commissions, schools,
Asylums, hospitals—he had her down,   780
With other ladies whom her starry lead
Persuaded from their spheres, to his country-place
In Shropshire, to the famed phalanstery
At Leigh Hall, Christianised from Fourier's own
(In which he has planted out his sapling stocks
Of knowledge into social nurseries),
And there, they say, she has tarried half a week,
And milked the cows, and churned, and pressed the curd,
And said "my sister" to the lowest drab
Of all the assembled castaways; such girls!   790
Ay, sided with them at the washing-tub—
Conceive, Sir Blaise, those naked perfect arms,

Round glittering arms, plunged elbow-deep in suds,
Like wild swans hid in lilies all a-shake.'

Lord Howe came up. 'What, talking poetry
So near the image of the unfavouring Muse?
That's you, Miss Leigh: I've watched you half an hour,
Precisely as I watched the statue called
A Pallas in the Vatican—you mind*
The face, Sir Blaise?—intensely calm and sad,   800
As wisdom cut it off from fellowship—
But *that* spoke louder. Not a word from *you*!
And these two gentlemen were bold, I marked,
And unabashed by even your silence.'

                                        'Ah,'
Said I, 'my dear Lord Howe, you shall not speak
To a printing woman who has lost her place
(The sweet safe corner of the household fire
Behind the heads of children), compliments,
As if she were a woman. We who have clipped
The curls before our eyes, may see at least   810
As plain as men do. Speak out, man to man;
No compliments, beseech you.'

                              'Friend to friend,
Let that be. We are sad tonight, I saw
(—Good night, Sir Blaise! ah, Smith—he has slipped away),
I saw you across the room, and stayed, Miss Leigh,
To keep a crowd of lion-hunters off,
With faces toward your jungle. There were three;
A spacious lady, five feet ten and fat,
Who has the devil in her (and there's room)
For walking to and fro upon the earth,   820
From Chipewa to China; she requires*
Your autograph upon a tinted leaf
'Twixt Queen Pomare's and Emperor Soulouque's.*
Pray give it; she has energies, though fat:
For me, I'd rather see a rick on fire
Than such a woman angry. Then a youth

Fresh from the backwoods, green as the underboughs,
Asks modestly, Miss Leigh, to kiss your shoe,
And adds, he has an epic in twelve parts,*
Which when you've read, you'll do it for his boot: 830
All which I saved you, and absorb next week
Both manuscript and man—because a lord
Is still more potent than a poetess
With any extreme republican. Ah, ah,
You smile, at last, then.'

                 'Thank you.'

                       'Leave the smile.
I'll lose the thanks for't—ay, and throw you in
My transatlantic girl, with golden eyes
That draw you to her splendid whiteness as
The pistil of a water-lily draws,
Adust with gold. Those girls across the sea 840
Are tyrannously pretty—and I swore
(She seemed to me an innocent, frank girl)
To bring her to you for a woman's kiss,
Not now, but on some other day or week:
—We'll call it perjury; I give her up.'

'No, bring her.'

              'Now,' said he, 'you make it hard
To touch such goodness with a grimy palm.
I thought to tease you well, and fret you cross,
And steel myself, when rightly vexed with you,
For telling you a thing to tease you more.' 850

'Of Romney?'

            'No, no; nothing worse,' he cried,
'Of Romney Leigh than what is buzzed about—
That *he* is taken in an eye-trap too,
Like many half as wise. The thing I mean
Refers to you, not him.'

                   'Refers to me.'

He echoed—'Me! You sound it like a stone
Dropped down a dry well very listlessly
By one who never thinks about the toad
Alive at the bottom. Presently perhaps
You'll sound your "me" more proudly—till I shrink.'   860

'Lord Howe's the toad, then, in this question?'
                                                    'Brief,
We'll take it graver. Give me sofa-room,
And quiet hearing. You know Eglinton,
John Eglinton, of Eglinton in Kent?'

'Is *he* the toad?—he's rather like the snail,
Known chiefly for the house upon his back:
Divide the man and house—you kill the man;
That's Eglinton of Eglinton, Lord Howe.'

He answered grave. 'A reputable man,
An excellent landlord of the olden stamp   870
If somewhat slack in new philanthropies,
Who keeps his birthdays with a tenants' dance,
Is hard upon them when they miss the church
Or hold their children back from catechism,
But not ungentle when the aged poor
Pick sticks at hedge-sides: nay, I've heard him say,
"The old dame has a twinge because she stoops;
That's punishment enough for felony."'

'O tender-hearted landlord! may I take
My long lease with him, when the time arrives   880
For gathering winter-faggots!'
                                    'He likes art,
Buys books and pictures . . . of a certain kind;
Neglects no patent duty; a good son' . . . .

'To a most obedient mother. Born to wear
His father's shoes, he wears her husband's too:

Indeed I've heard it's touching. Dear Lord Howe,
You shall not praise *me* so against your heart,
When I'm at worst for praise and faggots.'
                                  'Be
Less bitter with me, for . . . in short,' he said,
'I have a letter, which he urged me so   890
To bring you . . . I could scarcely choose but yield;
Insisting that a new love, passing through
The hand of an old friendship, caught from it
Some reconciling odour.'
                        'Love, you say?
My lord, I cannot love: I only find
The rhyme for love—and that's not love, my lord.
Take back your letter.'
                       'Pause: you'll read it first?'

'I will not read it: it is stereotyped;
The same he wrote to—anybody's name,
Anne Blythe the actress, when she died so true,   900
A duchess fainted in a private box:
Pauline the dancer, after the great *pas*
In which her little feet winked overhead
Like other fire-flies, and amazed the pit:
Or Baldinacci, when her F in alt
Had touched the silver tops of heaven itself
With such a pungent spirit-dart, the Queen
Laid softly, each to each, her white-gloved palms,
And sighed for joy: or else (I thank your friend)
Aurora Leigh—when some indifferent rhymes,   910
Like those the boys sang round the holy ox*
On Memphis-highway, chance perhaps to set
Our Apis-public lowing. Oh, he wants,
Instead of any worthy wife at home,
A star upon his stage of Eglinton?
Advise him that he is not over-shrewd
In being so little modest: a dropped star
Makes bitter waters, says a Book I've read—*

And there's his unread letter.'
                                        'My dear friend,'
Lord Howe began . . .
                              In haste I tore the phrase.   920
'You mean your friend of Eglinton, or me?'

'I mean you, you,' he answered with some fire.
'A happy life means prudent compromise;
The tare runs through the farmer's garnered sheaves,
And though the gleaner's apron holds pure wheat
We count her poorer. Tare with wheat, we cry,
And good with drawbacks. You, you love your art,
And, certain of vocation, set your soul
On utterance. Only, in this world we have made
(They say God made it first, but if He did   930
'Twas so long since, and, since we have spoiled it so,
He scarce would know it, if He looked this way,
From hells we preach of, with the flames blown out)
—In this bad, twisted, topsy-turvy world
Where all the heaviest wrongs get uppermost—
In this uneven, unfostering England here,
Where ledger-strokes and sword-strokes count indeed,
But soul-strokes merely tell upon the flesh
They strike from—it is hard to stand for art,
Unless some golden tripod from the sea*   940
Be fished up, by Apollo's divine chance,
To throne such feet as yours, my prophetess,
At Delphi. Think—the god comes down as fierce
As twenty bloodhounds, shakes you, strangles you,
Until the oracular shriek shall ooze in froth!
At best 'tis not all ease—at worst too hard:
A place to stand on is a 'vantage gained,
And here's your tripod. To be plain, dear friend,
You're poor, except in what you richly give;
You labour for your own bread painfully,   950
Or ere you pour our wine. For art's sake, pause.'

I answered slow—as some wayfaring man,
Who feels himself at night too far from home,
Makes steadfast face against the bitter wind.
'Is art so less a thing than virtue is,
That artists first must cater for their ease
Or ever they make issue past themselves
To generous use? alas, and is it so,
That we, who would be somewhat clean, must sweep
Our ways as well as walk them, and no friend   960
Confirm us nobly—"Leave results to God,
But you, be clean?" What! "prudent compromise
Makes acceptable life," you say instead,
You, you, Lord Howe?—in things indifferent, well.
For instance, compromise the wheaten bread
For rye, the meat for lentils, silk for serge,
And sleep on down, if needs, for sleep on straw;
But there, end compromise. I will not bate*
One artist-dream on straw or down, my lord,
Nor pinch my liberal soul, though I be poor,   970
Nor cease to love high, though I live thus low.'

So speaking, with less anger in my voice
Than sorrow, I rose quickly to depart;
While he, thrown back upon the noble shame
Of such high-stumbling natures, murmured words,
The right words after wrong ones. Ah, the man
Is worthy, but so given to entertain
Impossible plans of superhuman life—
He sets his virtues on so raised a shelf,
To keep them at the grand millennial height,   980
He has to mount a stool to get at them;
And, meantime, lives on quite the common way,
With everybody's morals.

                                As we passed,
Lord Howe insisting that his friendly arm
Should oar me across the sparkling brawling stream

Which swept from room to room—we fell at once
On Lady Waldemar. 'Miss Leigh,' she said,
And gave me such a smile, so cold and bright,
As if she tried it in a 'tiring glass*
And liked it; 'all tonight I've strained at you   990
As babes at baubles held up out of reach
By spiteful nurses ("Never snatch", they say),
And there you sat, most perfectly shut in
By good Sir Blaise and clever Mister Smith
And then our dear Lord Howe! at last indeed
I almost snatched. I have a world to speak
About your cousin's place in Shropshire where
I've been to see his work . . : our work—you heard
I went? . . . and of a letter yesterday,
In which if I should read a page or two   1000
You might feel interest, though you're locked of course
In literary toil.—You'll like to hear
Your last book lies at the phalanstery,
As judged innocuous for the elder girls
And younger women who still care for books.
We all must read, you see, before we live,
Till slowly the ineffable light comes up
And, as it deepens, drowns the written word—
So said your cousin, while we stood and felt
A sunset from his favourite beech-tree seat.   1010
He might have been a poet if he would,
But then he saw the higher thing at once
And climbed to it. I think he looks well now,
Has quite got over that unfortunate . . .
Ah, ah . . . I know it moved you. Tender-heart!
You took a liking to the wretched girl.
Perhaps you thought the marriage suitable,
Who knows? a poet hankers for romance,
And so on. As for Romney Leigh, 'tis sure
He never loved her—never. By the way,   1020
You have not heard of *her* . . . ? quite out of sight,
And out of saving? lost in every sense?'

She might have gone on talking half an hour,
And I stood still, and cold, and pale, I think,
As a garden-statue a child pelts with snow
For pretty pastime. Every now and then
I put in 'yes' or 'no', I scarce knew why;
The blind man walks wherever the dog pulls,
And so I answered. Till Lord Howe broke in;
'What penance takes the wretch who interrupts   1030
The talk of charming women? I, at last,
Must brave it. Pardon, Lady Waldemar!
The lady on my arm is tired, unwell,
And loyally I've promised she shall say
No harder word this evening, than . . . good-night;
The rest her face speaks for her.'—Then we went.

And I breathe large at home. I drop my cloak,
Unclasp my girdle, loose the band that ties
My hair . . . now could I but unloose my soul!
We are sepulchred alive in this close world,   1040
And want more room.
                    The charming woman there—
This reckoning up and writing down her talk
Affects me singularly. How she talked
To pain me! woman's spite.—You wear steel-mail;
A woman takes a housewife from her breast*
And plucks the delicatest needle out
As 'twere a rose, and pricks you carefully
'Neath nails, 'neath eyelids, in your nostrils—say,
A beast would roar so tortured—but a man,
A human creature, must not, shall not flinch,   1050
No, not for shame.
                    What vexes, after all,
Is just that such as she, with such as I,
Knows how to vex. Sweet heaven, she takes me up
As if she had fingered me and dog-eared me
And spelled me by the fireside half a life!
She knows my turns, my feeble points.—What then?

The knowledge of a thing implies the thing;
Of course, she found *that* in me, she saw *that*,
Her pencil underscored *this* for a fault,
And I, still ignorant. Shut the book up—close!   1060
And crush that beetle in the leaves.
                                        O heart,
At last we shall grow hard too, like the rest,
And call it self-defence because we are soft.

And after all, now . . . why should I be pained
That Romney Leigh, my cousin, should espouse
This Lady Waldemar? And, say, she held
Her newly blossomed gladness in my face . . .
'Twas natural surely, if not generous,
Considering how, when winter held her fast,
I helped the frost with mine, and pained her more   1070
Than she pains me. Pains me!—but wherefore pained?
'Tis clear my cousin Romney wants a wife—
So, good!—The man's need of the woman, here,
Is greater than the woman's of the man,
And easier served; for where the man discerns
A sex (ah, ah, the man can generalise,
Said he), we see but one, ideally
And really: where we yearn to lose ourselves
And melt like white pearls in another's wine,
He seeks to double himself by what he loves,   1080
And make his drink more costly by our pearls.
At board, at bed, at work and holiday,
It is not good for man to be alone,
And that's his way of thinking, first and last,
And thus my cousin Romney wants a wife.

But then my cousin sets his dignity
On personal virtue. If he understands
By love, like others, self-aggrandisement,
It is that he may verily be great
By doing rightly and kindly. Once he thought,   1090

For charitable ends set duly forth
In Heaven's white judgment-book, to marry ... ah,
We'll call her name Aurora Leigh, although
She's changed since then!—and once, for social ends,
Poor Marian Erle, my sister Marian Erle,
My woodland sister, sweet maid Marian,*
Whose memory moans on in me like the wind
Through ill-shut casements, making me more sad
Than ever I find reasons for. Alas,
Poor pretty plaintive face, embodied ghost!   1100
He finds it easy then, to clap thee off
From pulling at his sleeve and book and pen—
He locks thee out at night into the cold
Away from butting with thy horny eyes
Against his crystal dreams, that now he's strong
To love anew? that Lady Waldemar
Succeeds my Marian?
                    After all, why not?
He loved not Marian, more than once he loved
Aurora. If he loves at last that Third,
Albeit she prove as slippery as spilt oil   1110
On marble floors, I will not augur him
Ill-luck for that. Good love, howe'er ill-placed,
Is better for a man's soul in the end,
Than if he loved ill what deserves love well.
A pagan, kissing for a step of Pan
The wild goat's hoof-print on the loamy down,
Exceeds our modern thinker who turns back
The strata ... granite, limestone, coal, and clay,
Concluding coldly with, 'Here's law! where's God?'

And then at worst—if Romney loves her not—   1120
At worst—if he's incapable of love,
Which may be—then indeed, for such a man
Incapable of love, she's good enough;
For she, at worst too, is a woman still
And loves him ... as the sort of woman can.

My loose long hair began to burn and creep,
Alive to the very ends, about my knees:
I swept it backward as the wind sweeps flame,
With the passion of my hands. Ah, Romney laughed
One day (how full the memories come up!)   1130
'—Your Florence fire-flies live on in your hair,'
He said, 'it gleams so.' Well, I wrung them out,
My fire-flies; made a knot as hard as life
Of those loose, soft, impracticable curls,
And then sat down and thought . . . 'She shall not think
Her thought of me'—and drew my desk and wrote.

'Dear Lady Waldemar, I could not speak
With people round me, nor can sleep tonight,
And not speak, after the great news I heard
Of you and of my cousin. May you be   1140
Most happy; and the good he meant the world,
Replenish his own life. Say what I say,
And let my word be sweeter for your mouth,
As you are *you* . . . I only Aurora Leigh.'

That's quiet, guarded: though she hold it up
Against the light, she'll not see through it more
Than lies there to be seen. So much for pride;
And now for peace, a little. Let me stop
All writing back . . . 'Sweet thanks, my sweetest friend,
You've made more joyful my great joy itself.'   1150
—No, that's too simple! she would twist it thus,
'My joy would still be as sweet as thyme in drawers,
However shut up in the dark and dry;
But violets, aired and dewed by love like yours,
Outsmell all thyme: we keep that in our clothes,
But drop the other down our bosoms till
They smell like' . . . ah, I see her writing back
Just so. She'll make a nosegay of her words,
And tie it with blue ribbons at the end
To suit a poet—pshaw!

        And then we'll have   1160
The call to church, the broken, sad, bad dream
Dreamed out at last, the marriage-vow complete
With the marriage-breakfast; praying in white gloves,
Drawn off in haste for drinking pagan toasts
In somewhat stronger wine than any sipped
By gods since Bacchus had his way with grapes.

A postscript stops all that and rescues me.
'You need not write. I have been overworked,
And think of leaving London, England even,
And hastening to get nearer to the sun   1170
Where men sleep better. So, adieu.'—I fold
And seal—and now I'm out of all the coil;
I breathe now, I spring upward like a branch
The ten-years schoolboy with a crooked stick
May pull down to his level in search of nuts,
But cannot hold a moment. How we twang
Back on the blue sky, and assert our height,
While he stares after! Now, the wonder seems
That I could wrong myself by such a doubt.
We poets always have uneasy hearts,   1180
Because our hearts, large-rounded as the globe,
Can turn but one side to the sun at once.
We are used to dip our artist-hands in gall*
And potash, trying potentialities
Of alternated colour, till at last
We get confused, and wonder for our skin
How nature tinged it first. Well—here's the true
Good flesh-colour; I recognise my hand—
Which Romney Leigh may clasp as just a friend's,
And keep his clean.

        And now, my Italy.   1190
Alas, if we could ride with naked souls
And make no noise and pay no price at all,
I would have seen thee sooner, Italy,
For still I have heard thee crying through my life,

Thou piercing silence of ecstatic graves,
Men call that name!

              But even a witch today
Must melt down golden pieces in the nard
Wherewith to anoint her broomstick ere she rides;
And poets evermore are scant of gold,
And if they find a piece behind the door   1200
It turns by sunset to a withered leaf.
The Devil himself scarce trusts his patented
Gold-making art to any who make rhymes,
But culls his Faustus from philosophers,*
And not from poets. 'Leave my Job,' said God;*
And so the Devil leaves him without pence,
And poverty proves plainly special grace.
In these new, just, administrative times
Men clamour for an order of merit: why?
Here's black bread on the table and no wine!   1210

At least I am a poet in being poor,
Thank God. I wonder if the manuscript
Of my long poem, if 'twere sold outright,
Would fetch enough to buy me shoes to go
Afoot (thrown in, the necessary patch
For the other side the Alps)? It cannot be.
I fear that I must sell this residue
Of my father's books, although the Elzevirs*
Have fly-leaves overwritten by his hand
In faded notes as thick and fine and brown   1220
As cobwebs on a tawny monument
Of the old Greeks—*conferenda haec cum his—**
*Corruptè citat—lege potiùs,**
And so on, in the scholar's regal way
Of giving judgment on the parts of speech,
As if he sat on all twelve thrones up-piled,
Arraigning Israel. Ay, but books and notes
Must go together. And this Proclus too,*

In these dear quaint contracted Grecian types,
Fantastically crumpled like his thoughts   1230
Which would not seem too plain; you go round twice
For one step forward, then you take it back
Because you're somewhat giddy; there's the rule
For Proclus. Ah, I stained this middle leaf
With pressing in't my Florence iris-bell,
Long stalk and all: my father chided me
For that stain of blue blood—I recollect
The peevish turn his voice took—'Silly girls,
Who plant their flowers in our philosophy
To make it fine, and only spoil the book!   1240
No more of it, Aurora.' 'Yes—no more!
Ah, blame of love, that's sweeter than all praise
Of those who love not! 'tis so lost to me,
I cannot, in such beggared life, afford
To lose my Proclus—not for Florence even.

The kissing Judas, Wolff, shall go instead,*
Who builds us such a royal book as this
To honour a chief poet, folio-built,
And writes above, 'The house of Nobody!'
Who floats in cream, as rich as any sucked*   1250
From Juno's breasts, the broad Homeric lines,
And, while with their spondaic prodigious mouths
They lap the lucent margins as babe-gods,
Proclaims them bastards. Wolff's an atheist;
And if the Iliad fell out, as he says,
By mere fortuitous concourse of old songs,
Conclude as much too for the universe.

That Wolff, those Platos: sweep the upper shelves
As clean as this, and so I am almost rich,
Which means, not forced to think of being poor   1260
In sight of ends. Tomorrow: no delay.
I'll wait in Paris till good Carrington
Dispose of such and, having chaffered for

My book's price with the publisher, direct
All proceeds to me. Just a line to ask
His help.
      And now I come, my Italy,
My own hills! Are you 'ware of me, my hills,
How I burn toward you? do you feel tonight
The urgency and yearning of my soul,
As sleeping mothers feel the sucking babe   1270
And smile?—Nay, not so much as when in heat
Vain lightnings catch at your inviolate tops
And tremble while ye are steadfast. Still ye go
Your own determined, calm, indifferent way
Toward sunrise, shade by shade, and light by light,
Of all the grand progression nought left out,
As if God verily made you for yourselves
And would not interrupt your life with ours.

BOOK VI

The English have a scornful insular way
Of calling the French light. The levity
Is in the judgment only, which yet stands,
For say a foolish thing but oft enough
(And here's the secret of a hundred creeds,
Men get opinions as boys learn to spell,
By reiteration chiefly), the same thing
Shall pass at last for absolutely wise,
And not with fools exclusively. And so
We say the French are light, as if we said   10
The cat mews or the milch-cow gives us milk:
Say rather, cats are milked and milch-cows mew;
For what is lightness but inconsequence,
Vague fluctuation 'twixt effect and cause
Compelled by neither? Is a bullet light,
That dashes from the gun-mouth, while the eye
Winks and the heart beats one, to flatten itself
To a wafer on the white speck on a wall
A hundred paces off? Even so direct,
So sternly undivertible of aim,   20
Is this French people.
                        All, idealists
Too absolute and earnest, with them all
The idea of a knife cuts real flesh;
And still, devouring the safe interval
Which Nature placed between the thought and act
With those too fiery and impatient souls,
They threaten conflagration to the world,
And rush with most unscrupulous logic on
Impossible practice. Set your orators
To blow upon them with loud windy mouths   30

Through watchword phrases, jest or sentiment,
Which drive our burly brutal English mobs
Like so much chaff, whichever way they blow—
This light French people will not thus be driven.
They turn indeed—but then they turn upon
Some central pivot of their thought and choice,
And veer out by the force of holding fast.
That's hard to understand, for Englishmen
Unused to abstract questions, and untrained
To trace the involutions, valve by valve,   40
In each orbed bulb-root of a general truth,
And mark what subtly fine integument
Divides opposed compartments. Freedom's self
Comes concrete to us, to be understood,
Fixed in a feudal form incarnately
To suit our ways of thought and reverence,
The special form, with us, being still the thing.
With us, I say, though I'm of Italy
By mother's birth and grave, by father's grave
And memory; let it be—a poet's heart   50
Can swell to a pair of nationalities,
However ill-lodged in a woman's breast.

And so I am strong to love this noble France,
This poet of the nations, who dreams on
And wails on (while the household goes to wreck)
For ever, after some ideal good—
Some equal poise of sex, some unvowed love
Inviolate, some spontaneous brotherhood,
Some wealth that leaves none poor and finds none tired,
Some freedom of the many that respects   60
The wisdom of the few. Heroic dreams!
Sublime, to dream so; natural, to wake:
And sad, to use such lofty scaffoldings,
Erected for the building of a church,
To build instead a brothel or a prison—

May God save France!
                    And if at last she sighs
Her great soul up into a great man's face,*
To flush his temples out so gloriously
That few dare carp at Caesar for being bald,
What then?—this Caesar represents, not reigns,   70
And is no despot, though twice absolute:
This Head has all the people for a heart;
This purple's lined with the democracy—
Now let him see to it! for a rent within
Would leave irreparable rags without.

A serious riddle: find such anywhere
Except in France; and when 'tis found in France,
Be sure to read it rightly. So, I mused
Up and down, up and down, the terraced streets,
The glittering boulevards, the white colonnades   80
Of fair fantastic Paris, who wears trees
Like plumes, as if man made them, spire and tower
As if they had grown by nature, tossing up
Her fountains in the sunshine of the squares,
As if in beauty's game she tossed the dice,
Or blew the silver down-balls of her dreams
To sow futurity with seeds of thought
And count the passage of her festive hours.

The city swims in verdure, beautiful
As Venice on the waters, the sea-swan.   90
What bosky gardens dropped in close-walled courts*
Like plums in ladies' laps who start and laugh:
What miles of streets that run on after trees,
Still carrying all the necessary shops,
Those open caskets with the jewels seen!
And trade is art, and art's philosophy,
In Paris. There's a silk for instance, there,
As worth an artist's study for the folds,
As that bronze opposite! nay, the bronze has faults,

Art's here too artful—conscious as a maid   100
Who leans to mark her shadow on the wall
Until she lose a 'vantage in her step.
Yet Art walks forward, and knows where to walk;
The artists also are idealists,
Too absolute for nature, logical
To austerity in the application of
The special theory—not a soul content
To paint a crooked pollard and an ass,
As the English will because they find it so
And like it somehow.—There the old Tuileries*   110
Is pulling its high cap down on its eyes,
Confounded, conscience-stricken, and amazed
By the apparition of a new fair face
In those devouring mirrors. Through the grate
Within the gardens, what a heap of babes,
Swept up like leaves beneath the chestnut-trees
From every street and alley of the town,
By ghosts perhaps that blow too bleak this way
A-looking for their heads! dear pretty babes,
I wish them luck to have their ball-play out   120
Before the next change. Here the air is thronged
With statues poised upon their columns fine
As if to stand a moment were a feat,
Against that blue! What squares—what breathing-room
For a nation that runs fast—ay, runs against
The dentist's teeth at the corner in pale rows,*
Which grin at progress in an epigram.

I walked the day out, listening to the chink
Of the first Napoleon's bones in his second grave,*
By victories guarded 'neath the golden dome   130
That caps all Paris like a bubble. 'Shall*
These dry bones live,' thought Louis Philippe once,*
And lived to know. Herein is argument
For kings and politicians, but still more
For poets, who bear buckets to the well

Of ampler draught.
     These crowds are very good
For meditation (when we are very strong)
Though love of beauty makes us timorous,
And draws us backward from the coarse town-sights
To count the daisies upon dappled fields   140
And hear the streams bleat on among the hills
In innocent and indolent repose,
While still with silken elegiac thoughts
We wind out from us the distracting world
And die into the chrysalis of a man,
And leave the best that may, to come of us,
In some brown moth. I would be bold and bear
To look into the swarthiest face of things,
For God's sake who has made them.
           Six days' work;
The last day shutting 'twixt its dawn and eve 150
The whole work bettered of the previous five!
Since God collected and resumed in man*
The firmaments, the strata, and the lights,
Fish, fowl, and beast, and insect—all their trains
Of various life caught back upon His arm,
Reorganised, and constituted MAN,
The microcosm, the adding up of works—
Within whose fluttering nostrils, then at last
Consummating Himself the Maker sighed,
As some strong winner at the foot-race sighs 160
Touching the goal.
      Humanity is great;
And, if I would not rather pore upon
An ounce of common, ugly, human dust,
An artisan's palm or a peasant's brow,
Unsmooth, ignoble, save to me and God,
Than track old Nilus to his silver roots,*
Or wait on all the changes of the moon*
Among the mountain-peaks of Thessaly
(Until her magic crystal round itself

For many a witch to see in)—set it down   170
As weakness—strength by no means. How is this
That men of science, osteologists*
And surgeons, beat some poets in respect
For nature—count nought common or unclean,
Spend raptures upon perfect specimens
Of indurated veins, distorted joints,
Or beautiful new cases of curved spine,
While we, we are shocked at nature's falling off,
We dare to shrink back from her warts and blains,
We will not, when she sneezes, look at her,   180
Not even to say 'God bless her'? That's our wrong;
For that, she will not trust us often with
Her larger sense of beauty and desire,
But tethers us to a lily or a rose
And bids us diet on the dew inside,
Left ignorant that the hungry beggar-boy
(Who stares unseen against our absent eyes,
And wonders at the gods that we must be,
To pass so careless for the oranges!)
Bears yet a breastful of a fellow-world   190
To this world, undisparaged, undespoiled,
And (while we scorn him for a flower or two,
As being, Heaven help us, less poetical)
Contains himself both flowers and firmaments
And surging seas and aspectable stars
And all that we would push him out of sight
In order to see nearer. Let us pray
God's grace to keep God's image in repute,
That so, the poet and philanthropist
(Even I and Romney) may stand side by side,   200
Because we both stand face to face with men,
Contemplating the people in the rough,
Yet each so follow a vocation, his
And mine.

        I walked on, musing with myself
On life and art, and whether after all

A larger metaphysics might not help
Our physics, a completer poetry
Adjust our daily life and vulgar wants
More fully than the special outside plans,
Phalansteries, material institutes,   210
The civil conscriptions and lay monasteries*
Preferred by modern thinkers, as they thought
The bread of man indeed made all his life,*
And washing seven times in the 'People's Baths'*
Were sovereign for a people's leprosy,
Still leaving out the essential prophet's word
That comes in power. On which, we thunder down
We prophets, poets—Virtue's in the *word*!
The Maker burnt the darkness up with His,
To inaugurate the use of vocal life;   220
And, plant a poet's word even, deep enough
In any man's breast, looking presently
For offshoots, you have done more for the man
Than if you dressed him in a broadcloth coat
And warmed his Sunday pottage at your fire.
Yet Romney leaves me . . .
                              God! what face is that?
O Romney, O Marian!
                         Walking on the quays
And pulling thoughts to pieces leisurely,
As if I caught at grasses in a field
And bit them slow between my absent lips   230
And shred them with my hands . . .
                                     What face is that?
What a face, what a look, what a likeness! Full on mine
The sudden blow of it came down, till all
My blood swam, my eyes dazzled. Then I sprang . . .

It was as if a meditative man
Were dreaming out a summer afternoon
And watching gnats a-prick upon a pond,
When something floats up suddenly, out there,

Turns over . . . a dead face, known once alive . . .
So old, so new! it would be dreadful now   240
To lose the sight and keep the doubt of this:
He plunges—ha! he has lost it in the splash.

I plunged—I tore the crowd up, either side,
And rushed on, forward, forward, after her.
Her? whom?
                    A woman sauntered slow in front,
Munching an apple—she left off amazed
As if I had snatched it: that's not she, at least.
A man walked arm-linked with a lady veiled,
Both heads dropped closer than the need of talk:
They started; he forgot her with his face,   250
And she, herself, and clung to him as if
My look were fatal. Such a stream of folk,
And all with cares and business of their own!
I ran the whole quay down against their eyes;
No Marian; nowhere Marian. Almost, now,
I could call Marian, Marian, with the shriek
Of desperate creatures calling for the Dead.
Where is she, was she? was she anywhere?
I stood still, breathless, gazing, straining out
In every uncertain distance, till at last   260
A gentleman abstracted as myself
Came full against me, then resolved the clash
In voluble excuses—obviously
Some learned member of the Institute*
Upon his way there, walking, for his health,
While meditating on the last 'Discourse';
Pinching the empty air 'twixt finger and thumb,
From which the snuff being ousted by that shock
Defiled his snow-white waistcoat duly pricked
At the button-hole with honourable red;   270
'Madame, your pardon'—there he swerved from me
A metre, as confounded as he had heard
That Dumas would be chosen to fill up*

The next chair vacant, by his 'men *in us*.'
Since when was genius found respectable?
It passes in its place, indeed—which means
The seventh floor back, or else the hospital:
Revolving pistols are ingenious things,*
But prudent men (Academicians are)
Scarce keep them in the cupboard next the prunes.   280

And so, abandoned to a bitter mirth,
I loitered to my inn. O world, O world,
O jurists, rhymers, dreamers, what you please,
We play a weary game of hide-and-seek!
We shape a figure of our fantasy,
Call nothing something, and run after it
And lose it, lose ourselves too in the search,
Till clash against us comes a somebody
Who also has lost something and is lost,
Philosopher against philanthropist,   290
Academician against poet, man
Against woman, against the living the dead—
Then home, with a bad headache and worse jest!

To change the water for my heliotropes
And yellow roses. Paris has such flowers;
But England, also. 'Twas a yellow rose,
By that south window of the little house,
My cousin Romney gathered with his hand
On all my birthdays for me, save the last;
And then I shook the tree too rough, too rough,   300
For roses to stay after.
                    Now, my maps.
I must not linger here from Italy
Till the last nightingale is tired of song,
And the last fire-fly dies off in the maize.
My soul's in haste to leap into the sun
And scorch and seethe itself to a finer mood,
Which here, in this chill north, is apt to stand

Too stiffly in former moulds.

                            That face persists.
It floats up, it turns over in my mind,
As like to Marian, as one dead is like   310
The same alive. In very deed a face
And not a fancy, though it vanished so;
The small fair face between the darks of hair,
I used to liken, when I saw her first,
To a point of moonlit water down a well:
The low brow, the frank space between the eyes,
Which always had the brown pathetic look
Of a dumb creature who had been beaten once
And never since was easy with the world.
Ah, ah—now I remember perfectly   320
Those eyes, today—how over-large they seemed,
As if some patient passionate despair
(Like a coal dropped and forgot on tapestry,
Which slowly burns a widening circle out)
Had burnt them larger, larger. And those eyes
Today, I do remember, saw me too,
As I saw them, with conscious lids a-strain
In recognition. Now a fantasy,
A simple shade or image of the brain,
Is merely passive, does not retroact,   330
Is seen, but sees not.
                    'Twas a real face,
Perhaps a real Marian.
                        Which being so,
I ought to write to Romney, 'Marian's here;
Be comforted for Marian.'
                        My pen fell,
My hands struck sharp together, as hands do
Which hold at nothing. Can I write to *him*
A half truth? can I keep my own soul blind
To the other half . . . the worse? What are our souls,
If still, to run on straight a sober pace
Nor start at every pebble or dead leaf,   340

They must wear blinkers, ignore facts, suppress
Six-tenths of the road? Confront the truth, my soul!
And oh, as truly as that was Marian's face,
The arms of that same Marian clasped a thing
. . . Not hid so well beneath the scanty shawl,
I cannot name it now for what it was.

A child. Small business has a castaway
Like Marian with that crown of prosperous wives
At which the gentlest she grows arrogant
And says, 'my child.' Who finds an emerald ring   350
On a beggar's middle finger and requires
More testimony to convict a thief?
A child's too costly for so mere a wretch;
She filched it somewhere, and it means, with her,
Instead of honour, blessing, merely shame.

I cannot write to Romney, 'Here she is,
Here's Marian found! I'll set you on her track:
I saw her here, in Paris . . . and her child.
She put away your love two years ago,
But, plainly, not to starve. You suffered then;   360
And, now that you've forgot her utterly
As any last year's annual, in whose place
You've planted a thick-flowering evergreen,
I choose, being kind, to write and tell you this
To make you wholly easy—she's not dead,
But only . . . damned.'
                        Stop there: I go too fast;
I'm cruel like the rest—in haste to take
The first stir in the arras for a rat,
And set my barking, biting thoughts upon't.
—A child! what then? Suppose a neighbour's sick   370
And asked her, 'Marian, carry out my child
In this Spring air'—I punish her for that?
Or say, the child should hold her round the neck
For good child-reasons, that he liked it so

And would not leave her—she had winning ways—
I brand her therefore that she took the child?
Not so.
           I will not write to Romney Leigh.
For now he's happy—and she may indeed
Be guilty—and the knowledge of her fault
Would draggle his smooth time. But I, whose days   380
Are not so fine they cannot hear the rain,
And who moreover having seen her face
Must see it again . . . *will* see it, by my hopes
Of one day seeing heaven too. The police
Shall track her, hound her, ferret their own soil;
We'll dig this Paris to its catacombs,
But certainly we'll find her, have her out,
And save her, if she will or will not—child
Or no child—if a child, then one to save!

The long weeks passed on without consequence.   390
As easy find a footstep on the sand
The morning after spring-tide, as the trace
Of Marian's feet between the incessant surfs
Of this live flood. She may have moved this way—
But so the starfish does, and crosses out
The dent of her small shoe. The foiled police
Renounced me. 'Could they find a girl and child,
No other signalment but girl and child?
No data shown but noticeable eyes
And hair in masses, low upon the brow,   400
As if it were an iron crown and pressed?
Friends heighten, and suppose they specify:
Why, girls with hair and eyes are everywhere
In Paris; they had turned me up in vain
No Marian Erle indeed, but certainly
Mathildes, Justines, Victoires . . . or, if I sought
The English, Betsies, Saras, by the score.
They might as well go out into the fields
To find a speckled bean, that's somehow specked,

And somewhere in the pod.'—They left me so.   410
Shall *I* leave Marian? have I dreamed a dream?

—I thank God I have found her! I must say
'Thank God,' for finding her, although 'tis true
I find the world more sad and wicked for't.
But she—
        I'll write about her, presently.
My hand's a-tremble, as I had just caught up
My heart to write with, in the place of it.
At least you'd take these letters to be writ
At sea, in storm!—wait now . . .
                A simple chance
Did all. I could not sleep last night, and, tired   420
Of turning on my pillow and harder thoughts,
Went out at early morning, when the air
Is delicate with some last starry touch,
To wander through the Market-place of Flowers*
(The prettiest haunt in Paris), and make sure
At worst that there were roses in the world.
So wandering, musing, with the artist's eye,
That keeps the shade-side of the thing it loves,
Half absent, whole observing, while the crowd
Of young vivacious and black-braided heads   430
Dipped, quick as finches in a blossomed tree,
Among the nosegays, cheapening this and that
In such a cheerful twitter of rapid speech—
My heart leapt in me, startled by a voice
That slowly, faintly, with long breaths that marked
The interval between the wish and word,
Inquired in stranger's French, 'Would *that* be much,
That branch of flowering mountain-gorse?'—'So much?*
Too much for me, then!' turning the face round
So close upon me that I felt the sigh   440
It turned with.
          'Marian, Marian!'—face to face—
'Marian! I find you. Shall I let you go?'

I held her two slight wrists with both my hands;
'Ah Marian, Marian, can I let you go?'
—She fluttered from me like a cyclamen,
As white, which taken in a sudden wind
Beats on against the palisade.—'Let pass,'
She said at last. 'I will not,' I replied;
'I lost my sister Marian many days,
And sought her ever in my walks and prayers,   450
And, now I find her . . . do we throw away
The bread we worked and prayed for—crumble it
And drop it . . . to do even so by thee
Whom still I've hungered after more than bread,
My sister Marian?—can I hurt thee, dear?
Then why distrust me? Never tremble so.
Come with me rather where we'll talk and live
And none shall vex us. I've a home for you
And me and no one else' . . .
                                    She shook her head.
'A home for you and me and no one else   460
Ill suits one of us: I prefer to such,
A roof of grass on which a flower might spring,
Less costly to me than the cheapest here;
And yet I could not, at this hour, afford
A like home even. That you offer yours,
I thank you. You are as good as heaven itself—
As good as one I knew before . . . Farewell.'

I loosed her hands—'In *his* name, no farewell!'
(She stood as if I held her.) 'For his sake,
For his sake, Romney's! by the good he meant,   470
Ay, always! by the love he pressed for once—
And by the grief, reproach, abandonment,
He took in change' . . .
                        'He Romney! who grieved *him*?
Who had the heart for't? what reproach touched *him*?
Be merciful—speak quickly.'
                                'Therefore come,'

I answered with authority.—'I think
We dare to speak such things and name such names
In the open squares of Paris!'

              Not a word
She said, but in a gentle humbled way
(As one who had forgot herself in grief)   480
Turned round and followed closely where I went,
As if I led her by a narrow plank
Across devouring waters, step by step;
And so in silence we walked on a mile.

And then she stopped: her face was white as wax.
'We go much farther?'

                  'You are ill,' I asked,
'Or tired?'

          She looked the whiter for her smile.
'There's one at home,' she said, 'has need of me
By this time—and I must not let him wait.'

'Not even,' I asked, 'to hear of Romney Leigh?'   490

'Not even,' she said, 'to hear of Mister Leigh.'

'In that case,' I resumed, 'I go with you,
And we can talk the same thing there as here.
None waits for me: I have my day to spend.'

Her lips moved in a spasm without a sound—
But then she spoke. 'It shall be as you please;
And better so—'tis shorter seen than told:
And though you will not find me worth your pains,
That, even, may be worth some pains to know
For one as good as you are.'

                  Then she led   500
The way, and I, as by a narrow plank
Across devouring waters, followed her,
Stepping by her footsteps, breathing by her breath,

And holding her with eyes that would not slip;
And so, without a word, we walked a mile,
And so, another mile, without a word.

Until the peopled streets being all dismissed,
House-rows and groups all scattered like a flock,
The market-gardens thickened, and the long
White walls beyond, like spiders' outside threads,   510
Stretched, feeling blindly toward the country-fields
Through half-built habitations and half-dug
Foundations—intervals of trenchant chalk
That bit betwixt the grassy uneven turfs
Where goats (vine-tendrils trailing from their mouths)
Stood perched on edges of the cellarage
Which should be, staring as about to leap
To find their coming Bacchus. All the place
Seemed less a cultivation than a waste.
Men work here, only—scarce begin to live: 520
All's sad, the country struggling with the town,
Like an untamed hawk upon a strong man's fist,
That beats its wings and tries to get away,
And cannot choose be satisfied so soon
To hop through court-yards with its right foot tied,
The vintage plains and pastoral hills in sight.

We stopped beside a house too high and slim
To stand there by itself, but waiting till
Five others, two on this side, three on that,
Should grow up from the sullen second floor   530
They pause at now, to build it to a row.
The upper windows partly were unglazed
Meantime—a meagre, unripe house: a line
Of rigid poplars elbowed it behind,
And, just in front, beyond the lime and bricks
That wronged the grass between it and the road,
A great acacia with its slender trunk
And overpoise of multitudinous leaves

(In which a hundred fields might spill their dew
And intense verdure, yet find room enough) 540
Stood reconciling all the place with green.

I followed up the stair upon her step.
She hurried upward, shot across a face,
A woman's, on the landing—'How now, now!
Is no one to have holidays but you?
You said an hour, and stay three hours, I think,
And Julie waiting for your betters here?
Why if he had waked he might have waked, for me.'
—Just murmuring an excusing word she passed
And shut the rest out with the chamber-door, 550
Myself shut in beside her.

          'Twas a room
Scarce larger than a grave, and near as bare;
Two stools, a pallet-bed; I saw the room:
A mouse could find no sort of shelter in't,
Much less a greater secret; curtainless—
The window fixed you with its torturing eye,
Defying you to take a step apart
If peradventure you would hide a thing.
I saw the whole room, I and Marian there
Alone.

      Alone? She threw her bonnet off, 560
Then, sighing as 'twere sighing the last time,
Approached the bed, and drew a shawl away:
You could not peel a fruit you fear to bruise
More calmly and more carefully than so—
Nor would you find within, a rosier flushed
Pomegranate—

          There he lay upon his back,
The yearling creature, warm and moist with life
To the bottom of his dimples—to the ends
Of the lovely tumbled curls about his face;
For since he had been covered over-much 570
To keep him from the light-glare, both his cheeks

A.L. - 12

Were hot and scarlet as the first live rose*
The shepherd's heart-blood ebbed away into
The faster for his love. And love was here
As instant; in the pretty baby-mouth,
Shut close as if for dreaming that it sucked,
The little naked feet, drawn up the way
Of nestled birdlings; everything so soft
And tender—to the tiny hold-fast hands,
Which, closing on a finger into sleep,   580
Had kept the mould of 't.
                         While we stood there dumb,
For oh, that it should take such innocence
To prove just guilt, I thought, and stood there dumb—
The light upon his eyelids pricked them wide,
And, staring out at us with all their blue,
As half perplexed between the angelhood
He had been away to visit in his sleep,
And our most mortal presence, gradually
He saw his mother's face, accepting it
In change for heaven itself with such a smile   590
As might have well been learnt there—never moved,
But smiled on, in a drowse of ecstasy,
So happy (half with her and half with Heaven)
He could not have the trouble to be stirred,
But smiled and lay there. Like a rose, I said?
As red and still indeed as any rose,
That blows in all the silence of its leaves,
Content in blowing to fulfil its life.

She leaned above him (drinking him as wine)
In that extremity of love, 'twill pass   600
For agony or rapture, seeing that love
Includes the whole of nature, rounding it
To love . . . no more—since more can never be
Than just love. Self-forgot, cast out of self,
And drowning in the transport of the sight,
Her whole pale passionate face, mouth, forehead, eyes,

One gaze, she stood: then, slowly as he smiled
She smiled too, slowly, smiling unaware,
And drawing from his countenance to hers
A fainter red, as if she watched a flame   610
And stood in it a-glow. 'How beautiful,'
Said she.
            I answered, trying to be cold.
(Must sin have compensations, was my thought,
As if it were a holy thing like grief?
And is a woman to be fooled aside
From putting vice down, with that woman's toy
A baby?)—'Ay! the child is well enough,'
I answered. 'If his mother's palms are clean
They need be glad of course in clasping such;
But if not, I would rather lay my hand,   620
Were I she, on God's brazen altar-bars
Red-hot with burning sacrificial lambs,
Than touch the sacred curls of such a child.'

She plunged her fingers in his clustering locks,
As one who would not be afraid of fire;
And then with indrawn steady utterance said,
'My lamb, my lamb! although, through such as thou,
The most unclean got courage and approach
To God, once—now they cannot, even with men,
Find grace enough for pity and gentle words.'   630

'My Marian,' I made answer, grave and sad,
'The priest who stole a lamb to offer him,
Was still a thief. And if a woman steals
(Through God's own barrier-hedges of true love,
Which fence out licence in securing love)
A child like this, that smiles so in her face,
She is no mother but a kidnapper,
And he's a dismal orphan, not a son,
Whom all her kisses cannot feed so full
He will not miss hereafter a pure home   640

To live in, a pure heart to lean against,
A pure good mother's name and memory
To hope by, when the world grows thick and bad
And he feels out for virtue.'
                              'Oh,' she smiled
With bitter patience, 'the child takes his chance;
Not much worse off in being fatherless
Than I was, fathered. He will say, belike,
His mother was the saddest creature born;
He'll say his mother lived so contrary
To joy, that even the kindest, seeing her,   650
Grew sometimes almost cruel: he'll not say
She flew contrarious in the face of God
With bat-wings of her vices. Stole my child—
My flower of earth, my only flower on earth,
My sweet, my beauty!' ... Up she snatched the child,
And, breaking on him in a storm of tears,
Drew out her long sobs from their shivering roots,
Until he took it for a game, and stretched
His feet and flapped his eager arms like wings
And crowed and gurgled through his infant laugh: 660
'Mine, mine,' she said. 'I have as sure a right
As any glad proud mother in the world,
Who sets her darling down to cut his teeth
Upon her church-ring. If she talks of law,
I talk of law! I claim my mother-dues
By law—the law which now is paramount—
The common law, by which the poor and weak
Are trodden underfoot by vicious men,
And loathed for ever after by the good.*
Let pass! I did not filch—I found the child.'   670

'You found him, Marian?'
                              'Ay, I found him where
I found my curse—in the gutter, with my shame!
What have you, any of you, to say to that,
Who all are happy, and sit safe and high,

And never spoke before to arraign my right
To grief itself? What, what . . . being beaten down
By hoofs of maddened oxen into a ditch,
Half dead, whole mangled, when a girl at last
Breathes, sees . . . and finds there, bedded in her flesh
Because of the extremity of the shock,   680
Some coin of price! . . . and when a good man comes
(That's God! the best men are not quite as good)
And says, "I dropped the coin there: take it you,
And keep it—it shall pay you for the loss"—
You all put up your finger—"See the thief!
Observe what precious thing she has come to filch.
How bad those girls are!" Oh, my flower, my pet,
I dare forget I have you in my arms
And fly off to be angry with the world,
And fright you, hurt you with my tempers, till   690
You double up your lip? Why, that indeed
Is bad: a naughty mother!'
                    'You mistake,'
I interrupted; 'if I loved you not,
I should not, Marian, certainly be here.'

'Alas,' she said, 'you are so very good;
And yet I wish indeed you had never come
To make me sob until I vex the child.
It is not wholesome for these pleasure-plats
To be so early watered by our brine.
And then, who knows? he may not like me now   700
As well, perhaps, as ere he saw me fret—
One's ugly fretting! he has eyes the same
As angels, but he cannot see as deep,
And so I've kept for ever in his sight
A sort of smile to please him—as you place
A green thing from the garden in a cup,
To make believe it grows there. Look, my sweet,
My cowslip-ball! we've done with that cross face,
And here's the face come back you used to like.

Ah, ah! he laughs! he likes me. Ah, Miss Leigh,   710
You're great and pure; but were you purer still—
As if you had walked, we'll say, no otherwhere
Than up and down the New Jerusalem,*
And held your trailing lute-string up yourself
From brushing the twelve stones, for fear of some
Small speck as little as a needle-prick,
White stitched on white—the child would keep to *me*,
Would choose his poor lost Marian, like me best,
And, though you stretched your arms, cry back and cling,
As we do when God says it's time to die   720
And bids us go up higher. Leave us, then;
We two are happy. Does *he* push me off?
He's satisfied with me, as I with him.'

'So soft to one, so hard to others! Nay,'
I cried, more angry that she melted me,
'We make henceforth a cushion of our faults
To sit and practise easy virtues on?
I thought a child was given to sanctify
A woman—set her in the sight of all
The clear-eyed Heavens, a chosen minister   730
To do their business and lead spirits up
The difficult blue heights. A woman lives,
Not bettered, quickened toward the truth and good
Through being a mother? . . . then she's none! although
She damps her baby's cheeks by kissing them,
As we kill roses.'

                    'Kill! O Christ!' she said,
And turned her wild sad face from side to side
With most despairing wonder in it, 'What,
What have you in your souls against me then,
All of you? am I wicked, do you think?   740
God knows me, trusts me with the child; but you,
You think me really wicked?'

                              'Complaisant,'
I answered softly, 'to a wrong you've done,

Because of certain profits—which is wrong
Beyond the first wrong, Marian. When you left
The pure place and the noble heart, to take
The hand of a seducer' . . .

                  'Whom? whose hand?
I took the hand of' . . .

               Springing up erect
And lifting up the child at full arm's length,
As if to bear him like an oriflamme*   750
Unconquerable to armies of reproach—
'By *him*,' she said, 'my child's head and its curls,
By these blue eyes no woman born could dare
A perjury on, I make my mother's oath,
That if I left that Heart, to lighten it,
The blood of mine was still, except for grief!
No cleaner maid than I was, took a step
To a sadder end—no matron-mother now
Looks backward to her early maidenhood
Through chaster pulses. I speak steadily;   760
And if I lie so . . . if, being fouled in will
And paltered with in soul by devil's lust,*
I dared to bid this angel take my part . . .
Would God sit quiet, let us think, in heaven,
Nor strike me dumb with thunder? Yet I speak:
He clears me therefore. What, "seduced"'s your word?
Do wolves seduce a wandering fawn in France?
Do eagles, who have pinched a lamb with claws,
Seduce it into carrion? So with me.
I was not ever, as you say, seduced,   770
But simply, murdered.'

               There she paused, and sighed,
With such a sigh as drops from agony
To exhaustion—sighing while she let the babe
Slide down upon her bosom from her arms,
And all her face's light fell after him
Like a torch quenched in falling. Down she sank,
And sat upon the bedside with the child.

But I, convicted, broken utterly,
With woman's passion clung about her waist
And kissed her hair and eyes—'I have been wrong,   780
Sweet Marian' (weeping in a tender rage),
'Sweet holy Marian! And now, Marian, now,
I'll use your oath although my lips are hard,
And by the child, my Marian, by the child,
I swear his mother shall be innocent
Before my conscience, as in the open Book
Of Him who reads for judgment. Innocent,
My sister! let the night be ne'er so dark
The moon is surely somewhere in the sky;
So surely is your whiteness to be found   790
Through all dark facts. But pardon, pardon me,
And smile a little, Marian—for the child,
If not for me, my sister.'
                              The poor lip
Just motioned for the smile and let it go:
And then, with scarce a stirring of the mouth,
As if a statue spoke that could not breathe,
But spoke on calm between its marble lips—
'I'm glad, I'm very glad you clear me so.
I should be sorry that you set me down
With harlots, or with even a better name   800
Which misbecomes his mother. For the rest,
I am not on a level with your love,
Nor ever was, you know—but now am worse,
Because that word of yours has dealt with me
As when the hard sea bites and chews a stone
And changes the first form of it. I've marked
A shore of pebbles bitten to one shape
From all the various life of madrepores;*
And so, that little stone, called Marian Erle,
Picked up and dropped by you and another friend,   810
Was ground and tortured by the incessant sea
And bruised from what she was—changed! death's a
        change,

And she, I said, was murdered; Marian's dead.
What can you do with people when they are dead,
But, if you are pious, sing a hymn and go,
Or, if you are tender, heave a sigh and go,
But go by all means—and permit the grass
To keep its green feud up 'twixt them and you?
Then leave me—let me rest. I'm dead, I say,
And if, to save the child from death as well,   820
The mother in me has survived the rest,
Why, that's God's miracle you must not tax,
I'm not less dead for that: I'm nothing more
But just a mother. Only for the child
I'm warm, and cold, and hungry, and afraid,
And smell the flowers a little and see the sun,
And speak still, and am silent—just for him!
I pray you therefore to mistake me not
And treat me haply as I were alive;
For though you ran a pin into my soul,   830
I think it would not hurt nor trouble me.
Here's proof, dear lady—in the market-place
But now, you promised me to say a word
About . . . a friend, who once, long years ago,
Took God's place toward me, when He leans and loves
And does not thunder . . . whom at last I left,
As all of us leave God. You thought perhaps
I seemed to care for hearing of that friend?
Now, judge me! we have sat here half an hour
And talked together of the child and me,   840
And I not asked as much as, "What's the thing
You had to tell me of the friend . . . the friend?"
He's sad, I think you said—he's sick perhaps?
'Tis nought to Marian if he's sad or sick.
Another would have crawled beside your foot
And prayed your words out. Why, a beast, a dog,
A starved cat, if he had fed it once with milk,
Would show less hardness. But I'm dead, you see,
And that explains it.'

                    Poor, poor thing, she spoke
And shook her head, as white and calm as frost   850
On days too cold for raining any more,
But still with such a face, so much alive,
I could not choose but take it on my arm
And stroke the placid patience of its cheeks—
Then told my story out, of Romney Leigh,
How, having lost her, sought her, missed her still,
He, broken-hearted for himself and her,
Had drawn the curtains of the world awhile
As if he had done with morning. There I stopped,
For when she gasped, and pressed me with her eyes,   860
'And now . . . how is it with him? tell me now,'
I felt the shame of compensated grief,
And chose my words with scruple—slowly stepped
Upon the slippery stones set here and there
Across the sliding water. 'Certainly,
As evening empties morning into night,
Another morning takes the evening up
With healthful, providential interchange;
And, though he thought still of her'—
                              'Yes, she knew,
She understood: she had supposed indeed   870
That, as one stops a hole upon a flute,
At which a new note comes and shapes the tune,
Excluding her would bring a worthier in,
And, long ere this, that Lady Waldemar
He loved so' . . .
                'Loved,' I started—'loved her so!
Now tell me' . . .
                'I will tell you,' she replied:
'But, since we're taking oaths, you'll promise first
That he in England, he, shall never learn
In what a dreadful trap his creature here,
Round whose unworthy neck he had meant to tie   880
The honourable ribbon of his name,
Fell unaware and came to butchery:

Because—I know him—as he takes to heart
The grief of every stranger, he's not like
To banish mine as far as I should choose
In wishing him most happy. Now he leaves
To think of me, perverse, who went my way,
Unkind, and left him—but if once he knew . . .
Ah, then, the sharp nail of my cruel wrong
Would fasten me for ever in his sight,   890
Like some poor curious bird, through each spread wing
Nailed high up over a fierce hunter's fire,
To spoil the dinner of all tenderer folk
Come in by chance. Nay, since your Marian's dead,
You shall not hang her up, but dig a hole
And bury her in silence! ring no bells.'

I answered gaily, though my whole voice wept,
'We'll ring the joy-bells, not the funeral-bells,
Because we have her back, dead or alive.'

She never answered that, but shook her head;   900
Then low and calm, as one who, safe in heaven,
Shall tell a story of his lower life,
Unmoved by shame or anger—so she spoke.
She told me she had loved upon her knees,
As others pray, more perfectly absorbed
In the act and inspiration. She felt his
For just his uses, not her own at all,
His stool, to sit on or put up his foot,
His cup, to fill with wine or vinegar,
Whichever drink might please him at the chance   910
For that should please her always: let him write
His name upon her . . . it seemed natural;
It was most precious, standing on his shelf,
To wait until he chose to lift his hand.
Well, well—I saw her then, and must have seen
How bright her life went floating on her love,
Like wicks the housewives send afloat on oil
Which feeds them to a flame that lasts the night.

To do good seemed so much his business,
That, having done it, she was fain to think,   920
Must fill up his capacity for joy.
At first she never mooted with herself
If *he* was happy, since he made her so,
Or if he loved her, being so much beloved.
Who thinks of asking if the sun is light,
Observing that it lightens? who's so bold,
To question God of His felicity?
Still less. And thus she took for granted first
What first of all she should have put to proof,
And sinned against him so, but only so.   930
'What could you hope,' she said, 'of such as she?
You take a kid you like, and turn it out
In some fair garden: though the creature's fond
And gentle, it will leap upon the beds
And break your tulips, bite your tender trees;
The wonder would be if such innocence
Spoiled less: a garden is no place for kids.'

And, by degrees, when he who had chosen her
Brought in his courteous and benignant friends
To spend their goodness on her, which she took   940
So very gladly, as a part of his—
By slow degrees it broke on her slow sense
That she too in that Eden of delight
Was out of place, and, like the silly kid,
Still did most mischief where she meant most love.
A thought enough to make a woman mad
(No beast in this but she may well go mad),
That saying 'I am thine to love and use'
May blow the plague in her protesting breath
To the very man for whom she claims to die—   950
That, clinging round his neck, she pulls him down
And drowns him—and that, lavishing her soul,
She hales perdition on him. 'So, being mad,'

Said Marian . . .

        'Ah—who stirred such thoughts, you ask?
Whose fault it was, that she should have such thoughts?
None's fault, none's fault. The light comes, and we see:
But if it were not truly for our eyes,
There would be nothing seen, for all the light.
And so with Marian: if she saw at last,
The sense was in her—Lady Waldemar   960
Had spoken all in vain else.'

                      'O my heart,
O prophet in my heart,' I cried aloud,
'Then Lady Waldemar spoke!'

                  '*Did* she speak,'
Mused Marian softly, 'or did she only sign?
Or did she put a word into her face
And look, and so impress you with the word?
Or leave it in the foldings of her gown,
Like rosemary smells a movement will shake out
When no one's conscious? who shall say, or guess?
One thing alone was certain—from the day   970
The gracious lady paid a visit first,
She, Marian, saw things different—felt distrust
Of all that sheltering roof of circumstance
Her hopes were building into with clay nests:
Her heart was restless, pacing up and down
And fluttering, like dumb creatures before storms,
Not knowing wherefore she was ill at ease.'

'And still the lady came,' said Marian Erle,
'Much oftener than *he* knew it, Mister Leigh.
She bade me never tell him she had come,   980
She liked to love me better than he knew,
So very kind was Lady Waldemar:
And every time she brought with her more light,
And every light made sorrow clearer . . . Well,
Ah, well! we cannot give her blame for that;
'Twould be the same thing if an angel came,

Whose right should prove our wrong. And every time
The lady came, she looked more beautiful
And spoke more like a flute among green trees,
Until at last, as one, whose heart being sad   990
On hearing lovely music, suddenly
Dissolves in weeping, I brake out in tears
Before her, asked her counsel—"Had I erred
In being too happy? would she set me straight?
For she, being wise and good and born above
The flats I had never climbed from, could perceive
If such as I, might grow upon the hills;
And whether such poor herb sufficed to grow,
For Romney Leigh to break his fast upon't—
Or would he pine on such, or haply starve?"   1000
She wrapped me in her generous arms at once,
And let me dream a moment how it feels
To have a real mother, like some girls:
But when I looked, her face was younger . . . ay,
Youth's too bright not to be a little hard,
And beauty keeps itself still uppermost,
That's true!—Though Lady Waldemar was kind
She hurt me, hurt, as if the morning-sun
Should smite us on the eyelids when we sleep,
And wake us up with headache. Ay, and soon   1010
Was light enough to make my heart ache too:
She told me truths I asked for—'twas my fault—
"That Romney could not love me, if he would,
As men call loving: there are bloods that flow
Together like some rivers and not mix,
Through contraries of nature. He indeed
Was set to wed me, to espouse my class,
Act out a rash opinion—and, once wed,
So just a man and gentle could not choose
But make my life as smooth as marriage-ring,   1020
Bespeak me mildly, keep me a cheerful house,
With servants, brooches, all the flowers I liked,
And pretty dresses, silk the whole year round" . . .

At which I stopped her—"This for me. And now
For *him*"—She hesitated—truth grew hard;
She owned, "'Twas plain a man like Romney Leigh
Required a wife more level to himself.
If day by day he had to bend his height
To pick up sympathies, opinions, thoughts,
And interchange the common talk of life   1030
Which helps a man to live as well as talk,
His days were heavily taxed. Who buys a staff
To fit the hand, that reaches but the knee?
He'd feel it bitter to be forced to miss
The perfect joy of married suited pairs,
Who, bursting through the separating hedge
Of personal dues with that sweet eglantine
Of equal love, keep saying, 'So *we* think,
It strikes *us*—that's *our* fancy.'"—When I asked
If earnest will, devoted love, employed   1040
In youth like mine, would fail to raise me up
As two strong arms will always raise a child
To a fruit hung overhead, she sighed and sighed . . .
"That could not be," she feared. "You take a pink,
You dig about its roots and water it
And so improve it to a garden-pink,
But will not change it to a heliotrope,
The kind remains. And then, the harder truth—
This Romney Leigh, so rash to leap a pale,*
So bold for conscience, quick for martyrdom,   1050
Would suffer steadily and never flinch,
But suffer surely and keenly, when his class
Turned shoulder on him for a shameful match,
And set him up as nine-pin in their talk
To bowl him down with jestings."—There, she paused;
And when I used the pause in doubting that
We wronged him after all in what we feared—
"Suppose such things could never touch him more
In his high conscience (if the things should be)
Than, when the queen sits in an upper room,   1060

The horses in the street can spatter her!"—
A moment, hope came—but the lady closed
That door and nicked the lock and shut it out,
Observing wisely that, "the tender heart
Which made him over-soft to a lower class,
Would scarcely fail to make him sensitive
To a higher—how they thought and what they felt."'

'Alas, alas,' said Marian, rocking slow
The pretty baby who was near asleep,
The eyelids creeping over the blue balls—   1070
'She made it clear, too clear—I saw the whole!
And yet who knows if I had seen my way
Straight out of it by looking, though 'twas clear,
Unless the generous lady, 'ware of this,
Had set her own house all a-fire for me
To light me forwards? Leaning on my face
Her heavy agate eyes which crushed my will,
She told me tenderly (as when men come
To a bedside to tell people they must die),
"She knew of knowledge—ay, of knowledge knew,   1080
That Romney Leigh had loved *her* formerly.
And *she* loved *him*, she might say, now the chance
Was past—but that, of course, he never guessed—
For something came between them, something thin
As a cobweb, catching every fly of doubt
To hold it buzzing at the window-pane
And help to dim the daylight. Ah, man's pride
Or woman's—which is greatest? most averse
To brushing cobwebs? Well, but she and he
Remained fast friends; it seemed not more than so,   1090
Because he had bound his hands and could not stir.
An honourable man, if somewhat rash;
And she, not even for Romney, would she spill
A blot . . . as little even as a tear . . .
Upon his marriage-contract—not to gain
A better joy for two than came by that:

For, though I stood between her heart and heaven,
She loved me wholly."'
                    Did I laugh or curse?
I think I sat there silent, hearing all,
Ay, hearing double—Marian's tale, at once,   1100
And Romney's marriage-vow, '*I'll keep to* THEE,'
Which means that woman-serpent. Is it time
For church now?
                    'Lady Waldemar spoke more,'
Continued Marian, 'but, as when a soul
Will pass out through the sweetness of a song
Beyond it, voyaging the uphill road,
Even so mine wandered from the things I heard
To those I suffered. It was afterward
I shaped the resolution to the act.
For many hours we talked. What need to talk?   1110
The fate was clear and close; it touched my eyes;
But still the generous lady tried to keep
The case afloat, and would not let it go,
And argued, struggled upon Marian's side,
Which was not Romney's! though she little knew
What ugly monster would take up the end—
What griping death within the drowning death
Was ready to complete my sum of death.'

I thought—Perhaps he's sliding now the ring
Upon that woman's finger . . .
                    She went on: 1120
'The lady, failing to prevail her way,
Up-gathered my torn wishes from the ground
And pieced them with her strong benevolence;
And, as I thought I could breather freer air
Away from England, going without pause
Without farewell, just breaking with a jerk
The blossomed offshoot from my thorny life—
She promised kindly to provide the means,
With instant passage to the colonies

And full protection—"would commit me straight   1130
To one who once had been her waiting-maid
And had the customs of the world, intent
On changing England for Australia
Herself, to carry out her fortune so."
For which I thanked the Lady Waldemar,
As men upon their deathbeds thank last friends
Who lay the pillow straight: it is not much,
And yet 'tis all of which they are capable,
This lying smoothly in a bed to die.
And so, 'twas fixed—and so, from day to day,   1140
The woman named came in to visit me.'

Just then the girl stopped speaking—sat erect,
And stared at me as if I had been a ghost,
(Perhaps I looked as white as any ghost)
With large-eyed horror. 'Does God make,' she said,
'All sorts of creatures really, do you think?
Or is it that the Devil slavers them
So excellently, that we come to doubt
Who's stronger, He who makes, or he who mars?
I never liked the woman's face or voice   1150
Or ways: it made me blush to look at her;
It made me tremble if she touched my hand;
And when she spoke a fondling word I shrank
As if one hated me who had power to hurt;
And, every time she came, my veins ran cold
As somebody were walking on my grave.
At last I spoke to Lady Waldemar:
"Could such an one be good to trust?" I asked.
Whereat the lady stroked my cheek and laughed
Her silver laugh (one must be born to laugh,   1160
To put such music in it)—"Foolish girl,
Your scattered wits are gathering wool beyond
The sheep-walk reaches!—leave the thing to me."
And therefore, half in trust, and half in scorn

That I had heart still for another fear
In such a safe despair, I left the thing.

'The rest is short. I was obedient:
I wrote my letter which delivered *him*
From Marian to his own prosperities,
And followed that bad guide. The lady?—hush,   1170
I never blame the lady. Ladies who
Sit high, however willing to look down,
Will scarce see lower than their dainty feet;
And Lady Waldemar saw less than I,
With what a Devil's daughter I went forth
Along the swine's road, down the precipice,*
In such a curl of hell-foam caught and choked,
No shriek of soul in anguish could pierce through
To fetch some help. They say there's help in heaven
For all such cries. But if one cries from hell . . .   1180
What then?—the heavens are deaf upon that side.

'A woman . . . hear me, let me make it plain . . .
A woman . . . not a monster . . . both her breasts
Made right to suckle babes . . . she took me off
A woman also, young and ignorant
And heavy with my grief, my two poor eyes
Near washed away with weeping, till the trees,
The blessed unaccustomed trees and fields
Ran either side the train like stranger dogs
Unworthy of any notice—took me off   1190
So dull, so blind, so only half alive,
Not seeing by what road, nor by what ship,
Not toward what place, nor to what end of all.
Men carry a corpse thus—past the doorway, past
The garden-gate, the children's playground, up
The green lane—then they leave it in the pit,
To sleep and find corruption, cheek to cheek
With him who stinks since Friday.

                                        'But suppose;

To go down with one's soul into the grave,
To go down half dead, half alive, I say,   1200
And wake up with corruption . . . cheek to cheek
With him who stinks since Friday! There it is,
And that's the horror of 't, Miss Leigh.

                                        'You feel?
You understand?—no, do not look at me,
But understand. The blank, blind, weary way,
Which led, where'er it led, away at least;
The shifted ship, to Sydney or to France,
Still bound, wherever else, to another land;
The swooning sickness on the dismal sea,
The foreign shore, the shameful house, the night,   1210
The feeble blood, the heavy-headed grief . . .
No need to bring their damnable drugged cup,
And yet they brought it. Hell's so prodigal
Of devil's gifts, hunts liberally in packs,
Will kill no poor small creature of the wilds
But fifty red wide throats must smoke at it,
As HIS at me . . . when waking up at last . . .
I told you that I waked up in the grave.

'Enough so!—it is plain enough so. True,
We wretches cannot tell out all our wrong   1220
Without offence to decent happy folk.
I know that we must scrupulously hint
With half words, delicate reserves, the thing
Which no one scrupled we should feel in full.
Let pass the rest, then; only leave my oath
Upon this sleeping child—man's violence,
Not man's seduction, made me what I am,
As lost as . . . I told *him* I should be lost.
When mothers fail us, can we help ourselves?
That's fatal!—And you call it being lost,   1230
That down came next day's noon and caught me there
Half gibbering and half raving on the floor,
And wondering what had happened up in heaven,

That suns should dare to shine when God Himself
Was certainly abolished.
                              'I was mad,
How many weeks, I know not—many weeks.
I think they let me go when I was mad,
They feared my eyes and loosed me, as boys might
A mad dog which they had tortured. Up and down
I went, by road and village, over tracts   1240
Of open foreign country, large and strange,
Crossed everywhere by long thin poplar-lines
Like fingers of some ghastly skeleton Hand
Through sunlight and through moonlight evermore
Pushed out from hell itself to pluck me back,
And resolute to get me, slow and sure;
While every roadside Christ upon his cross
Hung reddening through his gory wounds at me,
And shook his nails in anger, and came down
To follow a mile after, wading up   1250
The low vines and green wheat, crying, "Take the girl!
She's none of mine from henceforth." Then I knew
(But this is somewhat dimmer than the rest)
The charitable peasants gave me bread
And leave to sleep in straw: and twice they tied,
At parting, Mary's image round my neck—
How heavy it seemed! as heavy as a stone;
A woman has been strangled with less weight:
I threw it in a ditch to keep it clean
And ease my breath a little, when none looked;   1260
I did not need such safeguards—brutal men
Stopped short, Miss Leigh, in insult, when they had seen
My face—I must have had an awful look.
And so I lived: the weeks passed on—I lived.
'Twas living my old tramp-life o'er again,
But, this time, in a dream, and hunted round
By some prodigious Dream-fear at my back,
Which ended yet: my brain cleared presently;
And there I sat, one evening, by the road,

I, Marian Erle, myself, alone, undone,
Facing a sunset low upon the flats
As if it were the finish of all time,
The great red stone upon my sepulchre,*
Which angels were too weak to roll away.'

BOOK VII

'THE woman's motive? shall we daub ourselves
With finding roots for nettles? 'tis soft clay
And easily explored. She had the means,
The monies, by the lady's liberal grace,
In trust for that Australian scheme and me,
Which so, that she might clutch with both her hands
And chink to her naughty uses undisturbed,*
She served me (after all it was not strange,
'Twas only what my mother would have done)
A motherly, right damnable good turn.*   10

'Well, after. There are nettles everywhere,
But smooth green grasses are more common still;
The blue of heaven is larger than the cloud;
A miller's wife at Clichy took me in
And spent her pity on me—made me calm
And merely very reasonably sad.
She found me a servant's place in Paris, where
I tried to take the cast-off life again,
And stood as quiet as a beaten ass
Who, having fallen through overloads, stands up   20
To let them charge him with another pack.

'A few months, so. My mistress, young and light,
Was easy with me, less for kindness than
Because she led, herself, an easy time
Betwixt her lover and her looking-glass,
Scarce knowing which way she was praised the most.
She felt so pretty and so pleased all day
She could not take the trouble to be cross,
But sometimes, as I stooped to tie her shoe,

Would tap me softly with her slender foot   30
Still restless with the last night's dancing in't,
And say, "Fie, pale-face! are you English girls
All grave and silent? mass-book still, and Lent?
And first-communion pallor on your cheeks,
Worn past the time for't? little fool, be gay!"
At which she vanished like a fairy, through
A gap of silver laughter.
                                'Came an hour
When all went otherwise. She did not speak,
But clenched her brows, and clipped me with her eyes
As if a viper with a pair of tongs,   40
Too far for any touch, yet near enough
To view the writhing creature—then at last,
"Stand still there, in the holy Virgin's name,
Thou Marian; thou'rt no reputable girl,
Although sufficient dull for twenty saints!
I think thou mock'st me and my house," she said;
"Confess thou'lt be a mother in a month,
Thou mask of saintship."
                                'Could I answer her?
The light broke in so. It meant *that* then, *that*?
I had not thought of that, in all my thoughts,   50
Through all the cold, numb aching of my brow,
Through all the heaving of impatient life
Which threw me on death at intervals—through all
The upbreak of the fountains of my heart
The rains had swelled too large: it could mean *that*?
Did God make mothers out of victims, then,
And set such pure amens to hideous deeds?
Why not? he overblows an ugly grave
With violets which blossom in the spring.
And *I* could be a mother in a month?   60
I hope it was not wicked to be glad.
I lifted up my voice and wept, and laughed,
To Heaven, not her, until it tore my throat.
"Confess, confess!"—what was there to confess,

Except man's cruelty, except my wrong?
Except this anguish, or this ecstasy?
This shame or glory? The light woman there
Was small to take it in: an acorn-cup
Would take the sea in sooner.

       ' "Good," she cried;
"Unmarried and a mother, and she laughs!   70
These unchaste girls are always impudent.
Get out, intriguer! leave my house and trot.
I wonder you should look me in the face,
With such a filthy secret."

        'Then I rolled
My scanty bundle up and went my way,
Washed white with weeping, shuddering head and foot
With blind hysteric passion, staggering forth
Beyond those doors. 'Twas natural of course
She should not ask me where I meant to sleep;
I might sleep well beneath the heavy Seine,   80
Like others of my sort; the bed was laid
For us. But any woman, womanly,
Had thought of him who should be in a month,
The sinless babe that should be in a month,
And if by chance he might be warmer housed
Than underneath such dreary dripping eaves.'

I broke on Marian there. 'Yet she herself,
A wife, I think, had scandals of her own,
A lover not her husband.'

        'Ay,' she said,
'But gold and meal are measured otherwise;   90
I learnt so much at school,' said Marian Erle.

'O crooked world,' I cried, 'ridiculous*
If not so lamentable! 'Tis the way
With these light women of a thrifty vice,
My Marian—always hard upon the rent
In any sister's virtue! while they keep
Their own so darned and patched with perfidy,

That, though a rag itself, it looks as well
Across a street, in balcony or coach,
As any perfect stuff might. For my part,   100
I'd rather take the wind-side of the stews
Than touch such women with my finger-end!
They top the poor street-walker by their lie
And look the better for being so much worse:
The devil's most devilish when respectable.
But you, dear, and your story.'

                   'All the rest
Is here,' she said, and signed upon the child.
'I found a mistress-sempstress who was kind
And let me sew in peace among her girls.
And what was better than to draw the threads   110
All day and half the night for him and him?
And so I lived for him, and so he lives,
And so I know, by this time, God lives too.'

She smiled beyond the sun and ended so,
And all my soul rose up to take her part
Against the world's successes, virtues, fames.
'Come with me, sweetest sister,' I returned,
'And sit within my house and do me good
From henceforth, thou and thine! ye are my own
From henceforth. I am lonely in the world,   120
And thou art lonely, and the child is half
An orphan. Come—and henceforth thou and I
Being still together will not miss a friend,
Nor he a father, since two mothers shall
Make that up to him. I am journeying south,
And in my Tuscan home I'll find a niche
And set thee there, my saint, the child and thee,
And burn the lights of love before thy face,
And ever at thy sweet look cross myself
From mixing with the world's prosperities;   130
That so, in gravity and holy calm,
We two may live on toward the truer life.'

She looked me in the face and answered not,
Nor signed she was unworthy, nor gave thanks,
But took the sleeping child and held it out
To meet my kiss, as if requiting me
And trusting me at once. And thus, at once,
I carried him and her to where I live;
She's there now, in the little room, asleep,
I hear the soft child-breathing through the door,   140
And all three of us, at tomorrow's break,
Pass onward, homeward, to our Italy.
Oh, Romney Leigh, I have your debts to pay,
And I'll be just and pay them.
                                But yourself!
To pay your debts is scarcely difficult,
To buy your life is nearly impossible,
Being sold away to Lamia. My head aches,
I cannot see my road along this dark;
Nor can I creep and grope, as fits the dark,
For these foot-catching robes of womanhood: 150
A man might walk a little . . . but I!—He loves
The Lamia-woman—and I, write to him
What stops his marriage, and destroys his peace—
Or what perhaps shall simply trouble him,
Until she only need to touch his sleeve
With just a finger's tremulous white flame,
Saying, 'Ah—Aurora Leigh! a pretty tale,
A very pretty poet! I can guess
The motive'—then, to catch his eyes in hers
And vow she does not wonder—and they two   160
To break in laughter as the sea along
A melancholy coast, and float up higher,
In such a laugh, their fatal weeds of love!
Ay, fatal, ay. And who shall answer me
Fate has not hurried tides—and if tonight
My letter would not be a night too late,
An arrow shot into a man that's dead,
To prove a vain intention? Would I show

The new wife vile, to make the husband mad?
No, Lamia! shut the shutters, bar the doors   170
From every glimmer on thy serpent-skin!
I will not let thy hideous secret out
To agonise the man I love—I mean
The friend I love . . . as friends love.

                            It is strange,
Today while Marian told her story like
To absorb most listeners, how I listened chief
To a voice not hers, nor yet that enemy's,
Nor God's in wrath . . . but one that mixed with mine
Long years ago among the garden-trees,
And said to *me*, to *me* too, 'Be my wife,   180
Aurora.' It is strange with what a swell
Of yearning passion, as a snow of ghosts
Might beat against the impervious door of heaven,
I thought, 'Now, if I had been a woman, such
As God made women, to save men by love—
By just my love I might have saved this man,
And made a nobler poem for the world
Than all I have failed in.' But I failed besides
In this; and now he's lost! through me alone!
And, by my only fault, his empty house   190
Sucks in, at this same hour, a wind from hell
To keep his hearth cold, make his casements creak
For ever to the tune of plague and sin—
O Romney, O my Romney, O my friend,
My cousin and friend! my helper, when I would,
My love, that might be! mine!

                         Why, how one weeps
When one's too weary! Were a witness by,
He'd say some folly . . . that I loved the man,
Who knows? . . . and make me laugh again for scorn.
At strongest, women are as weak in flesh,   200
As men, at weakest, vilest, are in soul:
So, hard for women to keep pace with men!
As well give up at once, sit down at once,

And weep as I do. Tears, tears! *why* we weep?
'Tis worth inquiry?—that we've shamed a life,
Or lost a love, or missed a world, perhaps?
By no means. Simply, that we've walked too far,
Or talked too much, or felt the wind i' the east—
And so we weep, as if both body and soul
Broke up in water—this way.

                   Poor mixed rags   210
Forsooth we're made of, like those other dolls
That lean with pretty faces into fairs.
It seems as if I had a man in me,
Despising such a woman.

                      Yet indeed,
To see a wrong or suffering moves us all
To undo it though we should undo ourselves,
Ay, all the more, that we undo ourselves;
That's womanly, past doubt, and not ill-moved.
A natural movement therefore, on my part,
To fill the chair up of my cousin's wife,   220
And save him from a devil's company!
We're all so—made so—'tis our woman's trade
To suffer torment for another's ease.
The world's male chivalry has perished out,
But women are knights-errant to the last;
And if Cervantes had been Shakespeare too,*
He had made his Don a Donna.

                      So it clears,
And so we rain our skies blue.

                    Put away
This weakness. If, as I have just now said,
A man's within me—let him act himself,   230
Ignoring the poor conscious trouble of blood
That's called the woman merely. I will write
Plain words to England—if too late, too late,
If ill-accounted, then accounted ill;
We'll trust the heavens with something.

                        'Dear Lord Howe,

You'll find a story on another leaf
Of Marian Erle—what noble friend of yours
She trusted once, through what flagitious means,*
To what disastrous ends—the story's true.
I found her wandering on the Paris quays,   240
A babe upon her breast—unnatural
Unseasonable outcast on such snow
Unthawed to this time. I will tax in this
Your friendship, friend, if that convicted She
Be not his wife yet, to denounce the facts
To himself—but, otherwise, to let them pass
On tiptoe like escaping murderers,
And tell my cousin merely—Marian lives,
Is found, and finds her home with such a friend,
Myself, Aurora. Which good news, "She's found,"   250
Will help to make him merry in his love:
I send it, tell him, for my marriage-gift,
As good as orange-water for the nerves,
Or perfumed gloves for headache—though aware
That he, except of love, is scarcely sick:
I mean the new love this time . . . since last year.
Such quick forgetting on the part of men!
Is any shrewder trick upon the cards
To enrich them? pray instruct me how 'tis done:
First, clubs—and while you look at clubs, 'tis spades;   260
That's prodigy. The lightning strikes a man,
And when we think to find him dead and charred . . .
Why, there he is on a sudden, playing pipes
Beneath the splintered elm-tree! Crime and shame
And all their hoggery trample your smooth world,*
Nor leave more foot-marks than Apollo's kine
Whose hoofs were muffled by the thieving god*
In tamarisk-leaves and myrtle. I'm so sad,
So weary and sad tonight, I'm somewhat sour—
Forgive me. To be blue and shrew at once,   270
Exceeds all toleration except yours,
But yours, I know, is infinite. Farewell.

Tomorrow we take train for Italy.
Speak gently of me to your gracious wife,
As one, however far, shall yet be near
In loving wishes to your house.'

                           I sign.
And now I loose my heart upon a page,
This—

         'Lady Waldemar, I'm very glad
I never liked you; which you knew so well
You spared me, in your turn, to like me much: 280
Your liking surely had done worse for me
Than has your loathing, though the last appears
Sufficiently unscrupulous to hurt,
And not afraid of judgment. Now, there's space
Between our faces—I stand off, as if
I judged a stranger's portrait and pronounced
Indifferently the type was good or bad.
What matter to me that the lines are false,
I ask you? did I ever ink my lips
By drawing your name through them as a friend's,   290
Or touch your hands as lovers do? Thank God
I never did: and since you're proved so vile,*
Ay, vile, I say—we'll show it presently—
I'm not obliged to nurse my friend in you,
Or wash out my own blots, in counting yours,
Or even excuse myself to honest souls
Who seek to press my lip or clasp my palm—
"Alas, but Lady Waldemar came first!"

''Tis true, by this time you may near me so
That you're my cousin's wife. You've gambled deep*   300
As Lucifer, and won the morning-star
In that case—and the noble house of Leigh
Must henceforth with its good roof shelter you:
I cannot speak and burn you up between
Those rafters, I who am born a Leigh—nor speak
And pierce your breast through Romney's, I who live

His friend and cousin—so, you're safe. You two
Must grow together like the tares and wheat*
<u>Till God's great fire.</u>—But make the best of time.

'And hide this letter: let it speak no more   310
Than I shall, how you tricked poor Marian Erle,
And set her own love digging its own grave
Within her green hope's pretty garden-ground—
Ay, sent her forth with someone of your sort
To a wicked house in France, from which she fled
With curses in her eyes and ears and throat,
Her whole soul choked with curses—mad in short,
And madly scouring up and down for weeks
The foreign hedgeless country, lone and lost—
So innocent, male-fiends might slink within   320
Remote hell-corners, seeing her so defiled.

'But you—you are a woman and more bold.
To do you justice, you'd not shrink to face . . .
We'll say, the unfledged life in the other room,
Which, treading down God's corn, you trod in sight
Of all the dogs, in reach of all the guns—
Ay, Marian's babe, her poor unfathered child,
Her yearling babe!—you'd face him when he wakes
And opens up his wonderful blue eyes:
You'd meet them and not wink perhaps, nor fear   330
God's triumph in them and supreme revenge
When righting His creation's balance-scale
(You pulled as low as Tophet) to the top
Of most celestial innocence. For me
Who am not as bold, I own those infant eyes
Have set me praying.

                    'While they look at Heaven,
No need of protestation in my words
Against the place you've made them! let them look.
They'll do your business with the Heavens, be sure:
I spare you common curses.

                                                     'Ponder this;   340
If haply you're the wife of Romney Leigh
(For which inheritance beyond your birth*
You sold that poisonous porridge called your soul),
I charge you, be his faithful and true wife!
Keep warm his hearth and clean his board, and, when
He speaks, be quick with your obedience;
Still grind your paltry wants and low desires
To dust beneath his heel; though, even thus,
The ground must hurt him—it was writ of old,*
"Ye shall not yoke together ox and ass,"   350
The nobler and ignobler. Ay, but you
Shall do your part as well as such ill things
Can do aught good. You shall not vex him—mark,
You shall not vex him, jar him when he's sad,
Or cross him when he's eager. Understand
To trick him with apparent sympathies,
Nor let him see thee in the face too near
And unlearn thy sweet seeming. Pay the price
Of lies, by being constrained to lie on still:
'Tis easy for thy sort: a million more   360
Will scarcely damn thee deeper.

                                    'Doing which
You are very safe from Marian and myself;
We'll breathe as softly as the infant here,
And stir no dangerous embers. Fail a point,
And show our Romney wounded, ill-content,
Tormented in his home, we open mouth,
And such a noise will follow, the last trump's
Will scarcely seem more dreadful, even to you;
You'll have no pipers after: Romney will
(I know him) push you forth as none of his,   370
All other men declaring it well done,
While women, even the worst, your like, will draw
Their skirts back, not to brush you in the street,
And so I warn you. I'm . . . Aurora Leigh.'

The letter written I felt satisfied.
The ashes, smouldering in me, were thrown out
By handfuls from me: I had writ my heart
And wept my tears, and now was cool and calm;
And, going straightway to the neighbouring room,
I lifted up the curtains of the bed   380
Where Marian Erle, the babe upon her arm,
Both faces leaned together like a pair
Of folded innocences self-complete,
Each smiling from the other, smiled and slept.
There seemed no sin, no shame, no wrath, no grief.
I felt she too had spoken words that night,
But softer certainly, and said to God,
Who laughs in heaven perhaps that such as I
Should make ado for such as she.—'Defiled'
I wrote? 'defiled' I thought her? Stoop,   390
Stoop lower, Aurora! get the angels' leave
To creep in somewhere, humbly, on your knees,
Within this round of sequestration white
In which they have wrapped earth's foundlings, heaven's
     elect.

The next day we took train to Italy
And fled on southward in the roar of steam.
The marriage-bells of Romney must be loud,
To sound so clear through all: I was not well,
And truly, though the truth is like a jest,
I could not choose but fancy, half the way,   400
I stood alone i' the belfry, fifty bells
Of naked iron, mad with merriment
(As one who laughs and cannot stop himself),
All clanking at me, in me, over me,
Until I shrieked a shriek I could not hear,
And swooned with noise—but still, along my swoon,
Was 'ware the baffled changes backward rang,
Prepared, at each emerging sense, to beat
And crash it out with clangour. I was weak;

I struggled for the posture of my soul   410
In upright consciousness of place and time,
But evermore, 'twixt waking and asleep,
Slipped somehow, staggered, caught at Marian's eyes
A moment (it is very good for strength
To know that someone needs you to be strong),
And so recovered what I called myself,
For that time.
           I just knew it when we swept
Above the old roofs of Dijon: Lyons dropped
A spark into the night, half trodden out
Unseen. But presently the winding Rhône   420
Washed out the moonlight large along his banks
Which strained their yielding curves out clear and clean
To hold it—shadow of town and castle blurred
Upon the hurrying river. Such an air
Blew thence upon the forehead—half an air
And half a water—that I leaned and looked,
Then, turning back on Marian, smiled to mark
That she looked only on her child, who slept,
His face toward the moon too.
                  So we passed
The liberal open country and the close,   430
And shot through tunnels, like a lightning-wedge
By great Thor-hammers driven through the rock,*
Which, quivering through the intestine blackness, splits,
And lets it in at once: the train swept in
A-throb with effort, trembling with resolve,
The fierce denouncing whistle wailing on
And dying off smothered in the shuddering dark,
While we, self-awed, drew troubled breath, oppressed
As other Titans underneath the pile*
And nightmare of the mountains. Out, at last,   440
To catch the dawn afloat upon the land!
—Hills, slung forth broadly and gauntly everywhere,
Not cramped in their foundations, pushing wide
Rich outspreads of the vineyards and the corn

(As if they entertained i' the name of France),
While, down their straining sides, streamed manifest
A soil as red as Charlemagne's knightly blood,
To consecrate the verdure. Someone said,
'Marseilles!' And lo, the city of Marseilles,
With all her ships behind her, and beyond,   450
The scimitar of ever-shining sea
For right-hand use, bared blue against the sky!

That night we spent between the purple heaven
And purple water: I think Marian slept;
But I, as a dog a-watch for his master's foot,
Who cannot sleep or eat before he hears,
I sat upon the deck and watched the night
And listened through the stars for Italy.
Those marriage-bells I spoke of, sounded far,
As some child's go-cart in the street beneath   460
To a dying man who will not pass the day,
And knows it, holding by a hand he loves.
I too sat quiet, satisfied with death,
Sat silent: I could hear my own soul speak,
And had my friend—for Nature comes sometimes
And says, 'I am ambassador for God.'
I felt the wind soft from the land of souls;
The old miraculous mountains heaved in sight,
One straining past another along the shore,
The way of grand dull Odyssean ghosts,*   470
A-thirst to drink the cool blue wine of seas
And stare on voyagers. Peak pushing peak
They stood: I watched, beyond that Tyrian belt*
Of intense sea betwixt them and the ship,
Down all their sides the misty olive-woods
Dissolving in the weak congenial moon
And still disclosing some brown convent-tower
That seems as if it grew from some brown rock,
Or many a little lighted village, dropped

Like a fallen star upon so high a point, 480
You wonder what can keep it in its place
From sliding headlong with the waterfalls
Which powder all the myrtle and orange-groves
With spray of silver. Thus my Italy
Was stealing on us. Genoa broke with day,
The Doria's long pale palace striking out,
From green hills in advance of the white town,
A marble finger dominant to ships,
Seen glimmering through the uncertain gray of dawn.

And then I did not think, 'my Italy,' 490
I thought, 'my father!' O my father's house,
Without his presence!—Places are too much
Or else too little, for immortal man—
Too little, when love's May o'ergrows the ground,
Too much, when that luxuriant robe of green
Is rustling to our ankles in dead leaves.
'Tis only good to be or here or there,
Because we had a dream on such a stone,
Or this or that—but, once being wholly waked
And come back to the stone without the dream, 500
We trip upon't, alas, and hurt ourselves;
Or else it falls on us and grinds us flat,
The heaviest gravestone on this burying earth.
—But while I stood and mused, a quiet touch
Fell light upon my arm, and turning round,
A pair of moistened eyes convicted mine.
'What, Marian! is the babe astir so soon?'
'He sleeps,' she answered; 'I have crept up thrice,
And seen you sitting, standing, still at watch.
I thought it did you good till now, but now' . . . 510
'But now,' I said, 'you leave the child alone.'
'And you're alone,' she answered—and she looked
As if I too were something. Sweet the help
Of one we have helped! Thanks, Marian, for such help.

I found a house at Florence on the hill
Of Bellosguardo. 'Tis a tower which keeps
A post of double observation o'er
That valley of Arno (holding as a hand
The outspread city), straight toward Fiesole
And Mount Morello and the setting sun,   520
The Vallombrosan mountains opposite,
Which sunrise fills as full as crystal cups
Turned red to the brim because their wine is red.
No sun could die nor yet be born unseen
By dwellers at my villa: morn and eve
Were magnified before us in the pure
Illimitable space and pause of sky,
Intense as angels' garments blanched with God,
Less blue than radiant. From the outer wall
Of the garden, drops the mystic floating gray   530
Of olive-trees (with interruptions green
From maize and vine), until 'tis caught and torn
Upon the abrupt black line of cypresses
Which signs the way to Florence. Beautiful
The city lies along the ample vale,
Cathedral, tower and palace, piazza and street,
The river trailing like a silver cord
Through all, and curling loosely, both before
And after, over the whole stretch of land
Sown whitely up and down its opposite slopes   540
With farms and villas.
                        Many weeks had passed,
No word was granted.—Last, a letter came
From Vincent Carrington—'My dear Miss Leigh,
You've been as silent as a poet should,
When any other man is sure to speak.
If sick, if vexed, if dumb, a silver piece
Will split a man's tongue—straight he speaks and says,
"Received that cheque." But you! . . . I sent you funds
To Paris, and you make no sign at all.
Remember I'm responsible and wait   550

A sign of you, Miss Leigh.

'Meantime your book
Is eloquent as if you were not dumb;
And common critics, ordinarily deaf
To such fine meanings, and, like deaf men, loath
To seem deaf, answering chance-wise, yes or no,
"It must be" or "it must not" (most pronounced
When least convinced), pronounce for once aright:
You'd think they really heard—and so they do . . .
The burr of three or four who really hear
And praise your book aright: Fame's smallest trump   560
Is a great ear-trumpet for the deaf as posts,
No other being effective. Fear not, friend;
We think here you have written a good book,
And you, a woman! It was in you—yes,
I felt 'twas in you: yet I doubted half
If that od-force of German Reichenbach,*
Which still from female finger-tips burns blue,
Could strike out as our masculine white heats
To quicken a man. Forgive me. All my heart
Is quick with yours since, just a fortnight since,   570
I read your book and loved it.

'Will you love
My wife, too? Here's my secret I might keep
A month more from you! but I yield it up
Because I know you'll write the sooner for't,
Most women (of your height even) counting love
Life's only serious business. Who's my wife
That shall be in a month, you ask? nor guess?
Remember what a pair of topaz eyes
You once detected, turned against the wall,
That morning in my London painting-room;   580
The face half sketched, and slurred; the eyes alone!
But you . . . you caught them up with yours, and said
"Kate Ward's eyes, surely."—Now I own the truth:
I had thrown them there to keep them safe from Jove,
They would so naughtily find out their way

To both the heads of both my Danaës
Where just it made me mad to look at them.
Such eyes! I could not paint or think of eyes
But those—and so I flung them into paint
And turned them to the wall's care. Ay, but now   590
I've let them out, my Kate's: I've painted her
(I change my style and leave mythologies),
The whole sweet face; it looks upon my soul
Like a face on water, to beget itself.
A half-length portrait, in a hanging cloak
Like one you wore once; 'tis a little frayed—
I pressed too for the nude harmonious arm—
But she, she'd have her way, and have her cloak;
She said she could be like you only so,
And would not miss the fortune. Ah, my friend,   600
You'll write and say she shall not miss your love
Through meeting mine? in faith, she would not change.
She has your books by heart more than my words,
And quotes you up against me till I'm pushed
Where, three months since, her eyes were: nay, in fact,
Nought satisfied her but to make me paint
Your last book folded in her dimpled hands
Instead of my brown palette as I wished,
And, grant me, the presentment had been newer;
She'd grant me nothing: I compounded for   610
The naming of the wedding-day next month,
And gladly too. 'Tis pretty, to remark
How women can love women of your sort,
And tie their hearts with love-knots to your feet,
Grow insolent about you against men
And put us down by putting up the lip,
As if a man—there *are* such, let us own,
Who write not ill—remains a man, poor wretch,
While you—! Write weaker than Aurora Leigh,
And there'll be women who believe of you   620
(Besides my Kate) that if you walked on sand
You would not leave a foot-print.

'Are you put
To wonder by my marriage, like poor Leigh?
"Kate Ward!" he said. "Kate Ward!" he said anew.
"I thought . . ." he said, and stopped—"I did not
    think . . ."
And then he dropped to silence.

                    'Ah, he's changed.
I had not seen him, you're aware, for long,
But went of course. I have not touched on this
Through all this letter—conscious of your heart,
And writing lightlier for the heavy fact,   630
As clocks are voluble with lead.

                   'How poor,
To say I'm sorry! dear Leigh, dearest Leigh.
In those old days of Shropshire—pardon me—
When he and you fought many a field of gold
On what you should do, or you should not do,
Make bread or verses (it just came to that),
I thought you'd one day draw a silken peace
Through a golden ring. I thought so: foolishly,
The event proved—for you went more opposite
To each other, month by month, and year by year,   640
Until this happened. God knows best, we say,
But hoarsely. When the fever took him first,
Just after I had writ to you in France,
They tell me Lady Waldemar mixed drinks
And counted grains, like any salaried nurse,
Excepting that she wept too. Then Lord Howe,
You're right about Lord Howe, Lord Howe's a trump,*
And yet, with such in his hand, a man like Leigh
May lose as *he* does. There's an end to all,
Yes, even this letter, though this second sheet   650
May find you doubtful. Write a word for Kate:
She reads my letters always, like a wife,
And if she sees her name I'll see her smile
And share the luck. So, bless you, friend of two!
I will not ask you what your feeling is

At Florence with my pictures; I can hear
Your heart a-flutter over the snow-hills:
And, just to pace the Pitti with you once,
I'd give a half-hour of tomorrow's walk
With Kate . . . I think so. Vincent Carrington.'   660

The noon was hot; the air scorched like the sun
And was shut out. The closed persiani threw*
Their long-scored shadows on my villa-floor,
And interlined the golden atmosphere
Straight, still—across the pictures on the wall,
The statuette on the console (of young Love
And Psyche made one marble by a kiss),
The low couch where I leaned, the table near,
The vase of lilies Marian pulled last night
(Each green leaf and each white leaf ruled in black   670
As if for writing some new text of fate)
And the open letter, rested on my knee,
But there the lines swerved, trembled, though I sat
Untroubled, plainly, reading it again
And three times. Well, he's married; that is clear.
No wonder that he's married, nor much more
That Vincent's therefore 'sorry'. Why, of course
The lady nursed him when he was not well,
Mixed drinks—unless nepenthe was the drink*
'Twas scarce worth telling. But a man in love   680
Will see the whole sex in his mistress' hood,
The prettier for its lining of fair rose,
Although he catches back and says at last,
'I'm sorry.' Sorry. Lady Waldemar
At prettiest, under the said hood, preserved
From such a light as I could hold to her face
To flare its ugly wrinkles out to shame,
Is scarce a wife for Romney, as friends judge,
Aurora Leigh or Vincent Carrington,
That's plain. And if he's 'conscious of my heart' . . .   690
It may be natural, though the phrase is strong

(One's apt to use strong phrases, being in love);
And even that stuff of 'fields of gold,' 'gold rings,'
And what he 'thought,' poor Vincent, what he 'thought,'
May never mean enough to ruffle me.
—Why, this room stifles. Better burn than choke;
Best have air, air, although it comes with fire—
Throw open blinds and windows to the noon
And take a blister on my brow instead
Of this dead weight! best, perfectly be stunned   700
By those insufferable cicale, sick
And hoarse with rapture of the summer-heat,
That sing, like poets, till their hearts break—sing
Till men say, 'It's too tedious.'
                              Books succeed,
And lives fail. Do I feel it so, at last?
Kate loves a worn-out cloak for being like mine,
While I live self-despised for being myself,
And yearn toward someone else, who yearns away
From what he is, in his turn. Strain a step
For ever, yet gain no step? Are we such,   710
We cannot, with our admirations even,
Our tiptoe aspirations, touch a thing
That's higher than we? is all a dismal flat,
And God alone above each, as the sun
O'er level lagoons, to make them shine and stink—
Laying stress upon us with immediate flame,
While we respond with our miasmal fog
And call it mounting higher because we grow
More highly fatal?
                  Tush, Aurora Leigh!
You wear your sackcloth looped in Caesar's way   720
And brag your failings as mankind's. Be still.
There *is* what's higher, in this very world,
Than you can live, or catch at. Stand aside,
And look at others—instance little Kate!
She'll make a perfect wife for Carrington.
She always has been looking round the earth

For something good and green to alight upon
And nestle into, with those soft-winged eyes,
Subsiding now beneath his manly hand
'Twixt trembling lids of inexpressive joy.   730
I will not scorn her, after all, too much,
That so much she should love me: a wise man
Can pluck a leaf, and find a lecture in't;
And I, too . . . God has made me—I've a heart
That's capable of worship, love, and loss;
We say the same of Shakespeare's. I'll be meek
And learn to reverence, even this poor myself.

The book, too—pass it. 'A good book,' says he,
'And you a woman.' I had laughed at that,
But long since. I'm a woman—it is true;   740
Alas, and woe to us, when we feel it most!
Then, least care have we for the crowns and goals
And compliments on writing our good books.

The book has some truth in it, I believe,
And truth outlives pain, as the soul does life.
I know we talk our Phaedons to the end,*
Through all the dismal faces that we make,
O'er-wrinkled with dishonouring agony
From decomposing drugs. I have written truth,
And I a woman—feebly, partially,   750
Inaptly in presentation, Romney'll add,
Because a woman. For the truth itself,
That's neither man's nor woman's, but just God's,
None else has reason to be proud of truth:
Himself will see it sifted, disenthralled,
And kept upon the height and in the light,
As far as and no farther than 'tis truth;
For, now He has left off calling firmaments
And strata, flowers and creatures, very good,
He says it still of truth, which is His own.   760

Truth, so far, in my book—the truth which draws
Through all things upwards—that a twofold world
Must go to a perfect cosmos. Natural things
And spiritual—who separates those two
In art, in morals, or the social drift,
Tears up the bond of nature and brings death,
Paints futile pictures, writes unreal verse,
Leads vulgar days, deals ignorantly with men,
Is wrong, in short, at all points. We divide
This apple of life, and cut it through the pips—   770
The perfect round which fitted Venus' hand*
Has perished as utterly as if we ate
Both halves. Without the spiritual, observe,
The natural's impossible—no form,
No motion: without sensuous, spiritual
Is inappreciable—no beauty or power:
And in this twofold sphere the twofold man
(For still the artist is intensely a man)
Holds firmly by the natural, to reach
The spiritual beyond it—fixes still   780
The type with mortal vision, to pierce through,
With eyes immortal, to the antetype
Some call the ideal—better called the real,
And certain to be called so presently
When things shall have their names. Look long enough
On any peasant's face here, coarse and lined,
You'll catch Antinous somewhere in that clay,*
As perfect featured as he yearns at Rome
From marble pale with beauty; then persist,
And, if your apprehension's competent,   790
You'll find some fairer angel at his back,
As much exceeding him as he the boor,
And pushing him with empyreal disdain*
For ever out of sight. Ay, Carrington
Is glad of such a creed: an artist must,
Who paints a tree, a leaf, a common stone
With just his hand, and finds it suddenly

A.L. - 14

A-piece with and conterminous to his soul.*
Why else do these things move him, leaf or stone?
The bird's not moved, that pecks at a spring-shoot;   800
Nor yet the horse, before a quarry a-graze:
But man, the twofold creature, apprehends
The twofold manner, in and outwardly,
And nothing in the world comes single to him,
A mere itself—cup, column, or candlestick,*
All patterns of what shall be in the Mount;
The whole temporal show related royally,
And built up to eterne significance
Through the open arms of God. 'There's nothing great
Nor small,' has said a poet of our day,*   810
Whose voice will ring beyond the curfew of eve
And not be thrown out by the matin's bell:
And truly, I reiterate, nothing's small!
No lily-muffled hum of a summer-bee,
But finds some coupling with the spinning stars;
No pebble at your foot, but proves a sphere;
No chaffinch, but implies the cherubim;
And (glancing on my own thin, veinèd wrist)
In such a little tremor of the blood
The whole strong clamour of a vehement soul   820
Doth utter itself distinct. Earth's crammed with heaven,
And every common bush afire with God;*
But only he who sees, takes off his shoes,
The rest sit round it and pluck blackberries,
And daub their natural faces unaware
More and more from the first similitude.

Truth, so far, in my book! a truth which draws
From all things upward. I, Aurora, still
Have felt it hound me through the wastes of life
As Jove did Io; and, until that Hand*   830
Shall overtake me wholly and on my head
Lay down its large unfluctuating peace,
The feverish gadfly pricks me up and down.

It must be. Art's the witness of what Is
Behind this show. If this world's show were all,
Then imitation would be all in Art;
There, Jove's hand grips us!—For we stand here, we,
If genuine artists, witnessing for God's
Complete, consummate, undivided work;
That every natural flower which grows on earth   840
Implies a flower upon the spiritual side,
Substantial, archetypal, all aglow
With blossoming causes—not so far away,
But we, whose spirit-sense is somewhat cleared,
May catch at something of the bloom and breath—
Too vaguely apprehended, though indeed
Still apprehended, consciously or not,
And still transferred to picture, music, verse,
For thrilling audient and beholding souls*
By signs and touches which are known to souls.   850
How known, they know not—why, they cannot find,
So straight call out on genius, say, 'A man
Produced this,' when much rather they should say,
''Tis insight and he saw this.'
                              Thus is Art
Self-magnified in magnifying a truth
Which, fully recognised, would change the world
And shift its morals. If a man could feel,
Not one day, in the artist's ecstasy,
But every day, feast, fast, or working-day,
The spiritual significance burn through   860
The hieroglyphic of material shows,
Henceforward he would paint the globe with wings,
And reverence fish and fowl, the bull, the tree,
And even his very body as a man—
Which now he counts so vile, that all the towns*
Make offal of their daughters for its use,
On summer-nights, when God is sad in heaven
To think what goes on in His recreant world
He made quite other; while that moon He made

To shine there, at the first love's covenant,　　　　870
Shines still, convictive as a marriage-ring
Before adulterous eyes.

　　　　　　　　　How sure it is,
That, if we say a true word, instantly
We feel 'tis God's, not ours, and pass it on
Like bread at sacrament we taste and pass
Nor handle for a moment, as indeed
We dared to set up any claim to such!
And I—my poem—let my readers talk.
I'm closer to it—I can speak as well:
I'll say with Romney, that the book is weak,　　　880
The range uneven, the points of sight obscure,
The music interrupted.

　　　　　　　　　　Let us go.
The end of woman (or of man, I think)
Is not a book. Alas, the best of books
Is but a word in Art, which soon grows cramped,
Stiff, dubious-statured with the weight of years,
And drops an accent or digamma down*
Some cranny of unfathomable time,
Beyond the critic's reaching. Art itself,
We've called the larger life, must feel the soul　　　890
Live past it. For more's felt than is perceived,
And more's perceived than can be interpreted,
And Love strikes higher with his lambent flame
Than Art can pile the faggots.

　　　　　　　　　　Is it so?
When Jove's hand meets us with composing touch,
And when at last we are hushed and satisfied,
Then Io does not call it truth, but love?

Well, well! my father was an Englishman:
My mother's blood in me is not so strong
That I should bear this stress of Tuscan noon　　　900
And keep my wits. The town, there, seems to seethe
In this Medaean boil-pot of the sun,*

And all the patient hills are bubbling round
As if a prick would leave them flat. Does heaven
Keep far off, not to set us in a blaze?
Not so—let drag your fiery fringes, heaven,
And burn us up to quiet. Ah, we know
Too much here, not to know what's best for peace;
We have too much light here, not to want more fire
To purify and end us. We talk, talk,   910
Conclude upon divine philosophies,
And get the thanks of men for hopeful books,
Whereat we take our own life up, and . . . pshaw!
Unless we piece it with another's life
(A yard of silk to carry out our lawn)*
As well suppose my little handkerchief
Would cover Samminiato, church and all,*
If out I threw it past the cypresses,
As, in this ragged, narrow life of mine,
Contain my own conclusions.
                            But at least   920
We'll shut up the persiani and sit down,
And when my head's done aching, in the cool,
Write just a word to Kate and Carrington.
May joy be with them! she has chosen well,
And he not ill.
            I should be glad, I think,
Except for Romney. Had *he* married Kate,
I surely, surely, should be very glad.
This Florence sits upon me easily,
With native air and tongue. My graves are calm,
And do not too much hurt me. Marian's good,   930
Gentle and loving—lets me hold the child,
Or drags him up the hills to find me flowers
And fill these vases ere I'm quite awake—
My grandiose red tulips, which grow wild,
Or Dante's purple lilies, which he blew*
To a larger bubble with his prophet breath,
Or one of those tall flowering reeds that stand

In Arno, like a sheaf of sceptres left
By some remote dynasty of dead gods
To suck the stream for ages and get green,   940
And blossom wheresoe'er a hand divine
Had warmed the place with ichor. Such I find*
At early morning laid across my bed,
And wake up pelted with a childish laugh
Which even Marian's low precipitous 'hush'
Has vainly interposed to put away—
While I, with shut eyes, smile and motion for
The dewy kiss that's very sure to come
From mouth and cheeks, the whole child's face at once
Dissolved on mine—as if a nosegay burst   950
Its string with the weight of roses overblown,
And dropped upon me. Surely I should be glad.
The little creature almost loves me now,
And calls my name, 'Alola,' stripping off
The *r*'s like thorns, to make it smooth enough
To take between his dainty, milk-fed lips,
God love him! I should certainly be glad,
Except, God help me, that I'm sorrowful
Because of Romney.

                    Romney, Romney! Well,
This grows absurd!—too like a tune that runs   960
I' the head, and forces all things in the world,
Wind, rain, the creaking gnat, or stuttering fly,
To sing itself and vex you—yet perhaps
A paltry tune you never fairly liked,
Some 'I'd be a butterfly', or 'C'est l'amour':*
We're made so—not such tyrants to ourselves
But still we are slaves to nature. Some of us
Are turned, too, over-much like some poor verse
With a trick of ritournelle: the same thing goes*
And comes back ever.

                    Vincent Carrington   970
Is 'sorry,' and I'm sorry; but *he*'s strong
To mount from sorrow to his heaven of love,

And when he says at moments, 'Poor, poor Leigh,
Who'll never call his own so true a heart,
So fair a face even'—he must quickly lose
The pain of pity, in the blush he makes
By his very pitying eyes. The snow, for him,
Has fallen in May and finds the whole earth warm,
And melts at the first touch of the green grass.

But Romney—he has chosen, after all.   980
I think he had as excellent a sun
To see by, as most others, and perhaps
Has scarce seen really worse than some of us
When all's said. Let him pass. I'm not too much
A woman, not to be a man for once
And bury all my Dead like Alaric,*
Depositing the treasures of my soul
In this drained watercourse, then letting flow
The river of life again with commerce-ships
And pleasure-barges full of silks and songs.   990
Blow, winds, and help us.
                            Ah, we mock ourselves
With talking of the winds; perhaps as much
With other resolutions. How it weighs,
This hot, sick air! and how I covet here
The Dead's provision on the river-couch,
With silver curtains drawn on tinkling rings!
Or else their rest in quiet crypts—laid by
From heat and noise—from those cicale, say,
And this more vexing heart-beat.
                                   So it is:
We covet for the soul, the body's part,   1000
To die and rot. Even so, Aurora, ends
Our aspiration who bespoke our place
So far in the east. The occidental flats
Had fed us fatter, therefore? we have climbed
Where herbage ends? we want the beast's part now,
And tire of the angel's?—Men define a man,

The creature who stands frontward to the stars,
The creature who looks inward to himself,
The tool-wright, laughing creature. 'Tis enough:
We'll say instead, the inconsequent creature, man,   1010
For that's his specialty. What creature else
Conceives the circle, and then walks the square?
Loves things proved bad, and leaves a thing proved good?
You think the bee makes honey half a year,
To loathe the comb in winter and desire
The little ant's food rather? But a man—
Note men!—they are but women after all,
As women are but Auroras!—there are men
Born tender, apt to pale at a trodden worm,
Who paint for pastime, in their favourite dream,   1020
Spruce auto-vestments flowered with crocus-flames:*
There are, too, who believe in hell, and lie;
There are, too, who believe in heaven, and fear:*
There are, who waste their souls in working out
Life's problem on these sands betwixt two tides,
Concluding—'Give us the oyster's part, in death.'*

Alas, long-suffering and most patient God,
Thou needst be surelier God to bear with us
Than even to have made us! thou aspire, aspire
From henceforth for me! thou who hast thyself   1030
Endured this fleshhood, knowing how as a soaked
And sucking vesture it can drag us down
And choke us in the melancholy Deep,
Sustain me, that with thee I walk these waves,
Resisting!—breathe me upward, thou in me
Aspiring who art the way, the truth, the life—*
That no truth henceforth seem indifferent,
No way to truth laborious, and no life,
Not even this life I live, intolerable!

The days went by. I took up the old days,   1040
With all their Tuscan pleasures worn and spoiled,

Like some lost book we dropped in the long grass
On such a happy summer-afternoon
When last we read it with a loving friend,
And find in autumn when the friend is gone,
The grass cut short, the weather changed, too late,
And stare at, as at something wonderful
For sorrow—thinking how two hands before
Had held up what is left to only one,
And how we smiled when such a vehement nail   1050
Impressed the tiny dint here which presents
This verse in fire for ever. Tenderly
And mournfully I lived. I knew the birds
And insects—which looked fathered by the flowers
And emulous of their hues: I recognised
The moths, with that great overpoise of wings
Which make a mystery of them how at all
They can stop flying; butterflies, that bear
Upon their blue wings such red embers round,
They seem to scorch the blue air into holes   1060
Each flight they take; and fire-flies, that suspire
In short soft lapses of transported flame
Across the tingling Dark, while overhead
The constant and inviolable stars
Outburn those light-of-love; melodious owls
(If music had but one note and was sad,
'Twould sound just so); and all the silent swirl
Of bats that seem to follow in the air
Some grand circumference of a shadowy dome
To which we are blind; and then the nightingales,   1070
Which pluck our heart across a garden-wall
(When walking in the town) and carry it
So high into the bowery almond-trees
We tremble and are afraid, and feel as if
The golden flood of moonlight unaware
Dissolved the pillars of the steady earth
And made it less substantial. And I knew
The harmless opal snakes, the large-mouthed frogs

(Those noisy vaunters of their shallow streams),
And lizards, the green lightnings of the wall,   1080
Which, if you sit down quiet, nor sigh aloud,
Will flatter you and take you for a stone,
And flash familiarly about your feet
With such prodigious eyes in such small heads!—
I knew them (though they had somewhat dwindled from
My childish imagery), and kept in mind
How last I sat among them equally,
In fellowship and mateship, as a child
Feels equal still toward insect, beast, and bird,
Before the Adam in him has forgone   1090
All privilege of Eden—making friends
And talk with such a bird or such a goat,
And buying many a two-inch-wide rush-cage
To let out the caged cricket on a tree,
Saying, 'Oh, my dear grillino, were you cramped?*
And are you happy with the ilex-leaves?
And do you love me who have let you go?
Say *yes* in singing, and I'll understand.'

But now the creatures all seemed farther off,
No longer mine, nor like me, only *there*,   1100
A gulf between us. I could yearn indeed,
Like other rich men, for a drop of dew
To cool this heat—a drop of the early dew,
The irrecoverable child-innocence
(Before the heart took fire and withered life)
When childhood might pair equally with birds;
But now . . . the birds were grown too proud for us!
Alas, the very sun forbids the dew.

And I, I had come back to an empty nest,
Which every bird's too wise for. How I heard   1110
My father's step on that deserted ground,
His voice along that silence, as he told
The names of bird and insect, tree and flower,

And all the presentations of the stars
Across Valdarno, interposing still
'My child,' 'my child.' When fathers say 'my child,'
'Tis easier to conceive the universe,
And life's transitions down the steps of law.

I rode once to the little mountain-house
As fast as if to find my father there,   1120
But, when in sight of 't, within fifty yards,
I dropped my horse's bridle on his neck
And paused upon his flank. The house's front
Was cased with lingots of ripe Indian corn
In tessellated order and device
Of golden patterns, not a stone of wall
Uncovered—not an inch of room to grow
A vine-leaf. The old porch had disappeared;
And right in the open doorway sat a girl
At plaiting straws, her black hair strained away   1130
To a scarlet kerchief caught beneath her chin
In Tuscan fashion—her full ebon eyes,
Which looked too heavy to be lifted so,
Still dropped and lifted toward the mulberry-tree
On which the lads were busy with their staves
In shout and laughter, stripping every bough
As bare as winter, of those summer leaves
My father had not changed for all the silk
In which the ugly silkworms hide themselves.
Enough. My horse recoiled before my heart;   1140
I turned the rein abruptly. Back we went
As fast, to Florence.
                    That was trial enough
Of graves. I would not visit, if I could,
My father's, or my mother's any more,
To see if stone-cutter or lichen beat
So early in the race, or throw my flowers,
Which could not outsmell heaven or sweeten earth.
They live too far above, that I should look

So far below to find them: let me think
That rather they are visiting my grave,   1150
Called life here (undeveloped yet to life),
And that they drop upon me, now and then,
For token or for solace, some small weed
Least odorous of the growths of paradise,
To spare such pungent scents as kill with joy.

My old Assunta, too, was dead, was dead—
O land of all men's past! for me alone,
It would not mix its tenses. I was past,
It seemed, like others—only not in heaven.
And many a Tuscan eve I wandered down   1160
The cypress alley like a restless ghost
That tries its feeble ineffectual breath
Upon its charred funeral-brands put out
Too soon, where black and stiff stood up the trees
Against the broad vermilion of the skies.
Such skies!—all clouds abolished in a sweep
Of God's skirt, with a dazzle to ghosts and men,
As down I went, saluting on the bridge
The hem of such before 'twas caught away
Beyond the peaks of Lucca. Underneath,   1170
The river, just escaping from the weight
Of that intolerable glory, ran
In acquiescent shadow murmurously;
While, up beside it, streamed the festa-folk*
With fellow-murmurs from their feet and fans,
And *issimo* and *ino* and sweet poise*
Of vowels in their pleasant scandalous talk;
Returning from the grand-duke's dairy-farm
Before the trees grew dangerous at eight
(For, 'trust no tree by moonlight,' Tuscans say),   1180
To eat their ice at Donay's tenderly—*
Each lovely lady close to a cavalier
Who holds her dear fan while she feeds her smile
On meditative spoonfuls of vanille

And listens to his hot-breathed vows of love
Enough to thaw her cream and scorch his beard.

'Twas little matter. I could pass them by
Indifferently, not fearing to be known.
No danger of being wrecked upon a friend,
And forced to take an iceberg for an isle!   1190
The very English, here, must wait and learn
To hang the cobweb of their gossip out
To catch a fly. I'm happy. It's sublime,
This perfect solitude of foreign lands!
To be, as if you had not been till then,
And were then, simply that you chose to be:
To spring up, not be brought forth from the ground,
Like grasshoppers at Athens, and skip thrice*
Before a woman makes a pounce on you
And plants you in her hair!—possess, yourself,   1200
A new world all alive with creatures new,
New sun, new moon, new flowers, new people—ah,
And be possessed by none of them! no right
In one, to call your name, inquire your where,
Or what you think of Mister Someone's book,
Or Mister Other's marriage or decease,
Or how's the headache which you had last week,
Or why you look so pale still, since it's gone?
—Such most surprising riddance of one's life
Comes next one's death; 'tis disembodiment   1210
Without the pang. I marvel, people choose
To stand stock-still like fakirs, till the moss
Grows on them and they cry out, self-admired,
'How verdant and how virtuous!' Well, I'm glad:
Or should be, if grown foreign to myself
As surely as to others.
                                   Musing so,
I walked the narrow unrecognising streets,
Where many a palace-front peers gloomily
Through stony vizors iron-barred (prepared

Alike, should foe or lover pass that way,   1220
For guest or victim), and came wandering out
Upon the churches with mild open doors
And plaintive wail of vespers, where a few,
Those chiefly women, sprinkled round in blots
Upon the dusky pavement, knelt and prayed
Toward the altar's silver glory. Oft a ray
(I liked to sit and watch) would tremble out,
Just touch some face more lifted, more in need,
(Of course a woman's)—while I dreamed a tale
To fit its fortunes. There was one who looked   1230
As if the earth had suddenly grown too large
For such a little humpbacked thing as she;
The pitiful black kerchief round her neck
Sole proof she had had a mother. One, again,
Looked sick for love—seemed praying some soft saint
To put more virtue in the new fine scarf
She spent a fortnight's meals on, yesterday,
That cruel Gigi might return his eyes
From Giuliana. There was one, so old,
So old, to kneel grew easier than to stand—   1240
So solitary, she accepts at last
Our Lady for her gossip, and frets on
Against the sinful world which goes its rounds
In marrying and being married, just the same
As when 'twas almost good and had the right
(Her Gian alive, and she herself eighteen).
'And yet, now even, if Madonna willed,
She'd win a tern in Thursday's lottery*
And better all things. Did she dream for nought,
That, boiling cabbage for the fast-day's soup,   1250
It smelt like blessed entrails? such a dream
For nought? would sweetest Mary cheat her so,
And lose that certain candle, straight and white
As any fair grand-duchess in her teens,
Which otherwise should flare here in a week?
Benigna sis, thou beauteous Queen of heaven!'*

I sat there musing, and imagining
Such utterance from such faces: poor blind souls
That writhe toward heaven along the devil's trail—
Who knows, I thought, but He may stretch his hand   1260
And pick them up? 'tis written in the Book*
He heareth the young ravens when they cry,
And yet they cry for carrion.—O my God,
And we, who make excuses for the rest,
We do it in our measure. Then I knelt,
And dropped my head upon the pavement too,
And prayed, since I was foolish in desire
Like other creatures, craving offal-food,
That He would stop his ears to what I said,
And only listen to the run and beat   1270
Of this poor, passionate, helpless blood—
                            And then
I lay, and spoke not: but He heard in heaven.

So many Tuscan evenings passed the same.
I could not lose a sunset on the bridge,
And would not miss a vigil in the church,
And liked to mingle with the outdoor crowd
So strange and gay and ignorant of my face,
For men you know not, are as good as trees.
And only once, at the Santissima,
I almost chanced upon a man I knew,   1280
Sir Blaise Delorme. He saw me certainly,
And somewhat hurried, as he crossed himself,
The smoothness of the action—then half bowed,
But only half, and merely to my shade,
I slipped so quick behind the porphyry plinth
And left him dubious if 'twas really I
Or peradventure Satan's usual trick
To keep a mounting saint uncanonised.
But he was safe for that time, and I too;
The argent angels in the altar-flare   1290
Absorbed his soul next moment. The good man!

In England we were scarce acquaintances,
That here in Florence he should keep my thought
Beyond the image on his eye, which came
And went: and yet his thought disturbed my life:
For, after that, I oftener sat at home
On evenings, watching how they fined themselves
With gradual conscience to a perfect night,
Until the moon, diminished to a curve,
Lay out there like a sickle for His hand   1300
Who cometh down at last to reap the earth.
At such times, ended seemed my trade of verse;
I feared to jingle bells upon my robe*
Before the four-faced silent cherubim:
With God so near me, could I sing of God?
I did not write, nor read, nor even think,
But sat absorbed amid the quickening glooms,
Most like some passive broken lump of salt
Dropped in by chance to a bowl of oenomel,*
To spoil the drink a little and lose itself,   1310
Dissolving slowly, slowly, until lost.

BOOK VIII

ONE eve it happened, when I sat alone,
Alone, upon the terrace of my tower,
A book upon my knees to counterfeit
The reading that I never read at all,
While Marian, in the garden down below,
Knelt by the fountain I could just hear thrill
The drowsy silence of the exhausted day,
And peeled a new fig from that purple heap
In the grass beside her, turning out the red
To feed her eager child (who sucked at it   10
With vehement lips across a gap of air
As he stood opposite, face and curls a-flame
With that last sun-ray, crying, 'give me, give,'
And stamping with imperious baby-feet,
We're all born princes)—something startled me—
The laugh of sad and innocent souls, that breaks
Abruptly, as if frightened at itself.
'Twas Marian laughed. I saw her glance above
In sudden shame that I should hear her laugh,
And straightway dropped my eyes upon my book,   20
And knew, the first time, 'twas Boccaccio's tale,*
The Falcon's, of the lover who for love
Destroyed the best that loved him. Some of us
Do it still, and then we sit and laugh no more.
Laugh *you*, sweet Marian—you've the right to laugh,
Since God himself is for you, and a child!
For me there's somewhat less—and so I sigh.

The heavens were making room to hold the night,
The sevenfold heavens unfolding all their gates
To let the stars out slowly (prophesied   30

In close-approaching advent, not discerned),
While still the cue-owls from the cypresses
Of the Poggio called and counted every pulse*
Of the skyey palpitation. Gradually
The purple and transparent shadows slow
Had filled up the whole valley to the brim,
And flooded all the city, which you saw
As some drowned city in some enchanted sea,
Cut off from nature—drawing you who gaze
With passionate desire, to leap and plunge   40
And find a sea-king with a voice of waves,
And treacherous soft eyes, and slippery locks
You cannot kiss but you shall bring away
Their salt upon your lips. The duomo-bell*
Strikes ten, as if it struck ten fathoms down,
So deep; and twenty churches answer it
The same, with twenty various instances.
Some gaslights tremble along squares and streets;
The Pitti's palace-front is drawn in fire;
And, past the quays, Maria Novella Place,   50
In which the mystic obelisks stand up
Triangular, pyramidal, each based
Upon its four-square brazen tortoises,
To guard that fair church, Buonarroti's Bride,*
That stares out from her large blind dial-eyes
(Her quadrant and armillary dials, black
With rhythms of many suns and moons) in vain
Inquiry for so rich a soul as his.
Methinks I have plunged, I see it all so clear . . .
And, O my heart . . . the sea-king!

                                   In my ears   60
The sound of waters. There he stood, my king!

I felt him, rather than beheld him. Up
I rose, as if he were my king indeed,
And then sat down, in trouble at myself,
And struggling for my woman's empery.*

'Tis pitiful; but women are so made:
We'll die for you perhaps—'tis probable;
But we'll not spare you an inch of our full height:
We'll have our whole just stature—five feet four,
Though laid out in our coffins: pitiful.   70
—'You, Romney!—Lady Waldemar is here?'

He answered in a voice which was not his.
'I have her letter; you shall read it soon.
But first, I must be heard a little, I,
Who have waited long and travelled far for that.
Although you thought to have shut a tedious book
And farewell. Ah, you dog-eared such a page,
And here you find me.'
                        Did he touch my hand,
Or but my sleeve? I trembled, hand and foot—
He must have touched me.—'Will you sit?' I asked,   80
And motioned to a chair; but down he sat,
A little slowly, as a man in doubt,
Upon the couch beside me—couch and chair
Being wheeled upon the terrace.
                                'You are come,
My cousin Romney?—this is wonderful.
But all is wonder on such summer-nights;
And nothing should surprise us any more,
Who see that miracle of stars. Behold.'

I signed above, where all the stars were out,
As if an urgent heat had started there   90
A secret writing from a sombre page,
A blank, last moment, crowded suddenly
With hurrying splendours.
                        'Then you do not know'—
He murmured.
            'Yes, I know,' I said, 'I know.
I had the news from Vincent Carrington.
And yet I did not think you'd leave the work

In England, for so much even—though of course
You'll make a work-day of your holiday,
And turn it to our Tuscan people's use—
Who much need helping since the Austrian boar*   100
(So bold to cross the Alp to Lombardy
And dash his brute front unabashed against
The steep snow-bosses of that shield of God
Who soon shall rise in wrath and shake it clear)
Came hither also, raking up our grape
And olive-gardens with his tyrannous tusk,
And rolling on our maize with all his swine.'

'You had the news from Vincent Carrington,'
He echoed—picking up the phrase beyond,
As if he knew the rest was merely talk   110
To fill a gap and keep out a strong wind;
'You had, then, Vincent's personal news?'

                            'His own,'
I answered. 'All that ruined world of yours
Seems crumbling into marriage. Carrington
Has chosen wisely.'

                'Do you take it so?'
He cried, 'and is it possible at last' . . .
He paused there—and then, inward to himself,
'Too much at last, too late!—yet certainly' . . .
(And there his voice swayed as an Alpine plank
That feels a passionate torrent underneath)   120
'The knowledge, had I known it first or last,
Could scarce have changed the actual case for *me*.
And best for *her* at this time.'

                        Nay, I thought,
He loves Kate Ward, it seems, now, like a man,
Because he has married Lady Waldemar!
Ah, Vincent's letter said how Leigh was moved
To hear that Vincent was betrothed to Kate.
With what cracked pitchers go we to deep wells
In this world! Then I spoke—'I did not think,

My cousin, you had ever known Kate Ward.'   130

'In fact I never knew her. 'Tis enough
That Vincent did, and therefore chose his wife
For other reasons than those topaz eyes
We've heard of. Not to undervalue them,
For all that. One takes up the world with eyes.'

—Including Romney Leigh, I thought again,
Albeit he knows them only by repute.
How vile must all men be, since *he's* a man.

His deep pathetic voice, as if he guessed
I did not surely love him, took the word;   140
'You never got a letter from Lord Howe
A month back, dear Aurora?'
                                      'None,' I said.

'I felt it was so,' he replied: 'yet, strange!
Sir Blaise Delorme has passed through Florence?'
                                               'Ay,
By chance I saw him in Our Lady's church
(I saw him, mark you, but he saw not me),
Clean-washed in holy water from the count
Of things terrestrial—letters, and the rest;
He had crossed us out together with his sins.*
Ay, strange; but only strange that good Lord Howe   150
Preferred him to the post because of pauls.*
For me I'm sworn to never trust a man—
At least with letters.'
                          'There were facts to tell,
To smooth with eye and accent. Howe supposed . . .
Well, well, no matter! there was dubious need;
You heard the news from Vincent Carrington.
And yet perhaps you had been startled less
To see me, dear Aurora, if you had read

That letter.'
                    —Now he sets me down as vexed.
I think I've draped myself in woman's pride   160
To a perfect purpose. Oh, I'm vexed, it seems!
My friend Lord Howe deputes his friend Sir Blaise
To break as softly as a sparrow's egg
That lets a bird out tenderly, the news
Of Romney's marriage to a certain saint;
To *smooth with eye and accent*—indicate
His possible presence. Excellently well
You've played your part, my Lady Waldemar—
As I've played mine.
                    'Dear Romney,' I began,
'You did not use, of old, to be so like   170
A Greek king coming from a taken Troy,
'Twas needful that precursors spread your path
With three-piled carpets, to receive your foot
And dull the sound of 't. For myself, be sure,
Although it frankly grinds the gravel here,
I still can bear it. Yet I'm sorry too
To lose this famous letter, which Sir Blaise
Has twisted to a lighter absently
To fire some holy taper: dear Lord Howe
Writes letters good for all things but to lose;   180
And many a flower of London gossipry
Has dropped wherever such a stem broke off.
Of course I feel that, lonely among my vines,
Where nothing's talked of, save the blight again,
And no more Chianti! Still the letter's use*
As preparation . . . Did I start indeed?
Last night I started at a cockchafer,*
And shook a half-hour after. Have you learnt
No more of women, 'spite of privilege,
Than still to take account too seriously   190
Of such weak flutterings? Why, we like it, sir,
We get our powers and our effects that way:
The trees stand stiff and still at time of frost,

If no wind tears them; but, let summer come,
When trees are happy—and a breath avails
To set them trembling through a million leaves
In luxury of emotion. Something less
It takes to move a woman: let her start
And shake at pleasure—nor conclude at yours,
The winter's bitter—but the summer's green.'   200

He answered, 'Be the summer ever green
With you, Aurora!—though you sweep your sex
With somewhat bitter gusts from where you live
Above them—whirling downward from your heights
Your very own pine-cones, in a grand disdain
Of the lowland burrs with which you scatter them.
So high and cold to others and yourself,
A little less to Romney were unjust,
And thus, I would not have you. Let it pass:
I feel content so. You can bear indeed   210
My sudden step beside you: but for me,
'Twould move me sore to hear your softened voice—
Aurora's voice—if softened unaware
In pity of what I am.'
                          Ah friend, I thought,
As husband of the Lady Waldemar
You're granted very sorely pitiable!
And yet Aurora Leigh must guard her voice
From softening in the pity of your case,
As if from lie or licence. Certainly
We'll soak up all the slush and soil of life   220
With softened voices, ere we come to *you*.

At which I interrupted my own thought
And spoke out calmly. 'Let us ponder, friend:
Whate'er our state we must have made it first;
And though the thing displease us, ay, perhaps
Displease us warrantably, never doubt
That other states, thought possible once, and then

Rejected by the instinct of our lives,
If then adopted had displeased us more
Than this on which the choice, the will, the love,   230
Has stamped the honour of a patent act
From henceforth. What we choose may not be good,
But, that we choose it, proves it good for *us*
Potentially, fantastically, now
Or last year, rather than a thing we saw,
And saw no need for choosing. Moths will burn
Their wings—which proves that light is good for moths,
Who else had flown not where they agonise.'

'Ay, light is good,' he echoed, and there paused;
And then abruptly . . . 'Marian. Marian's well?'   240

I bowed my head but found no word. 'Twas hard
To speak of *her* to Lady Waldemar's
New husband. How much did he know, at last?
How much? how little?—He would take no sign,
But straight repeated—'Marian. Is she well?'

'She's well,' I answered.

                              She was there in sight
An hour back, but the night had drawn her home,
Where still I heard her in an upper room,
Her low voice singing to the child in bed,
Who, restless with the summer-heat and play   250
And slumber snatched at noon, was long sometimes
In falling off, and took a score of songs
And mother-hushes ere she saw him sound.

'She's well,' I answered.

                              'Here?' he asked.
                                        'Yes, here.'

He stopped and sighed. 'That shall be presently,
But now this must be. I have words to say,
And would be alone to say them, I with you,
And no third troubling.'

         'Speak then,' I returned,
'She will not vex you.'

         At which, suddenly
He turned his face upon me with its smile   260
As if to crush me. 'I have read your book,
Aurora.'
        'You have read it,' I replied,
'And I have writ it—we have done with it.
And now the rest?'
        'The rest is like the first,'
He answered—'for the book is in my heart,
Lives in me, wakes in me, and dreams in me:
My daily bread tastes of it—and my wine
Which has no smack of it, I pour it out,
It seems unnatural drinking.'
            Bitterly
I took the word up; 'Never waste your wine.   270
The book lived in me ere it lived in you;
I know it closer than another does,
And how it's foolish, feeble, and afraid,
And all unworthy so much compliment.
Beseech you, keep your wine—and, when you drink,
Still wish some happier fortune to a friend,
Than even to have written a far better book.'

He answered gently, 'That is consequent:
The poet looks beyond the book he has made,
Or else he had not made it. If a man   280
Could make a man, he'd henceforth be a god
In feeling what a little thing is man:
It is not my case. And this special book,

I did not make it, to make light of it:
It stands above my knowledge, draws me up;
'Tis high to me. It may be that the book
Is not so high, but I so low, instead;
Still high to me. I mean no compliment:
I will not say there are not, young or old,
Male writers, ay, or female, let it pass,   290
Who'll write us richer and completer books.
A man may love a woman perfectly,
And yet by no means ignorantly maintain
A thousand women have not larger eyes:
Enough that she alone has looked at him
With eyes that, large or small, have won his soul.
And so, this book, Aurora—so, your book.'

'Alas,' I answered, 'is it so, indeed?'
And then was silent.
                    'Is it so, indeed,'
He echoed, 'that *alas* is all your word?'   300

I said—'I'm thinking of a far-off June,
When you and I, upon my birthday once,
Discoursed of life and art, with both untried.
I'm thinking, Romney, how 'twas morning then,
And now 'tis night.'

                    'And now,' he said, ''tis night.'

'I'm thinking,' I resumed, ''tis somewhat sad,
That if I had known, that morning in the dew,
My cousin Romney would have said such words
On such a night at close of many years,
In speaking of a future book of mine,   310
It would have pleased me better as a hope,
Than as an actual grace it can at all:
That's sad, I'm thinking.'

                    'Ay,' he said, ''tis night.'

'And there,' I added lightly, 'are the stars!
And here, we'll talk of stars and not of books.'

'You have the stars,' he murmured—'it is well:
Be like them! shine, Aurora, on my dark,
Though high and cold and only like a star,
And for this short night only—you, who keep
The same Aurora of the bright June day   320
That withered up the flowers before my face,
And turned me from the garden evermore
Because I was not worthy. Oh, deserved,
Deserved! that I, who verily had not learnt
God's lesson half, attaining as a dunce
To obliterate good words with fractious thumbs
And cheat myself of the context—*I* should push
Aside, with male ferocious impudence,
The world's Aurora who had conned her part
On the other side the leaf! ignore her so,   330
Because she was a woman and a queen,
And had no beard to bristle through her song,
My teacher, who has taught me with a book,
My Miriam, whose sweet mouth, when nearly drowned*
I still heard singing on the shore! Deserved,
That here I should look up unto the stars
And miss the glory' . . .

                    'Can I understand?'
I broke in. 'You speak wildly, Romney Leigh,
Or I hear wildly. In that morning-time
We recollect, the roses were too red,   340
The trees too green, reproach too natural
If one should see not what the other saw:
And now, it's night, remember; we have shades
In place of colours; we are now grown cold,
And old, my cousin Romney. Pardon me—
I'm very happy that you like my book,
And very sorry that I quoted back
A ten years' birthday. 'Twas so mad a thing

In any woman, I scarce marvel much
You took it for a venturous piece of spite,   350
Provoking such excuses as indeed
I cannot call you slack in.'

                                        'Understand,'
He answered sadly, 'something, if but so.
This night is softer than an English day,
And men may well come hither when they're sick,
To draw in easier breath from larger air.
'Tis thus with me; I come to you—to you,
My Italy of women, just to breathe
My soul out once before you, ere I go,
As humble as God makes me at the last   360
(I thank Him), quite out of the way of men
And yours, Aurora—like a punished child,
His cheeks all blurred with tears and naughtiness,
To silence in a corner. I am come
To speak, beloved' . . .

                        'Wisely, cousin Leigh,
And worthily of us both!'

                                'Yes, worthily;
For this time I must speak out and confess
That I, so truculent in assumption once,
So absolute in dogma, proud in aim,
And fierce in expectation—I, who felt   370
The whole world tugging at my skirts for help,
As if no other man than I could pull,
Nor woman, but I led her by the hand,
Nor cloth hold, but I had it in my coat,
Do know myself tonight for what I was
On that June day, Aurora. Poor bright day,
Which meant the best . . . a woman and a rose,
And which I smote upon the cheek with words
Until it turned and rent me! Young you were,
That birthday, poet, but you talked the right: 380
While I . . . I built up follies like a wall
To intercept the sunshine and your face.

Your face! that's worse.'
                              'Speak wisely, cousin Leigh.'

'Yes, wisely, dear Aurora, though too late:
But then, not wisely. I was heavy then,
And stupid, and distracted with the cries
Of tortured prisoners in the polished brass
Of that Phalarian bull, society,*
Which seems to bellow bravely like ten bulls,
But, if you listen, moans and cries instead   390
Despairingly, like victims tossed and gored
And trampled by their hoofs. I heard the cries
Too close: I could not hear the angels lift
A fold of rustling air, nor what they said
To help my pity. I beheld the world
As one great famishing carnivorous mouth—
A huge, deserted, callow, blind bird Thing,
With piteous open beak that hurt my heart,
Till down upon the filthy ground I dropped,
And tore the violets up to get the worms.   400
Worms, worms, was all my cry: an open mouth,
A gross want, bread to fill it to the lips,
No more. That poor men narrowed their demands
To such an end, was virtue, I supposed,
Adjudicating that to see it so
Was reason. Oh, I did not push the case
Up higher, and ponder how it answers when
The rich take up the same cry for themselves,
Professing equally—"An open mouth
A gross need, food to fill us, and no more."   410
Why that's so far from virtue, only vice
Can find excuse for't! that makes libertines,
And slurs our cruel streets from end to end
With eighty thousand women in one smile,*
Who only smile at night beneath the gas.
The body's satisfaction and no more
Is used for argument against the soul's

Here too; the want, here too, implies the right.
—How dark I stood that morning in the sun,
My best Aurora (though I saw your eyes),   420
When first you told me . . . oh, I recollect
The sound, and how you lifted your small hand,
And how your white dress and your burnished curls
Went greatening round you in the still blue air,
As if an inspiration from within
Had blown them all out when you spoke the words,
Even these—"You will not compass your poor ends*
Of barley-feeding and material ease,
Without the poet's individualism
To work your universal. It takes a soul,   430
To move a body—it takes a high-souled man,
To move the masses, even to a cleaner sty:
It takes the ideal, to blow an inch inside
The dust of the actual: and your Fouriers failed,
Because not poets enough to understand
That life develops from within." I say
Your words—I could say other words of yours,
For none of all your words will let me go;
Like sweet verbena which, being brushed against,
Will hold us three hours after by the smell   440
In spite of long walks upon windy hills.
But these words dealt in sharper perfume—these
Were ever on me, stinging through my dreams,
And saying themselves for ever o'er my acts
Like some unhappy verdict. That I failed,
Is certain. Sty or no sty, to contrive
The swine's propulsion toward the precipice,
Proved easy and plain. I subtly organised
And ordered, built the cards up high and higher,
Till, someone breathing, all fell flat again;   450
In setting right society's wide wrong,
Mere life's so fatal. So I failed indeed
Once, twice, and oftener—hearing through the rents
Of obstinate purpose, still those words of yours,

"*You will not compass your poor ends, not you!*"
But harder than you said them; every time
Still farther from your voice, until they came
To overcrow me with triumphant scorn
Which vexed me to resistance. Set down this
For condemnation—I was guilty here;   460
I stood upon my deed and fought my doubt,
As men will—for I doubted—till at last
My deed gave way beneath me suddenly
And left me what I am:—the curtain dropped,
My part quite ended, all the footlights quenched,
My own soul hissing at me through the dark,
I ready for confession—I was wrong,
I've sorely failed, I've slipped the ends of life,
I yield, you have conquered.'

                          'Stay,' I answered him;
'I've something for your hearing, also. I   470
Have failed too.'

                  'You!' he said, 'you're very great;
The sadness of your greatness fits you well:
As if the plume upon a hero's casque
Should nod a shadow upon his victor face.'

I took him up austerely—'You have read
My book, but not my heart; for recollect,
'Tis writ in Sanskrit which you bungle at.
I've surely failed, I know, if failure means
To look back sadly on work gladly done—
To wander on my mountains of Delight,   480
So called (I can remember a friend's words
As well as you, sir), weary and in want
Of even a sheep-path, thinking bitterly . . .
Well, well! no matter. I but say so much,
To keep you, Romney Leigh, from saying more,
And let you feel I am not so high indeed,
That I can bear to have you at my foot—
Or safe, that I can help you. That June day,

Too deeply sunk in craterous sunsets now
For you or me to dig it up alive—   490
To pluck it out all bleeding with spent flame
At the roots, before those moralising stars
We have got instead—that poor lost day, you said
Some words as truthful as the thing of mine
You cared to keep in memory; and I hold
If I, that day, and, being the girl I was,
Had shown a gentler spirit, less arrogance,
It had not hurt me. You will scarce mistake
The point here: I but only think, you see,
More justly, that's more humbly, of myself,   500
Than when I tried a crown on and supposed . . .
Nay, laugh, sir—I'll laugh with you!—pray you, laugh.
I've had so many birthdays since that day
I've learnt to prize mirth's opportunities,
Which come too seldom. Was it you who said
I was not changed? the same Aurora? Ah,
We could laugh there, too! Why, Ulysses' dog*
Knew *him*, and wagged his tail and died: but if
I had owned a dog, I too, before my Troy,
And if you brought him here . . . I warrant you   510
He'd look into my face, bark lustily,
And live on stoutly, as the creatures will
Whose spirits are not troubled by long loves.
A dog would never know me, I'm so changed,
Much less a friend . . . except that you're misled
By the colour of the hair, the trick of the voice,
Like that Aurora Leigh's.'
                              'Sweet trick of voice!
I would be a dog for this, to know it at last,
And die upon the falls of it. O love,
O best Aurora! are you then so sad   520
You scarcely had been sadder as my wife?'

'Your wife, sir! I must certainly be changed,
If I, Aurora, can have said a thing

So light, it catches at the knightly spurs
Of a noble gentleman like Romney Leigh
And trips him from his honourable sense
Of what befits' . . .
                    'You wholly misconceive,'
He answered.
                    I returned—'I'm glad of it.
But keep from misconception, too, yourself:
I am not humbled to so low a point,   530
Nor so far saddened. If I am sad at all,
Ten layers of birthdays on a woman's head
Are apt to fossilise her girlish mirth,
Though ne'er so merry: I'm perforce more wise,
And that, in truth, means sadder. For the rest,
Look here, sir: I was right upon the whole   *Perversion*
That birthday morning. 'Tis impossible
To get at men excepting through their souls,
However open their carnivorous jaws;
And poets get directlier at the soul,   540
Than any of your economists—for which
You must not overlook the poet's work
When scheming for the world's necessities.
The soul's the way. Not even Christ Himself
Can save man else than as He holds man's soul;
And therefore did He come into our flesh,
As some wise hunter creeping on his knees
With a torch, into the blackness of a cave,
To face and quell the beast there—take the soul,
And so possess the whole man, body and soul.   550
I said, so far, right, yes; not farther, though:
We both were wrong that June day—both as wrong
As an east wind had been. I who talked of art,
And you who grieved for all men's griefs . . . what then?
We surely made too small a part for God
In these things. What we are, imports us more
Than what we eat; and life, you've granted me,
Develops from within. But innermost

Of the inmost, most interior of the interne,
God claims His own, Divine humanity   560
Renewing nature—or the piercingest verse,
Pressed in by subtlest poet, still must keep
As much upon the outside of a man
As the very bowl in which he dips his beard.
—And then . . . the rest; I cannot surely speak:
Perhaps I doubt more than you doubted then,
If I, the poet's veritable charge,
Have borne upon my forehead. If I have,
It might feel somewhat liker to a crown,
The foolish green one even.—Ah, I think,   570
And chiefly when the sun shines, that I've failed.
But what then, Romney? Though we fail indeed,
You . . . I . . . a score of such weak workers . . . He
Fails never. If He cannot work by us,
He will work over us. Does He want a man,
Much less a woman, think you? Every time
The star winks there, so many souls are born,
Who all shall work too. Let our own be calm:
We should be ashamed to sit beneath those stars,
Impatient that we're nothing.'

                                'Could we sit   580
Just so for ever, sweetest friend,' he said,
'My failure would seem better than success.
And yet indeed your book has dealt with me
More gently, cousin, than you ever will!
Your book brought down entire the bright June day,
And set me wandering in the garden-walks,
And let me watch the garland in a place
You blushed so . . . nay, forgive me, do not stir—
I only thank the book for what it taught,
And what permitted. Poet, doubt yourself,   590
But never doubt that you're a poet to me
From henceforth. You have written poems, sweet,
Which moved me in secret, as the sap is moved
In still March branches, signless as a stone:

But this last book o'ercame me like soft rain
Which falls at midnight, when the tightened bark
Breaks out into unhesitating buds
And sudden protestations of the Spring.
In all your other books, I saw but *you*:
A man may see the moon so, in a pond,   600
And not be nearer therefore to the moon,
Nor use the sight . . . except to drown himself:
And so I forced my heart back from the sight,
For what had *I*, I thought, to do with *her*,
Aurora . . . Romney? But, in this last book,
You showed me something separate from yourself,
Beyond you, and I bore to take it in
And let it draw me. You have shown me truths,
O June-day friend, that help me now at night
When June is over! truths not yours, indeed,   610
But set within my reach by means of you,
Presented by your voice and verse the way
To take them clearest. Verily I was wrong;
And verily many thinkers of this age,
Ay, many Christian teachers, half in heaven,
Are wrong in just my sense who understood
Our natural world too insularly, as if
No spiritual counterpart completed it
Consummating its meaning, rounding all
To justice and perfection, line by line,   620
Form by form, nothing single nor alone,
The great below clenched by the great above,
Shade here authenticating substance there,
The body proving spirit, as the effect
The cause: we meantime being too grossly apt
To hold the natural, as dogs a bone
(Though reason and nature beat us in the face),
So obstinately, that we'll break our teeth
Or ever we let go. For everywhere
We're too materialistic—eating clay   630
(Like men of the west) instead of Adam's corn

And Noah's wine, clay by handfuls, clay by lumps,
Until we're filled up to the throat with clay,
And grow the grimy colour of the ground
On which we are feeding. Ay, materialist
The age's name is. God Himself, with some,
Is apprehended as the bare result
Of what His hand materially has made,
Expressed in such an algebraic sign
Called God—that is, to put it otherwise,   640
They add up nature to a nought of God
And cross the quotient. There are many even,
Whose names are written in the Christian church
To no dishonour, diet still on mud
And splash the altars with it. You might think
The clay Christ laid upon their eyelids when,*
Still blind, he called them to the use of sight,
Remained there to retard its exercise
With clogging incrustations. Close to heaven,
They see for mysteries, through the open doors,   650
Vague puffs of smoke from pots of earthenware;
And fain would enter, when their time shall come,
With quite another body than Saint Paul*
Has promised—husk and chaff, the whole barleycorn,
Or where's the resurrection?'
                              'Thus it is,'
I sighed. And he resumed with mournful face.
'Beginning so, and filling up with clay
The wards of this great key, the natural world,*
And fumbling vainly therefore at the lock
Of the spiritual, we feel ourselves shut in   660
With all the wild-beast roar of struggling life,
The terrors and compunctions of our souls,
As saints with lions—we who are not saints,
And have no heavenly lordship in our stare
To awe them backward. Ay, we are forced, so pent,
To judge the whole too partially . . . confound
Conclusions. Is there any common phrase

Significant, with the adverb heard alone,
The verb being absent, and the pronoun out?
But we, distracted in the roar of life,   670
Still insolently at God's adverb snatch,
And bruit against Him that His thought is void,*
His meaning hopeless—cry, that everywhere
The government is slipping from his hand,
Unless some other Christ (say Romney Leigh)
Come up and toil and moil and change the world,
Because the First has proved inadequate,
However we talk bigly of His work
And piously of His person. We blaspheme
At last, to finish our doxology,*   680
Despairing on the earth for which He died.'

'So now,' I asked, 'you have more hope of men?'

'I hope,' he answered. 'I am come to think
That God will have His work done, as you said,
And that we need not be disturbed too much
For Romney Leigh or others having failed
With this or that quack nostrum—recipes
For keeping summits by annulling depths,
For wrestling with luxurious lounging sleeves,
And acting heroism without a scratch.   690
We fail—what then? Aurora, if I smiled
To see you, in your lovely morning-pride,
Try on the poet's wreath which suits the noon
(Sweet cousin, walls must get the weather-stain
Before they grow the ivy!), certainly
I stood myself there worthier of contempt,
Self-rated, in disastrous arrogance,
As competent to sorrow for mankind
And even their odds. A man may well despair,
Who counts himself so needful to success.   700
I failed: I throw the remedy back on God,
And sit down here beside you, in good hope.'

'And yet take heed,' I answered, 'lest we lean
Too dangerously on the other side,
And so fail twice. Be sure, no earnest work
Of any honest creature, howbeit weak,
Imperfect, ill-adapted, fails so much,
It is not gathered as a grain of sand
To enlarge the sum of human action used
For carrying out God's end. No creature works   710
So ill, observe, that therefore he's cashiered.*
The honest earnest man must stand and work,
The woman also—otherwise she drops
At once below the dignity of man,
Accepting serfdom. Free men freely work.
Whoever fears God, fears to sit at ease.'

He cried, 'True. After Adam, work was curse;
The natural creature labours, sweats, and frets.
But, after Christ, work turns to privilege,
And henceforth, one with our humanity,   720
The Six-day Worker working still in us
Has called us freely to work on with Him
In high companionship. So, happiest!
I count that Heaven itself is only work
To a surer issue. Let us work, indeed,
But no more work as Adam—nor as Leigh
Erewhile, as if the only man on earth,
Responsible for all the thistles blown
And tigers couchant, struggling in amaze
Against disease and winter, snarling on   730
For ever that the world's not paradise.
O cousin, let us be content, in work,
To do the thing we can, and not presume
To fret because it's little. 'Twill employ*
Seven men, they say, to make a perfect pin;
Who makes the head, content to miss the point,
Who makes the point, agreed to leave the join:
And if a man should cry, "I want a pin,

And I must make it straightway, head and point,"
His wisdom is not worth the pin he wants.   740
Seven men to a pin—and not a man too much!
Seven generations, haply, to this world,
To right it visibly a finger's breadth,
And mend its rents a little. Oh, to storm
And say, "This world here is intolerable;
I will not eat this corn, nor drink this wine,
Nor love this woman, flinging her my soul
Without a bond for't as a lover should,
Nor use the generous leave of happiness
As not too good for using generously"   750
(Since virtue kindles at the touch of joy
Like a man's cheek laid on a woman's hand,
And God, who knows it, looks for quick returns
From joys)—to stand and claim to have a life
Beyond the bounds of the individual man,
And raze all personal cloisters of the soul
To build up public stores and magazines,
As if God's creatures otherwise were lost,
The builder surely saved by any means!
To think—I have a pattern on my nail,   760
And I will carve the world new after it
And solve so these hard social questions—nay,
Impossible social questions, since their roots
Strike deep in Evil's own existence here
Which God permits because the question's hard
To abolish evil nor attaint free-will.
Ay, hard to God, but not to Romney Leigh!
For Romney has a pattern on his nail
(Whatever may be lacking on the Mount)*
And, not being over-nice to separate   770
What's element from what's convention, hastes
By line on line to draw you out a world,
Without your help indeed, unless you take
His yoke upon you and will learn of him,
So much he has to teach! so good a world!

The same, the whole creation's groaning for!
No rich nor poor, no gain nor loss nor stint;
No pottage in it able to exclude
A brother's birthright, and no right of birth,
The pottage—both secured to every man,   780
And perfect virtue dealt out like the rest
Gratuitously, with the soup at six,
To whoso does not seek it.'

                           'Softly, sir,'
I interrupted—'I had a cousin once
I held in reverence. If he strained too wide,
It was not to take honour but give help;
The gesture was heroic. If his hand
Accomplished nothing . . . (well, it is not proved)
That empty hand thrown impotently out
Were sooner caught, I think, by One in Heaven,   790
Than many a hand that reaped a harvest in
And keeps the scythe's glow on it. Pray you, then,
For my sake merely, use less bitterness
In speaking of my cousin.'

                        'Ah,' he said,
'Aurora! when the prophet beats the ass,*
The angel intercedes.' He shook his head—
'And yet to mean so well and fail so foul,
Expresses ne'er another beast than man;
The antithesis is human. Hearken, dear;
There's too much abstract willing, purposing,   800
In this poor world. We talk by aggregates,
And think by systems, and, being used to face
Our evils in statistics, are inclined
To cap them with unreal remedies
Drawn out in haste on the other side the slate.'

'That's true,' I answered, fain to throw up thought
And make a game of 't—'Yes, we generalise
Enough to please you. If we pray at all,
We pray no longer for our daily bread

But next centenary's harvests. If we give, 810
Our cup of water is not tendered till
We lay down pipes and found a Company
With Branches. Ass or angel, 'tis the same:
A woman cannot do the thing she ought,
Which means whatever perfect thing she can,
In life, in art, in science, but she fears
To let the perfect action take her part,
And rest there: she must prove what she can do
Before she does it, prate of woman's rights,
Of woman's mission, woman's function, till 820
The men (who are prating too on their side) cry,
"A woman's function plainly is . . . to talk."
Poor souls, they are very reasonably vexed;
They cannot hear each other talk.'
                                        'And you,
An artist, judge so?'
                        'I, an artist—yes:
Because, precisely, I'm an artist, sir,
And woman, if another sat in sight,
I'd whisper—Soft, my sister! not a word!
By speaking we prove only we can speak,
Which he, the man here, never doubted. What 830
He doubts is, whether we can *do* the thing
With decent grace we've not yet done at all.
Now, do it; bring your statue—you have room!
He'll see it even by the starlight here;
And if 'tis e'er so little like the god
Who looks out from the marble silently
Along the track of his own shining dart
Through the dusk of ages, there's no need to speak;
The universe shall henceforth speak for you,
And witness, "She who did this thing was born 840
To do it—claims her licence in her work."
And so with more works. Whoso cures the plague,
Though twice a woman, shall be called a leech:*
Who rights a land's finances, is excused

For touching coppers, though her hands be white—
But we, we talk!'
                              'It is the age's mood,'
He said; 'we boast, and do not. We put up
Hostelry signs where'er we lodge a day,
Some red colossal cow with mighty paps
A Cyclops' fingers could not strain to milk—   850
Then bring out presently our saucerful
Of curds. We want more quiet in our works,
More knowledge of the bounds in which we work;
More knowledge that each individual man
Remains an Adam to the general race,
Constrained to see, like Adam, that he keep
His personal state's condition honestly,
Or vain all thoughts of his to help the world,
Which still must be developed from its *one*
If bettered in its many. We indeed,   860
Who think to lay it out new like a park,
We take a work on us which is not man's,
For God alone sits far enough above
To speculate so largely. None of us
(Not Romney Leigh) is mad enough to say,
We'll have a grove of oaks upon that slope
And sink the need of acorns. Government,
If veritable and lawful, is not given
By imposition of the foreign hand,
Nor chosen from a pretty pattern-book   870
Of some domestic idealogue who sits
And coldly chooses empire, where as well
He might republic. Genuine government
Is but the expression of a nation, good
Or less good—even as all society,
Howe'er unequal, monstrous, crazed and cursed,
Is but the expression of men's single lives,
The loud sum of the silent units. What,
We'd change the aggregate and yet retain
Each separate figure? whom do we cheat by that?   880

Now, not even Romney.'
                'Cousin, you are sad.
Did all your social labour at Leigh Hall
And elsewhere, come to nought then?'
                        'It *was* nought,'
He answered mildly. 'There is room indeed
For statues still, in this large world of God's,
But not for vacuums—so I am not sad;
Not sadder than is good for what I am.
My vain phalanstery dissolved itself;
My men and women of disordered lives
I brought in orderly to dine and sleep,   890
Broke up those waxen masks I made them wear,
With fierce contortions of the natural face—
And cursed me for my tyrannous constraint
In forcing crooked creatures to live straight;
And set the country hounds upon my back
To bite and tear me for my wicked deed
Of trying to do good without the church
Or even the squires, Aurora. Do you mind
Your ancient neighbours? The great book-club teems
With "sketches," "summaries," and "last tracts" but
     twelve,   900
On socialistic troublers of close bonds
Betwixt the generous rich and grateful poor.
The vicar preached from "Revelations" (till
The doctor woke), and found me with "the frogs"*
On three successive Sundays; ay, and stopped
To weep a little (for he's getting old)
That such perdition should o'ertake a man
Of such fair acres—in the parish, too!
He printed his discourses "by request,"
And if your book shall sell as his did, then   910
Your verses are less good than I suppose.
The women of the neighbourhood subscribed,
And sent me a copy bound in scarlet silk,
Tooled edges, blazoned with the arms of Leigh:

I own that touched me.'
                              'What, the pretty ones?
Poor Romney!'
                              'Otherwise the effect was small:
I had my windows broken once or twice
By liberal peasants naturally incensed
At such a vexer of Arcadian peace,
Who would not let men call their wives their own   920
To kick like Britons, and made obstacles
When things went smoothly as a baby drugged,
Toward freedom and starvation—bringing down
The wicked London tavern-thieves and drabs
To affront the blessed hillside drabs and thieves
With mended morals, quotha—fine new lives!—
My windows paid for't. I was shot at, once,
By an active poacher who had hit a hare
From the other barrel (tired of springeing game
So long upon my acres, undisturbed,   930
And restless for the country's virtue—yet
He missed me); ay, and pelted very oft
In riding through the village. "There he goes
Who'd drive away our Christian gentlefolks,
To catch us undefended in the trap
He baits with poisonous cheese, and lock us up
In that pernicious prison of Leigh Hall
With all his murderers! Give another name
And say Leigh Hell, and burn it up with fire."
And so they did, at last, Aurora.'
                              'Did?'   940

'You never heard it, cousin? Vincent's news
Came stinted, then.'
                              'They did? they burnt Leigh Hall?'

'You're sorry, dear Aurora? Yes indeed,
They did it perfectly: a thorough work,
And not a failure, this time. Let us grant

'Tis somewhat easier, though, to burn a house
Than build a system—yet that's easy, too,
In a dream. Books, pictures—ay, the pictures! what,
You think your dear Vandykes would give them pause?
Our proud ancestral Leighs, with those peaked beards,   950
Or bosoms white as foam thrown up on rocks
From the old-spent wave. Such calm defiant looks
They flared up with! now nevermore to twit
The bones in the family vault with ugly death.
Not one was rescued, save the Lady Maud,
Who threw you down, that morning you were born,
The undeniable lineal mouth and chin
To wear for ever for her gracious sake,
For which good deed I saved her; the rest went:
And you, you're sorry, cousin. Well, for me,   960
With all my phalansterians safely out
(Poor hearts, they helped the burners, it was said,
And certainly a few clapped hands and yelled),
The ruin did not hurt me as it might—
As when for instance I was hurt one day
A certain letter being destroyed. In fact,
To see the great house flare so . . . oaken floors,
Our fathers made so fine with rushes once
Before our mothers furbished them with trains,
Carved wainscoats, panelled walls, the favourite slide   970
For draining off a martyr (or a rogue),
The echoing galleries, half a half-mile long,
And all the various stairs that took you up
And took you down, and took you round about
Upon their slippery darkness, recollect,
All helping to keep up one blazing jest!
The flames through all the casements pushing forth
Like red-hot devils crinkled into snakes,
All signifying—"Look you, Romney Leigh,
We save the people from your saving, here,   980
Yet so as by fire! we make a pretty show
Besides—and that's the best you've ever done."

—To see this, almost moved myself to clap!
The "vale et plaude" came too with effect*
When in the roof fell, and the fire that paused,
Stunned momently beneath the stroke of slates
And tumbling rafters, rose at once and roared,
And wrapping the whole house (which disappeared
In a mounting whirlwind of dilated flame)
Blew upward, straight, its drift of fiery chaff   990
In the face of Heaven, which blenched, and ran up higher.'

'Poor Romney!'
                    'Sometimes when I dream,' he said,
'I hear the silence after, 'twas so still.
For all those wild beasts, yelling, cursing round,
Were suddenly silent, while you counted five,
So silent, that you heard a young bird fall
From the top nest in the neighbouring rookery,
Through edging over-rashly toward the light.
The old rooks had already fled too far,
To hear the screech they fled with, though you saw   1000
Some flying still, like scatterings of dead leaves
In autumn-gusts, seen dark against the sky—
All flying—ousted, like the House of Leigh.'

'Dear Romney!'
                    'Evidently 'twould have been
A fine sight for a poet, sweet, like you,
To make the verse blaze after. I myself,
Even I, felt something in the grand old trees,
Which stood that moment like brute Druid gods
Amazed upon the rim of ruin, where,
As into a blackened socket, the great fire   1010
Had dropped—still throwing up splinters now and then
To show them gray with all their centuries,
Left there to witness that on such a day
The House went out.'

                              'Ah!'
                                    'While you counted five,
I seemed to feel a little like a Leigh—
But then it passed, Aurora. A child cried,
And I had enough to think of what to do
With all those houseless wretches in the dark,
And ponder where they'd dance the next time, they
Who had burnt the viol.'
                              'Did you think of that?   1020
Who burns his viol will not dance, I know,
To cymbals, Romney.'
                            'O my sweet sad voice,'
He cried—'O voice that speaks and overcomes!
The sun is silent, but Aurora speaks.'

'Alas,' I said, 'I speak I know not what:
I'm back in childhood, thinking as a child,
A foolish fancy—will it make you smile?
I shall not from the window of my room
Catch sight of those old chimneys any more.'

'No more,' he answered. 'If you pushed one day   1030
Through all the green hills to our fathers' house,
You'd come upon a great charred circle, where
The patient earth was singed an acre round;
With one stone stair, symbolic of my life,
Ascending, winding, leading up to nought!
'Tis worth a poet's seeing. Will you go?'

I made no answer. Had I any right
To weep with this man, that I dared to speak?
A woman stood between his soul and mine,
And waved us off from touching evermore,   1040
With those unclean white hands of hers. Enough.
We had burnt our viols and were silent.
                                            So,
The silence lengthened till it pressed. I spoke,
To breathe: 'I think you were ill afterward.'

'More ill,' he answered, 'had been scarcely ill.
I hoped this feeble fumbling at life's knot
Might end concisely—but I failed to die,
As formerly I failed to live—and thus
Grew willing, having tried all other ways,
To try just God's. Humility's so good,   1050
When pride's impossible. Mark us, how we make
Our virtues, cousin, from our worn-out sins,
Which smack of them from henceforth. Is it right,
For instance, to wed here while you love there?
And yet because a man sins once, the sin
Cleaves to him, in necessity to sin,
That if he sin not *so*, to damn himself,
He sins *so*, to damn others with himself:
And thus, to wed here, loving there, becomes
A duty. Virtue buds a dubious leaf   1060
Round mortal brows; your ivy's better, dear.
—Yet she, 'tis certain, is my very wife,
The very lamb left mangled by the wolves
Through my own bad shepherding: and could I choose
But take her on my shoulder past this stretch
Of rough, uneasy wilderness, poor lamb,
Poor child, poor child?—Aurora, my beloved
I will not vex you any more tonight,
But, having spoken what I came to say,
The rest shall please you. What she can, in me—   1070
Protection, tender liking, freedom, ease,
She shall have surely, liberally, for her
And hers, Aurora. Small amends they'll make
For hideous evils which she had not known
Except by me, and for this imminent loss,
This forfeit presence of a gracious friend,
Which also she must forfeit for my sake,
Since . . . drop your hand in mine a moment, sweet,
We're parting!—ah, my snowdrop, what a touch,
As if the wind had swept it off! you grudge   1080
Your gelid sweetness on my palm but so,

A moment? angry, that I could not bear
You . . . speaking, breathing, living, side by side
With someone called my wife . . . and live, myself?
Nay, be not cruel—you must understand!
Your lightest footfall on a floor of mine
Would shake the house, my lintel being uncrossed
'Gainst angels: henceforth it is night with me,
And so, henceforth, I put the shutters up:
Auroras must not come to spoil my dark.'   1090

He smiled so feebly, with an empty hand
Stretched sideway from me—as indeed he looked
To any one but me to give him help;
And, while the moon came suddenly out full,
The double-rose of our Italian moons,
Sufficient plainly for the heaven and earth
(The stars struck dumb and washed away in dews
Of golden glory, and the mountains steeped
In divine languor), he, the man, appeared
So pale and patient, like the marble man   1100
A sculptor puts his personal sadness in
To join his grandeur of ideal thought—
As if his mallet struck me from my height
Of passionate indignation, I who had risen
Pale, doubting paused . . . Was Romney mad indeed?
Had all this wrong of heart made sick the brain?

Then quiet, with a sort of tremulous pride,
'Go, cousin,' I said coldly; 'a farewell
Was sooner spoken 'twixt a pair of friends
In those old days, than seems to suit you now.   1110
Howbeit, since then, I've writ a book or two,
I'm somewhat dull still in the manly art
Of phrase and metaphrase. Why, any man*
Can carve a score of white Loves out of snow,*
As Buonarroti in my Florence there,
And set them on the wall in some safe shade,

As safe, sir, as your marriage! very good;
Though if a woman took one from the ledge
To put it on the table by her flowers
And let it mind her of a certain friend,   1120
'Twould drop at once (so better), would not bear
Her nail-mark even, where she took it up
A little tenderly—so best, I say:
For me, I would not touch the fragile thing
And risk to spoil it half an hour before
The sun shall shine to melt it: leave it there.
I'm plain at speech, direct in purpose: when
I speak, you'll take the meaning as it is,
And not allow for puckerings in the silk
By clever stitches—I'm a woman, sir,   1130
I use the woman's figures naturally,
As you the male licence. So, I wish you well.
I'm simply sorry for the griefs you've had,
And not for your sake only, but mankind's.
This race is never grateful: from the first,
One fills their cup at supper with pure wine,*
Which back they give at cross-time on a sponge,
In vinegar and gall.'
                       'If gratefuller,'
He murmured, 'by so much less pitiable!
God's self would never have come down to die,   1140
Could man have thanked him for it.'
                                    'Happily
'Tis patent that, whatever,' I resumed,
'You suffered from this thanklessness of men,
You sink no more than Moses' bulrush-boat
When once relieved of Moses—for you're light,
You're light, my cousin! which is well for you,
And manly. For myself—now mark me, sir,
They burnt Leigh Hall; but if, consummated
To devils, heightened beyond Lucifers,
They had burnt, instead, a star or two of those   1150
We saw above there just a moment back,

Before the moon abolished them—destroyed
And riddled them in ashes through a sieve
On the head of the foundering universe—what then?
If you and I remained still you and I,
It could not shift our places as mere friends,
Nor render decent you should toss a phrase
Beyond the point of actual feeling!—Nay,
You shall not interrupt me: as you said,
We're parting. Certainly, not once nor twice   1160
Tonight you've mocked me somewhat, or yourself,
And I, at least, have not deserved it so
That I should meet it unsurprised. But now,
Enough: we're parting . . . parting. Cousin Leigh,
I wish you well through all the acts of life
And life's relations, wedlock not the least,
And it shall "please me," in your words, to know
You yield your wife, protection, freedom, ease,
And very tender liking. May you live
So happy with her, Romney, that your friends   1170
Shall praise her for it. Meantime some of us
Are wholly dull in keeping ignorant
Of what she has suffered by you, and what debt
Of sorrow your rich love sits down to pay:
But if 'tis sweet for love to pay its debt,
'Tis sweeter still for love to give its gift,
And you, be liberal in the sweeter way,
You can, I think. At least, as touches me,
You owe her, cousin Romney, no amends.
She is not used to hold my gown so fast,   1180
You need entreat her now to let it go;
The lady never was a friend of mine,
Nor capable—I thought you knew as much—
Of losing for your sake so poor a prize
As such a worthless friendship. Be content,
Good cousin, therefore, both for her and you!
I'll never spoil your dark, nor dull your noon,
Nor vex you when you're merry, or at rest:

You shall not need to put a shutter up
To keep out this Aurora—though your north   1190
Can make Auroras which vex nobody,
Scarce known from night, I fancied! let me add,
My larks fly higher than some windows. Well,
You've read your Leighs. Indeed 'twould shake a house,
If such as I came in with outstretched hand
Still warm and thrilling from the clasp of one . . .
Of one we know . . . to acknowledge, palm to palm,
As mistress there, the Lady Waldemar.

'Now God be with us' . . . with a sudden clash
Of voice he interrupted—'what name's that?   1200
You spoke a name, Aurora.'
                                        'Pardon me;
I would that, Romney, I could name your wife
Nor wound you, yet be worthy.'
                                        'Are we mad?'
He echoed—'wife! mine! Lady Waldemar!
I think you said my wife.' He sprang to his feet,
And threw his noble head back toward the moon
As one who swims against a stormy sea,
Then laughed with such a helpless, hopeless scorn,
I stood and trembled.
                              'May God judge me so,'
He said at last—'I came convicted here,   1210
And humbled sorely if not enough. I came,
Because this woman from her crystal soul
Had shown me something which a man calls light:
Because too, formerly, I sinned by her
As then and ever since I have, by God,
Through arrogance of nature—though I loved . . .*
Whom best, I need not say, since that is writ
Too plainly in the book of my misdeeds:
And thus I came here to abase myself,
And fasten, kneeling, on her regent brows   1220
A garland which I startled thence one day

Of her beautiful June youth. But here again
I'm baffled—fail in my abasement as
My aggrandisement: there's no room left for me
At any woman's foot who misconceives
My nature, purpose, possible actions. What!
Are you the Aurora who made large my dreams
To frame your greatness? you conceive so small?
You stand so less than woman, through being more,
And lose your natural instinct (like a beast)   1230
Through intellectual culture? since indeed
I do not think that any common she
Would dare adopt such monstrous forgeries
For the legible life-signature of such
As I, with all my blots—with all my blots!
At last then, peerless cousin, we are peers,
At last we're even. Ah, you've left your height,
And here upon my level we take hands,
And here I reach you to forgive you, sweet,
And that's a fall, Aurora. Long ago   1240
You seldom understood me—but before,
I could not blame you. Then, you only seemed
So high above, you could not see below;
But now I breathe—but now I pardon!—nay,
We're parting. Dearest, men have burnt my house,
Maligned my motives—but not one, I swear,
Has wronged my soul as this Aurora has
Who called the Lady Waldemar my wife.'

'Not married to her! yet you said' . . . .
                                        'Again?
Nay, read the lines' (he held a letter out)   1250
'She sent you through me.'
                          By the moonlight there,
I tore the meaning out with passionate haste
Much rather than I read it. Thus it ran.

BOOK IX

EVEN thus. I pause to write it out at length,
The letter of the Lady Waldemar.

'I prayed your cousin Leigh to take you this,
He says he'll do it. After years of love,
Or what is called so, when a woman frets
And fools upon one string of a man's name,
And fingers it for ever till it breaks—
He may perhaps do for her such a thing,
And she accept it without detriment
Although she should not love him any more.   10
And I, who do not love him, nor love you,
Nor you, Aurora—choose you shall repent
Your most ungracious letter and confess,
Constrained by his convictions (he's convinced),
You've wronged me foully. Are you made so ill,
You woman—to impute such ill to *me*?
We both had mothers—lay in their bosom once.
And after all, I thank you, Aurora Leigh,
For proving to myself that there are things
I would not do—not for my life, nor him,   20
Though something I have somewhat overdone—
For instance, when I went to see the gods
One morning on Olympus, with a step
That shook the thunder from a certain cloud,
Committing myself vilely. Could I think,
The Muse I pulled my heart out from my breast
To soften, had herself a sort of heart,
And loved my mortal? He at least loved her,
I heard him say so—'twas my recompense,
When, watching at his bedside fourteen days,   30

He broke out ever like a flame at whiles
Between the heats of fever—"Is it thou?
Breathe closer, sweetest mouth!" and when at last
The fever gone, the wasted face extinct,
As if it irked him much to know me there,
He said, "'Twas kind, 'twas good, 'twas womanly"
(And fifty praises to excuse no love),
"But was the picture safe he had ventured for?"
And then, half wandering—"I have loved her well,
Although she could not love me."—"Say instead,"   40
I answered, "she does love you."—'Twas my turn
To rave: I would have married him so changed,
Although the world had jeered me properly
For taking up with Cupid at his worst,
The silver quiver worn off on his hair.
"No, no," he murmured, "no, she loves me not;
Aurora Leigh does better: bring her book
And read it softly, Lady Waldemar,
Until I thank your friendship more for that
Than even for harder service." So I read   50
Your book, Aurora, for an hour that day:
I kept its pauses, marked its emphasis;
My voice, impaled upon its hooks of rhyme,*
Not once would writhe, nor quiver, nor revolt;
I read on calmly—calmly shut it up,
Observing, "There's some merit in the book;
And yet the merit in't is thrown away,
As chances still with women if we write
Or write not: we want string to tie our flowers,
So drop them as we walk, which serves to show   60
The way we went. Good morning, Mister Leigh;
You'll find another reader the next time.
A woman who does better than to love,
I hate; she will do nothing very well:
Male poets are preferable, straining less
And teaching more." I triumphed o'er you both,
And left him.

            'When I saw him afterward
I had read your shameful letter, and my heart.
He came with health recovered, strong though pale,
Lord Howe and he, a courteous pair of friends,   70
To say what men dare say to women, when
Their debtors. But I stopped them with a word,
And proved I had never trodden such a road
To carry so much dirt upon my shoe.
Then, putting into it something of disdain,
I asked forsooth his pardon, and my own,
For having done no better than to love,
And that not wisely—though 'twas long ago,
And had been mended radically since.
I told him, as I tell you now, Miss Leigh,   80
And proved, I took some trouble for his sake
(Because I knew he did not love the girl)
To spoil my hands with working in the stream
Of that poor bubbling nature—till she went,
Consigned to one I trusted, my own maid
Who once had lived full five months in my house
(Dressed hair superbly) with a lavish purse
To carry to Australia where she had left
A husband, said she. If the creature lied,
The mission failed, we all do fail and lie   90
More or less—and I'm sorry—which is all
Expected from us when we fail the most
And go to church to own it. What I meant,
Was just the best for him, and me, and her . . .
Best even for Marian!—I am sorry for't,
And very sorry. Yet my creature said
She saw her stop to speak in Oxford Street
To one . . . no matter! I had sooner cut
My hand off (though 'twere kissed the hour before,
And promised a duke's troth-ring for the next)   100
Than crush her silly head with so much wrong.
Poor child! I would have mended it with gold,
Until it gleamed like Saint Sophia's dome*

When all the faithful troop to morning-prayer:
But he, he nipped the bud of such a thought
With that cold Leigh look which I fancied once,
And broke in, "Henceforth she was called his wife:
His wife required no succour: he was bound
To Florence, to resume this broken bond;
Enough so. Both were happy, he and Howe,   110
To acquit me of the heaviest charge of all"—
At which I shot my tongue against my fly
And struck him; "Would he carry—he was just,
A letter from me to Aurora Leigh,
And ratify from his authentic mouth
My answer to her accusation?"—"Yes,
If such a letter were prepared in time."
—He's just, your cousin—ay, abhorrently:
He'd wash his hands in blood, to keep them clean.
And so, cold, courteous, a mere gentleman,   120
He bowed, we parted.
                    'Parted. Face no more,
Voice no more, love no more! wiped wholly out
Like some ill scholar's scrawl from heart and slate—
Ay, spit on and so wiped out utterly
By some coarse scholar! I have been too coarse,
Too human. Have we business, in our rank,
With blood i' the veins? I will have henceforth none,
Not even to keep the colour at my lip:
A rose is pink and pretty without blood,
Why not a woman? When we've played in vain   130
The game, to adore—we have resources still,
And can play on at leisure, being adored:
Here's Smith already swearing at my feet
That I'm the typic She. Away with Smith!—
Smith smacks of Leigh—and henceforth I'll admit
No socialist within three crinolines,
To live and have his being. But for you,
Though insolent your letter and absurd,
And though I hate you frankly—take my Smith!

For when you have seen this famous marriage tied,   140
A most unspotted Erle to a noble Leigh
(His love astray on one he should not love),
Howbeit you may not want his love, beware,
You'll want some comfort. So I leave you Smith,
Take Smith!—he talks Leigh's subjects, somewhat worse;
Adopts a thought of Leigh's, and dwindles it;
Goes leagues beyond, to be no inch behind;
Will mind you of him, as a shoe-string may
Of a man: and women, when they are made like you,
Grow tender to a shoe-string, footprint even,   150
Adore averted shoulders in a glass,
And memories of what, present once, was loathed.
And yet, you loathed not Romney—though you played
At "fox and goose" about him with your soul;*
Pass over fox, you rub out fox—ignore
A feeling, you eradicate it—the act's
Identical.

      'I wish you joy, Miss Leigh,
You've made a happy marriage for your friend,
And all the honour, well-assorted love,
Derives from you who love him, whom he loves!   160
You need not wish *me* joy to think of it;
I have so much. Observe, Aurora Leigh,
Your droop of eyelid is the same as his,
And, but for you, I might have won his love,
And, to you, I have shown my naked heart;
For which three things, I hate, hate, hate you. Hush
Suppose a fourth!—I cannot choose but think
That, with him, I were virtuouser than you
Without him: so I hate you from this gulf
And hollow of my soul, which opens out   170
To what, except for you, had been my heaven,
And is, instead, a place to curse by! LOVE.'

An active kind of curse. I stood there cursed,
Confounded. I had seized and caught the sense

Of the letter, with its twenty stinging snakes,
In a moment's sweep of eyesight, and I stood
Dazed.—'Ah! not married.'

                          'You mistake,' he said,
'I'm married. Is not Marian Erle my wife?
As God sees things, I have a wife and child;
And I, as I'm a man who honours God,   180
Am here to claim them as my child and wife.'

I felt it hard to breathe, much less to speak.
Nor word of mine was needed. Someone else
Was there for answering. 'Romney,' she began,
'My great good angel, Romney.'

                          Then at first,
I knew that Marian Erle was beautiful.
She stood there, still and pallid as a saint,
Dilated, like a saint in ecstasy,
As if the floating moonshine interposed
Betwixt her foot and the earth, and raised her up   190
To float upon it. 'I had left my child,
Who sleeps,' she said, 'and having drawn this way
I heard you speaking . . . friend!—Confirm me now.
You take this Marian, such as wicked men
Have made her, for your honourable wife?'

The thrilling, solemn, proud, pathetic voice.
He stretched his arms out toward that thrilling voice,
As if to draw it on to his embrace.
—'I take her as God made her, and as men
Must fail to unmake her, for my honoured wife.'   200

She never raised her eyes, nor took a step,
But stood there in her place, and spoke again.
—'You take this Marian's child, which is her shame
In sight of men and women, for your child,
Of whom you will not ever feel ashamed?'

The thrilling, tender, proud, pathetic voice.
He stepped on toward it, still with outstretched arms,
As if to quench upon his breast that voice.
—'May God so father me, as I do him,
And so forsake me, as I let him feel   210
He's orphaned haply. Here I take the child
To share my cup, to slumber on my knee,
To play his loudest gambol at my foot,
To hold my finger in the public ways,
Till none shall need inquire, "Whose child is this?"
The gesture saying so tenderly, "My own."'

She stood a moment silent in her place;
Then turning toward me very slow and cold—
'And you—what say you?—will you blame me much,
If, careful for that outcast child of mine,   220
I catch this hand that's stretched to me and him,
Nor dare to leave him friendless in the world
Where men have stoned me? Have I not the right
To take so mere an aftermath from life,*
Else found so wholly bare? Or is it wrong
To let your cousin, for a generous bent,
Put out his ungloved fingers among briars
To set a tumbling bird's nest somewhat straight?
You will not tell him, though we're innocent,
We are not harmless . . . and that both our harms   230
Will stick to his good smooth noble life like burrs,
Never to drop off though he shakes the cloak?
You've been my friend: you will not now be his?
You've known him that he's worthy of a friend,
And you're his cousin, lady, after all,
And therefore more than free to take his part,
Explaining, since the nest is surely spoilt
And Marian what you know her—though a wife,
The world would hardly understand her case
Of being just hurt and honest; while, for him,   240
'Twould ever twit him with his bastard child
And married harlot. Speak, while yet there's time:

You would not stand and let a good man's dog
Turn round and rend him, because his, and reared
Of a generous breed—and will you let his act,
Because it's generous? Speak. I'm bound to you,
And I'll be bound by only you, in this.'

The thrilling, solemn voice, so passionless,
Sustained, yet low, without a rise or fall,
As one who had authority to speak,   250
And not as Marian.
          I looked up to feel
If God stood near me, and beheld His heaven
As blue as Aaron's priestly robe appeared*
To Aaron when he took it off to die.
And then I spoke—'Accept the gift, I say,
My sister Marian, and be satisfied.
The hand that gives, has still a soul behind
Which will not let it quail for having given,
Though foolish worldlings talk they know not what
Of what they know not. Romney's strong enough   260
For this: do you be strong to know he's strong:
He stands on Right's side; never flinch for him,
As if he stood on the other. You'll be bound
By me? I am a woman of repute;
No fly-blow gossip ever specked my life;
My name is clean and open as this hand,
Whose glove there's not a man dares blab about
As if he had touched it freely. Here's my hand
To clasp your hand, my Marian, owned as pure!
As pure—as I'm a woman and a Leigh!—   270
And, as I'm both, I'll witness to the world
That Romney Leigh is honoured in his choice
Who chooses Marian for his honoured wife.'

Her broad wild woodland eyes shot out a light,
Her smile was wonderful for rapture. 'Thanks,
My great Aurora.' Forward then she sprang,
And dropping her impassioned spaniel head

With all its brown abandonment of curls
On Romney's feet, we heard the kisses drawn
Through sobs upon the foot, upon the ground—   280
'O Romney! O my angel! O unchanged,
Though since we've parted I have passed the grave!
But Death itself could only better *thee*,
Not change thee!—*Thee* I do not thank at all:
I but thank God who made thee what thou art,
So wholly godlike.'
                              When he tried in vain
To raise her to his embrace, escaping thence
As any leaping fawn from a huntsman's grasp,
She bounded off and 'lighted beyond reach,
Before him, with a staglike majesty   290
Of soft, serene defiance—as she knew
He could not touch her, so was tolerant
He had cared to try. She stood there with her great
Drowned eyes, and dripping cheeks, and strange sweet
    smile
That lived through all, as if one held a light
Across a waste of waters—shook her head
To keep some thoughts down deeper in her soul—
Then, white and tranquil like a summer-cloud
Which, having rained itself to a tardy peace,
Stands still in Heaven as if it ruled the day,   300
Spoke out again—'Although, my generous friend,
Since last we met and parted you're unchanged,
And, having promised faith to Marian Erle,
Maintain it, as she were not changed at all;
And though that's worthy, though that's full of balm
To any conscious spirit of a girl
Who once has loved you as I loved you once—
Yet still it will not make her . . . if she's dead,
And gone away where none can give or take
In marriage—able to revive, return   310
And wed you—will it, Romney? Here's the point;
My friend, we'll see it plainer: you and I

Must never, never, never join hands so.
Nay, let me say it—for I said it first
To God, and placed it, rounded to an oath,
Far, far above the moon there, at His feet,
As surely as I wept just now at yours—
We never, never, never join hands so.
And now, be patient with me; do not think
I'm speaking from a false humility.
The truth is, I am grown so proud with grief,*   320
And He has said so often through His nights
And through His mornings, "Weep a little still,
Thou foolish Marian, because women must,
But do not blush at all except for sin"—
That I, who felt myself unworthy once
Of virtuous Romney and his high-born race,
Have come to learn—a woman, poor or rich,
Despised or honoured, is a human soul,
And what her soul is, that she is herself,   330
Although she should be spit upon of men,
As is the pavement of the churches here,
Still good enough to pray in. And being chaste
And honest, and inclined to do the right,
And love the truth, and live my life out green
And smooth beneath his steps, I should not fear
To make him thus a less uneasy time
Than many a happier woman. Very proud
You see me. Pardon, that I set a trap
To hear a confirmation in your voice,   340
Both yours and yours. It is so good to know
'Twas really God who said the same before;
And thus it is in Heaven, that first God speaks,
And then His angels. Oh, it does me good,
It wipes me clean and sweet from devil's dirt,
That Romney Leigh should think me worthy still
Of being his true and honourable wife!
Henceforth I need not say, on leaving earth,
I had no glory in it. For the rest,

The reason's ready (master, angel, friend,   350
Be patient with me) wherefore you and I
Can never, never, never join hands so.
I know you'll not be angry like a man
(For *you* are none) when I shall tell the truth,
Which is, I do not love you, Romney Leigh,
I do not love you. Ah well! catch my hands,
Miss Leigh, and burn into my eyes with yours—
I swear I do not love him. Did I once?
'Tis said that women have been bruised to death
And yet, if once they loved, that love of theirs   360
Could never be drained out with all their blood:
I've heard such things and pondered. Did I indeed
Love once; or did I only worship? Yes,
Perhaps, O friend, I set you up so high
Above all actual good or hope of good
Or fear of evil, all that could be mine,
I haply set you above love itself,
And out of reach of these poor woman's arms,
Angelic Romney. What was in my thought?
To be your slave, your help, your toy, your tool.   370
To be your love . . . I never thought of that:
To give you love . . . still less. I gave you love?
I think I did not give you anything;
I was but only yours—upon my knees,
All yours, in soul and body, in head and heart,
A creature you had taken from the ground
Still crumbling through your fingers to your feet
To join the dust she came from. Did I love,
Or did I worship? judge, Aurora Leigh!
But, if indeed I loved, 'twas long ago—   380
So long! before the sun and moon were made,
Before the hells were open—ah, before
I heard my child cry in the desert night,
And knew he had no father. It may be
I'm not as strong as other women are,
Who, torn and crushed, are not undone from love.

It may be I am colder than the dead,
Who, being dead, love always. But for me,
Once killed, this ghost of Marian loves no more,
No more . . . except the child! . . . no more at all. 390
I told your cousin, sir, that I was dead;
And now, she thinks I'll get up from my grave,
And wear my chin-cloth for a wedding-veil,*
And glide along the churchyard like a bride
While all the dead keep whispering through the withes,*
"You would be better in your place with us,
You pitiful corruption!" At the thought,
The damps break out on me like leprosy
Although I'm clean. Ay, clean as Marian Erle!
As Marian Leigh, I know, I were not clean: 400
Nor have I so much life that I should love,
Except the child. Ah God! I could not bear
To see my darling on a good man's knees,
And know, by such a look, or such a sigh,
Or such a silence, that he thought sometimes,
"This child was fathered by some cursed wretch" . . .
For, Romney—angels are less tender-wise
Than God and mothers: even *you* would think
What *we* think never. He is ours, the child;
And we would sooner vex a soul in Heaven 410
By coupling with it the dead body's thought,
It left behind it in a last month's grave,
Than, in my child, see other than . . . my child.
We only, never call him fatherless
Who has God and his mother. O my babe,
My pretty, pretty blossom, an ill-wind
Once blew upon my breast! can any think
I'd have another—one called happier,
A fathered child, with father's love and race
That's worn as bold and open as a smile, 420
To vex my darling when he's asked his name
And has no answer? What! a happier child
Than mine, my best—who laughed so loud tonight

He could not sleep for pastime? Nay, I swear
By life and love, that, if I lived like some,
And loved like . . . *some,* ay, loved you, Romney Leigh,
As some love (eyes that have wept so much, see clear),
I've room for no more children in my arms,
My kisses are all melted on one mouth,
I would not push my darling to a stool   430
To dandle babies. Here's a hand shall keep*
For ever clean without a marriage-ring,
To tend my boy until he cease to need
One steadying finger of it, and desert
(Not miss) his mother's lap, to sit with men.
And when I miss him (not he me) I'll come
And say, "Now give me some of Romney's work,
To help your outcast orphans of the world
And comfort grief with grief." For you, meantime,
Most noble Romney, wed a noble wife,   440
And open on each other your great souls—
I need not farther bless you. If I dared
But strain and touch her in her upper sphere
And say, "Come down to Romney—pay my debt!"
I should be joyful with the stream of joy
Sent through me. But the moon is in my face . . .
I dare not—though I guess the name he loves;
I'm learned with my studies of old days,
Remembering how he crushed his under-lip
When someone came and spoke, or did not come: 450
Aurora, I could touch her with my hand,
And fly because I dare not.'
                              She was gone.

He smiled so sternly that I spoke in haste.
'Forgive her—she sees clearly for herself:
Her instinct's holy.'
                    '*I* forgive!' he said,
'I only marvel how she sees so sure,
While others' . . . there he paused—then hoarse, abrupt—

'Aurora! you forgive us, her and me?
For her, the thing she sees, poor loyal child,
If once corrected by the thing I know,   460
Had been unspoken, since she loves you well,
Has leave to love you—while for me, alas,
If once or twice I let my heart escape
This night . . . Remember, where hearts slip and fall
They break beside: we're parting—parting—ah,
You do not love, that you should surely know
What that word means. Forgive, be tolerant;
It had not been, but that I felt myself
So safe in impuissance and despair,*
I could not hurt you though I tossed my arms   470
And sighed my soul out. The most utter wretch
Will choose his postures when he comes to die,
However in the presence of a queen;
And you'll forgive me some unseemly spasms
Which meant no more than dying. Do you think
I had ever come here in my perfect mind,
Unless I had come here in my settled mind
Bound Marian's, bound to keep the bond and give
My name, my house, my hand, the things I could,
To Marian? For even *I* could give as much: 480
Even I, affronting her exalted soul
By a supposition that she wanted these,
Could act the husband's coat and hat set up
To creak i' the wind and drive the world-crows off
From pecking in her garden. Straw can fill
A hole to keep out vermin. Now, at last,
I own Heaven's angels round her life suffice
To fight the rats of our society,
Without this Romney: I can see it at last;
And here is ended my pretension which   490
The most pretended. Over-proud of course,
Even so!—but not so stupid . . . blind . . . that I,
Whom thus the great Taskmaster of the world*
Has set to meditate mistaken work,

My dreary face against a dim blank wall
Throughout man's natural life-time—could pretend
Or wish . . . O love, I have loved you! O my soul,
I have lost you!—but I swear by all yourself,
And all you might have been to me these years
If that June morning had not failed my hope—   500
I'm not so bestial, to regret that day
This night—this night, which still to you is fair!
Nay, not so blind, Aurora. I attest
Those stars above us which I cannot see . . .'

'You cannot' . . .

                     'That if Heaven itself should stoop,
Remix the lots, and give me another chance,
I'd say, "No other!"—I'd record my blank.
Aurora never should be wife of mine.'

'Not see the stars?'

                     ''Tis worse still, not to see
To find your hand, although we're parting, dear.   510
A moment let me hold it ere we part;
And understand my last words—these, at last!
I would not have you thinking when I'm gone
That Romney dared to hanker for your love
In thought or vision, if attainable
(Which certainly for me it never was),
And wished to use it for a dog today
To help the blind man stumbling. God forbid!
And now I know He held you in His palm,
And kept you open-eyed to all my faults,   520
To save you at last from such a dreary end.
Believe me, dear, that, if I had known like Him
What loss was coming on me, I had done
As well in this as He has.—Farewell you
Who are still my light—farewell! How late it is:
I know that, now. You've been too patient, sweet.
I will but blow my whistle toward the lane,
And someone comes—the same who brought me here.

Get in—Good-night.'
                    'A moment. Heavenly Christ!
A moment. Speak once, Romney. 'Tis not true.   530
I hold your hands, I look into your face—
You see me?'
             'No more than the blessed stars.
Be blessed too, Aurora. Nay, my sweet,
You tremble. Tender-hearted! Do you mind
Of yore, dear, how you used to cheat old John,
And let the mice out slyly from his traps,
Until he marvelled at the soul in mice
Which took the cheese and left the snare? The same
Dear soft heart always! 'Twas for this I grieved
Howe's letter never reached you. Ah, you had heard   540
Of illness—not the issue, not the extent:
My life long sick with tossings up and down,
The sudden revulsion in the blazing house,
The strain and struggle both of body and soul,
Which left fire running in my veins for blood:
Scarce lacked that thunderbolt of the falling beam
Which nicked me on the forehead as I passed
The gallery-door with a burden. Say heaven's bolt,
Not William Erle's, not Marian's father's—tramp
And poacher, whom I found for what he was,   550
And, eager for her sake to rescue him,
Forth swept from the open highway of the world,
Road-dust and all—till, like a woodland boar
Most naturally unwilling to be tamed,
He notched me with his tooth. But not a word
To Marian! and I do not think, besides,
He turned the tilting of the beam my way—
And if he laughed, as many swear, poor wretch,
Nor he nor I supposed the hurt so deep.
We'll hope his next laugh may be merrier,   560
In a better cause.'
              'Blind, Romney?'
                        'Ah, my friend,

You'll learn to say it in a cheerful voice.
I, too, at first desponded. To be blind,
Turned out of nature, mulcted as a man,*
Refused the daily largesse of the sun
To humble creatures! When the fever's heat
Dropped from me, as the flame did from my house,
And left me ruined like it, stripped of all
The hues and shapes of aspectable life,
A mere bare blind stone in the blaze of day,*   570
A man, upon the outside of the earth,
As dark as ten feet under, in the grave—
Why that seemed hard.'
                              'No hope?'
                                      'A tear! you weep,
Divine Aurora? tears upon my hand!
I've seen you weeping for a mouse, a bird—
But, weep for me, Aurora? Yes, there's hope.
Not hope of sight—I could be learned, dear,
And tell you in what Greek and Latin name
The visual nerve is withered to the root,*
Though the outer eyes appear indifferent,   580
Unspotted in their crystals. But there's hope.
The spirit, from behind this dethroned sense,
Sees, waits in patience till the walls break up
From which the bas-relief and fresco have dropped:
There's hope. The man here, once so arrogant
And restless, so ambitious, for his part,
Of dealing with statistically packed
Disorders (from a pattern on his nail),
And packing such things quite another way—
Is now contented. From his personal loss   590
He has come to hope for others when they lose,
And wear a gladder faith in what we gain . . .
Through bitter experience, compensation sweet,
Like that tear, sweetest. I am quiet now,
As tender surely for the suffering world,
But quiet—sitting at the wall to learn,

Content henceforth to do the thing I can:
For, though as powerless, said I, as a stone,
A stone can still give shelter to a worm,
And it is worth while being a stone for that: 600
There's hope, Aurora.'
                    'Is there hope for me?
For me?—and is there room beneath the stone
For such a worm?—And if I came and said . . .
What all this weeping scarce will let me say,
And yet what women cannot say at all
But weeping bitterly . . . (the pride keeps up,
Until the heart breaks under it) . . . I love—
I love you, Romney' . . .
                    'Silence!' he exclaimed.
'A woman's pity sometimes makes her mad.
A man's distraction must not cheat his soul   610
To take advantage of it. Yet, 'tis hard—
Farewell, Aurora.'
                    'But I love you, sir;
And when a woman says she loves a man,
The man must hear her, though he love her not,
Which . . . hush! . . . he has leave to answer in his turn;
She will not surely blame him. As for me,
You call it pity—think I'm generous?
'Twere somewhat easier, for a woman proud
As I am, and I'm very vilely proud,
To let it pass as such, and press on you   620
Love born of pity—seeing that excellent loves
Are born so, often, nor the quicklier die—
And this would set me higher by the head
Than now I stand. No matter: let the truth
Stand high; Aurora must be humble: no,
My love's not pity merely. Obviously
I'm not a generous woman, never was,
Or else, of old, I had not looked so near
To weights and measures, grudging you the power
To give, as first I scorned your power to judge   630

For me, Aurora. I would have no gifts
Forsooth, but God's—and I would use *them* too
According to my pleasure and my choice,
As He and I were equals, you below,
Excluded from that level of interchange
Admitting benefaction. You were wrong
In much? you said so. I was wrong in most.
Oh, most! You only thought to rescue men
By half means, halfway, seeing half their wants,
While thinking nothing of your personal gain.   640
But I who saw the human nature broad
At both sides, comprehending too the soul's,
And all the high necessities of Art,*
Betrayed the thing I saw, and wronged my own life
For which I pleaded. Passioned to exalt
The artist's instinct in me at the cost
Of putting down the woman's, I forgot
No perfect artist is developed here
From any imperfect woman. Flower from root,
And spiritual from natural, grade by grade   650
In all our life. A handful of the earth
To make God's image! the despised poor earth,
The healthy odorous earth—I missed with it
The divine Breath that blows the nostrils out
To ineffable inflatus—ay, the breath
Which love is. Art is much, but love is more.
O Art, my Art, thou'rt much, but Love is more!
Art symbolises heaven, but Love is God
And makes heaven. I, Aurora, fell from mine.
I would not be a woman like the rest,   660
A simple woman who believes in love
And owns the right of love because she loves,
And, hearing she's beloved, is satisfied
With what contents God: I must analyse,
Confront, and question; just as if a fly
Refused to warm itself in any sun
Till such was *in leone*: I must fret*

Forsooth because the month was only May,
Be faithless of the kind of proffered love,
And captious, lest it miss my dignity, 670
And scornful, that my lover sought a wife
To use . . . to use! O Romney, O my love,
I am changed since then, changed wholly—for indeed
If now you'd stoop so low to take my love
And use it roughly, without stint or spare,
As men use common things with more behind
(And, in this, ever would be more behind)
To any mean and ordinary end—
The joy would set me like a star, in heaven,
So high up, I should shine because of height 680
And not of virtue. Yet in one respect,
Just one, beloved, I am in nowise changed:
I love you, loved you . . . I loved you first and last,
And love you on for ever. Now I know
I loved you always, Romney. She who died
Knew that, and said so; Lady Waldemar
Knows that . . . and Marian. I had known the same,
Except that I was prouder than I knew,
And not so honest. Ay, and, as I live,
I should have died so, crushing in my hand 690
This rose of love, the wasp inside and all,
Ignoring ever to my soul and you
Both rose and pain—except for this great loss,
This great despair—to stand before your face
And know you do not see me where I stand.
You think, perhaps, I am not changed from pride,
And that I chiefly bear to say such words,
Because you cannot shame me with your eyes?
O calm, grand eyes, extinguished in a storm,
Blown out like lights o'er melancholy seas, 700
Though shrieked for by the shipwrecked—O my Dark,
My Cloud—to go before me every day*
While I go ever toward the wilderness—
I would that you could see me bare to the soul!

If this be pity, 'tis so for myself,
And not for Romney! *he* can stand alone;
A man like *him* is never overcome:
No woman like me, counts him pitiable
While saints applaud him. He mistook the world;
But I mistook my own heart, and that slip   710
Was fatal. Romney—will you leave me here?
So wrong, so proud, so weak, so unconsoled,
So mere a woman!—and I love you so,
I love you, Romney—'
                    Could I see his face,
I wept so? Did I drop against his breast,
Or did his arms constrain me? were my cheeks
Hot, overflooded, with my tears or his?
And which of our two large explosive hearts
So shook me? That, I know not. There were words
That broke in utterance . . . melted, in the fire—   720
Embrace, that was convulsion . . . then a kiss
As long and silent as the ecstatic night,
And deep, deep, shuddering breaths, which meant beyond
Whatever could be told by word or kiss.

But what he said . . . I have written day by day,
With somewhat even writing. Did I think
That such a passionate rain would intercept
And dash this last page? What he said, indeed,
I fain would write it down here like the rest,
To keep in my eyes, as in my ears,   730
The heart's sweet scripture, to be read at night
When weary, or at morning when afraid,
And lean my heaviest oath on when I swear
That, when all's done, all tried, all counted here,
All great arts, and all good philosophies,
This love just puts its hand out in a dream
And straight outreaches all things.
                      What he said,
I fain would write. But if an angel spoke

In thunder, should we haply know much more
Than that it thundered? If a cloud came down   740
And wrapped us wholly, could we draw its shape,
As if on the outside and not overcome?
And so he spake. His breath against my face
Confused his words, yet made them more intense
(As when the sudden finger of the wind
Will wipe a row of single city-lamps
To a pure white line of flame, more luminous
Because of obliteration), more intense,
The intimate presence carrying in itself
Complete communication, as with souls   750
Who, having put the body off, perceive
Through simply being. Thus 'twas granted me
To know he loved me to the depth and height
Of such large natures, ever competent,
With grand horizons by the sea or land,
To love's grand sunrise. Small spheres hold small fires,
But he loved largely, as a man can love
Who, baffled in his love, dares live his life,
Accept the ends which God loves, for his own,
And lift a constant aspect.

               From the day   760
I brought to England my poor searching face
(An orphan even of my father's grave),
He had loved me, watched me, watched his soul in mine,
Which in me grew and heightened into love.
For he, a boy still, had been told the tale
Of how a fairy bride from Italy
With smells of oleanders in her hair,
Was coming through the vines to touch his hand;
Whereat the blood of boyhood on the palm
Made sudden heats. And when at last I came,   770
And lived before him, lived, and rarely smiled,
He smiled and loved me for the thing I was,
As every child will love the year's first flower
(Not certainly the fairest of the year,

But, in which, the complete year seems to blow),
The poor sad snowdrop—growing between drifts,
Mysterious medium 'twixt the plant and frost,
So faint with winter while so quick with spring,
And doubtful if to thaw itself away
With that snow near it. Not that Romney Leigh   780
Had loved me coldly. If I thought so once,
It was as if I had held my hand in fire
And shook for cold. But now I understood
For ever, that the very fire and heat
Of troubling passion in him burnt him clear,
And shaped, to dubious order, word and act:
That, just because he loved me over all,
All wealth, all lands, all social privilege,
To which chance made him unexpected heir,
And, just because on all these lesser gifts,   790
Constrained by conscience and the sense of wrong,
He had stamped with steady hand God's arrow-mark
Of dedication to the human need,
He thought it should be so too, with his love.
He, passionately loving, would bring down
His love, his life, his best (because the best),
His bride of dreams, who walked so still and high
Through flowery poems as through meadow-grass,
The dust of golden lilies on her feet,
That *she* should walk beside him on the rocks   800
In all that clang and hewing out of men,
And help the work of help which was his life,
And prove he kept back nothing—not his soul.
And when I failed him—for I failed him, I,
And when it seemed he had missed my love, he thought
'Aurora makes room for a working-noon,'
And so, self-girded with torn strips of hope,
Took up his life as if it were for death
(Just capable of one heroic aim),
And threw it in the thickest of the world—   810
At which men laughed as if he had drowned a dog.

No wonder—since Aurora failed him first!
The morning and the evening made his day.

But oh, the night! oh, bitter-sweet! oh, sweet!
O dark, O moon and stars, O ecstasy
Of darkness! O great mystery of love,
In which absorbed, loss, anguish, treason's self
Enlarges rapture—as a pebble dropped
In some full wine-cup overbrims the wine!
While we two sat together, leaned that night   820
So close my very garments crept and thrilled
With strange electric life, and both my cheeks
Grew red, then pale, with touches from my hair
In which his breath was—while the golden moon
Was hung before our faces as the badge
Of some sublime inherited despair,
Since ever to be seen by only one—
A voice said, low and rapid as a sigh,
Yet breaking, I felt conscious, from a smile,
'Thank God, who made me blind, to make me see!   830
Shine on, Aurora, dearest light of souls,
Which rul'st for evermore both day and night!
I am happy.'
                    I flung closer to his breast,
As sword that, after battle, flings to sheath;
And, in that hurtle of united souls,
The mystic motions which in common moods
Are shut beyond our sense, broke in on us,
And, as we sat, we felt the old earth spin,
And all the starry turbulence of worlds
Swing round us in their audient circles, till,   840
If that same golden moon were overhead
Or if beneath our feet, we did not know.

And then calm, equal, smooth with weights of joy,
His voice rose, as some chief musician's song
Amid the old Jewish temple's Selah-pause,*

And bade me mark how we two met at last
Upon this moon-bathed promontory of earth,
To give up much on each side, then take all.
'Beloved,' it sang, 'we must be here to work;
And men who work can only work for men,   850
And, not to work in vain, must comprehend
Humanity and so work humanly,
And raise men's bodies still by raising souls,
As God did first.'
            'But stand upon the earth,'
I said, 'to raise them (this is human too,
There's nothing high which has not first been low,
My humbleness, said One, has made me great!),*
As God did last.'
            'And work all silently
And simply,' he returned, 'as God does all;
Distort our nature never for our work,   860
Nor count our right hands stronger for being hoofs.
The man most man, with tenderest human hands,
Works best for men—as God in Nazareth.'

He paused upon the word, and then resumed;
'Fewer programmes, we who have no prescience.
Fewer systems, we who are held and do not hold.
Less mapping out of masses to be saved,
By nations or by sexes. Fourier's void,*
And Comte absurd—and Cabet puerile.*
Subsist no rules of life outside of life,   870
No perfect manners without Christian souls:
The Christ himself had been no Lawgiver
Unless He had given the life, too, with the law.'

I echoed thoughtfully—'The man, most man,
Works best for men, and, if most man indeed,
He gets his manhood plainest from his soul:
While obviously this stringent soul itself
Obeys the old law of development,

The Spirit ever witnessing in ours,
And Love, the soul of soul, within the soul, 880
Evolving it sublimely. First, God's love.'

'And next,' he smiled, 'the love of wedded souls,
Which still presents that mystery's counterpart.
Sweet shadow-rose, upon the water of life,
Of such a mystic substance, Sharon gave*
A name to! human, vital, fructuous rose,
Whose calyx holds the multitude of leaves,
Loves filial, loves fraternal, neighbour-loves
And civic—all fair petals, all good scents,
All reddened, sweetened from one central Heart!' 890

'Alas,' I cried, 'it was not long ago,
You swore this very social rose smelt ill.'

'Alas,' he answered, 'is it a rose at all?
The filial's thankless, the fraternal's hard,
The rest is lost. I do but stand and think,
Across the waters of a troubled life
This Flower of Heaven so vainly overhangs,
What perfect counterpart would be in sight
If tanks were clearer. Let us clean the tubes,
And wait for rains. O poet, O my love, 900
Since *I* was too ambitious in my deed
And thought to distance all men in success
(Till God came on me, marked the place and said,
"Ill-doer, henceforth keep within this line,
Attempting less than others"—and I stand
And work among Christ's little ones, content),
Come thou, my compensation, my dear sight,
My morning-star, my morning—rise and shine,
And touch my hills with radiance not their own.
Shine out for two, Aurora, and fulfil 910
My falling-short that must be! work for two,
As I, though thus restrained, for two shall love!

Gaze on, with inscient vision toward the sun,*
And, from his visceral heat, pluck out the roots
Of light beyond him. Art's a service—mark:*
A silver key is given to thy clasp,
And thou shalt stand unwearied, night and day,
And fix it in the hard, slow-turning wards,
To open, so, that intermediate door
Betwixt the different planes of sensuous form   920
And form insensuous, that inferior men
May learn to feel on still through these to those,
And bless thy ministration. The world waits
For help. Beloved, let us love so well,
Our work shall still be better for our love,
And still our love be sweeter for our work,
And both commended, for the sake of each,
By all true workers and true lovers born.
Now press the clarion on thy woman's lip
(Love's holy kiss shall still keep consecrate)   930
And breathe thy fine keen breath along the brass,
And blow all class-walls level as Jericho's*
Past Jordan—crying from the top of souls
To souls, that, here assembled on earth's flats,
They get them to some purer eminence
Than any hitherto beheld for clouds!
What height we know not—but the way we know,
And how by mounting ever, we attain,
And so climb on. It is the hour for souls,
That bodies, leavened by the will and love,   940
Be lightened to redemption. The world's old,
But the old world waits the time to be renewed,
Toward which, new hearts in individual growth
Must quicken, and increase to multitude
In new dynasties of the race of men;
Developed whence, shall grow spontaneously
New churches, new economies, new laws
Admitting freedom, new societies
Excluding falsehood: HE shall make all new.'*

My Romney!—Lifting up my hand in his, 950
As wheeled by Seeing spirits toward the east,
He turned instinctively, where, faint and far,
Along the tingling desert of the sky,
Beyond the circle of the conscious hills,
Were laid in jasper-stone as clear as glass
The first foundations of that new, near Day
Which should be builded out of Heaven to God.
He stood a moment with erected brows
In silence, as a creature might who gazed—
Stood calm, and fed his blind, majestic eyes 960
Upon the thought of perfect noon: and when
I saw his soul saw—'Jasper first,' I said,*
'And second, sapphire; third, chalcedony;
The rest in order—last, an amethyst.'

Book IX
950
My Romney! — I drag up my hand in his,
As wheeled by Science aside toward the east,
He turned in horror where, blind and far,
Along the ...
beyond me are ... of the contagious hills.

EXPLANATORY NOTES

A number of the following annotations depend upon an approximate dating of the events in the poem. Book I summarizes Aurora Leigh's first twenty years; the action of Book II takes place on her twentieth birthday and shortly thereafter; she is 27 in Books III and IV. (ii. 1238: 'it is seven years since'), and two years older in Books V, VI, and VII (v. 572–3: 'I have not seen Romney Leigh | Full eighteen months . . . add six, you get two years'); in Books VIII and IX her age is 30 (viii. 347–8: 'I quoted back | A ten years' birthday'; 532: 'Ten layers of birthdays on a woman's head'). In her description of Paris in Book VI Aurora Leigh speaks of Eugénie, wife of Napoleon III, as 'a new fair face' (113) in the Tuileries. Eugénie married the French ruler in January 1853; one can therefore roughly date Aurora's stay in Paris as occurring in 1853 or 1854. If Aurora Leigh was 29 or 30 in 1853–4, she was born c.1824. Other internal evidence is consistent with this dating (though there are anachronisms: e.g. 'Australian gold', mentioned in conversation in Book II, was not discovered until 1851). The most noteworthy aspect of the time-frame is that the action of eight of the poem's nine books takes place between 1844 and 1854—the ten years during which the genesis, germination, and much of the composition of *Aurora Leigh* occurred. This is just what one would expect of a poem that flaunts its contemporaneity and that its author laboured to make 'intensely modern, crammed from the times . . . as far as my strength will allow' (*Letters*, ed. Frederic G. Kenyon (London, 1898), ii. 112).

I am much indebted to the work of Charlotte Porter and Helen A. Clarke in their edition of the poem in volumes 4 and 5 of their *Complete Works of Elizabeth Barrett Browning* (New York, 1900). James M. W. Borg's 'The Fashioning of Elizabeth Barrett Browning's *Aurora Leigh*' (Ph.D. diss. Northwestern, 1979) was also helpful. Margaret Reynolds's edition (Athens, Oh., 1992) appeared too late for me to make much use of it, though in several places I have benefited from her work. Her edition supplies a much more complete identification of biblical allusions and echoes than is here offered.

Dedication

Kenyon: a wealthy and generous dilettante, well known in the London literary world, Kenyon (1784–1856) was a distant cousin of Elizabeth Barrett Browning and devoted to her. He encouraged her courtship with Robert Browning, and after their marriage helped to manage their business affairs. *Aurora Leigh* was completed at his London house in Devonshire Place.

Book I

1 *Of writing many books there is no end*: see Ecclesiastes 12: 12.

10–13 *I have ... in their sleep*: recalling Wordsworth's 'Ode, Intimations of Immortality', stanza 9; see also *The Prelude* (1850), ii. 234–40.

outer Infinite: 'infinite wonder = sea' in Wellesley MS.

24 *scudi*: Italian coins.

45 *I, Aurora Leigh*: 'One day at dinner Mrs. Browning said in half-soliloquy, "I wonder which is the best name, Laura Leigh or Aurora Leigh?" and asked both of us our opinions. Browning gave his vote in favor of Aurora, and I not knowing at all to what she referred and thinking merely of the sound, said "Oh, Aurora, Laura Leigh lacks backbone." When the book was published Mrs. Browning remembering this casual remark sent me a copy with the message that she "hoped it contained backbone".' (Harriet Hosmer, *Letters and Memories*, ed. Cornelia Carr (New York, 1912), 99.)

53 *corals to cut life upon*: toys of polished coral given to teething infants.

57 *as in a rose-bush*: recalling the burning bush in Exodus 3: 2.

72 *Da Vinci's drains*: Leonardo da Vinci (1452–1519) was born near Florence and worked there during the 1470s and the early 1500s. Among his engineering achievements are designs for a variety of pumps and aquaducts.

74–5 *Some English question ... The unpopular but necessary tax*: income tax was first imposed during the Napoleonic wars; it was reintroduced by Sir Robert Peel in 1842.

111 *Pelago*: village three miles from Florence.

114–16 *Pan's white goats ... his own*: white goats were sacred to Pan, the god of nature. The father hopes that a natural bond will compensate his daughter for the loss of maternal sustenance.

130 *cameriera*: maid.

132 *Pitti*: Florentine palace.

156 *loving Psyche who loses sight of Love*: Psyche's beloved Cupid (Love), who visited her only at night, had charged her to make no attempt to gaze on him. When she disobeyed, he left her.

160 *Our Lady ... stabbed with swords*: in Italy the Virgin Mary is sometimes represented thus; the swords symbolize her Seven Sorrows.

161 *Lamia*: serpent woman, recalling Keats's poem of that name; described at the moment when her transformation from human to reptile begins.

178 *chin-bands*: used to hold closed the mouths of corpses; see John 11: 44.

222 *tormented scorpion*: scorpions were thought to sting themselves to death when surrounded by a ring of fire.

286 *ruth*: pity.

295 *apothecary*: medical practitioner.

305 *A sort of cage-bird life*: 'Confined, then, in cages like the feathered race, they have nothing to do but to plume themselves, and stalk with mock majesty from perch to perch. It is true they are provided with food and raiment, for which they neither toil nor spin; but health, liberty, and virtue are given in exchange.' (Mary Wollstonecraft, *A Vindication of the Rights of Woman* (1792), ed. Miriam Kramnick (Harmondsworth, 1975), 146.)

342 *Tuscan*: Tuscany is the region of Italy that includes Florence.

348 *pored*: thought intently upon.

390 *'Bene' or 'Che che'*: common Italian exclamations, the former of agreement or approbation, the latter of astonishment or protest.

394 *The Articles, the Tracts 'against' the times*: the Thirty-nine articles were the key doctrinal formulae of the Anglican

Church. *Tracts for the Times* were produced from 1833 onwards by J. H. Newman, John Keble, and other members of the Oxford Movement, who were attempting to combat the spread of rationalism and liberalism in the Anglican Church.

395 *Buonaventure's 'Prick of Love'*: St Bonaventure, the thirteenth-century Franciscan theologian, stressed the superiority of love and desire to the reasoning faculties in coming to know God.

400 *Balzac and neologism*: the novels of Balzac (1799–1850) were not only modern; they were also widely regarded in England as immoral. Neologism can refer both to the coining of new words and to the adoption of rationalistic moral and religious views.

408 *Oviedo*: Spanish historian of the sixteenth century.

410–13 *Mount Chimborazo ... Tenerife ... Lara ... Klagen-furt*: Chimborazo, the highest peak in the Ecuadorian Andes, is almost twice the height of the principal peak on Tenerife, one of the Canary Islands. Lara is a town in Spain; Klagenfurt a provincial city in Austria.

416 *in Johnson's day*: Samuel Johnson (1709–84) remarked of the performance of a celebrated violinist: 'Difficult do you call it, Sir? I wish it were impossible.'

420 *Tophet*: hell.

424 *Cellarius*: slow waltz of Parisian origin, named for the Austrian dancing-master who brought the polka to Paris in 1840.

427 *I read a score of books on womanhood*: beginning in the last decades of the eighteenth century, a stream of publications giving advice on the education and conduct of ladies were published in Britain. These manuals, books of etiquette, educational tracts, and collections of sermons and letters disseminated to the upper and middle classes the traditional view that women were weaker than men in body and mind, and that their role was essentially passive and self-abnegating. Among the most widely read advice books in early Victorian England were those of Sarah Stickney Ellis, including *The Women of England: Their Social Duties and Domestic Habits* (1838), and *The Wives of England: Their Relative Duties, Domestic Influence and Social Obligations* (1843).

430 *that boldly assert*: 'demonstrating' in first edition.

454–5 *the tortoise-shell | Which slew the tragic poet*: Aeschylus is said to have died as a result of an eagle dropping on his head a tortoise that it was attempting to crack.

467 *Brinvilliers*: the Marquise de Brinvilliers (1630–76) plotted with her lover to poison her father and brothers. After her arrest, she was tortured by having gallons of water forced down her throat before being beheaded.

527–8 *The goats ... God's separative judgment-hour*: alluding to Matthew 25: 32–3, 41.

612 *Giotto's background*: gold is the background colour in the pictures of the Florentine painter Giotto (*c.*1267–1337).

616 *Vallombrosa*: valley near Pelago.

647 *holpen*: helped.

712 *Theophrast*: Theophrastus, a Greek philosopher of the fourth century BC; pupil of Aristotle.

714 *Aelian*: Roman writer (*c.*170–235) noted for his collection of excerpts and anecdotes of a moralizing character.

716 *game of fives*: a form of handball using a three-sided court.

723–4 *as did the women formerly | By young Achilles*: to prevent his joining the Greeks in their war against Troy, Achilles' mother sent her son to the court of King Lycomedes, where he was disguised as a girl, given a female name, and lived among the king's daughters.

736–8 *Ah babe i' the wood ... like the red-breast bird, | Flies back to cover ... with leaves*: the old ballad 'The Children in the Wood' (or 'Babes in the Wood') was very popular in England during the eighteenth and early nineteenth centuries. To obtain their inheritance, the uncle of two orphaned siblings arranged to have them killed. But the young girl and her brother came to be abandoned in the woods instead:

> Thus wandered these poor innocents,
>   Till deathe did end their grief,
> In one anothers armes they dyed,
>   As wanting due relief:
> No burial this pretty pair
>   Of any man receives,

> Till Robin-red-breast piously
> Did cover them with leaves.

(Thomas Percy, *Reliques of Ancient English Poetry* [1765] (London, 1854), iii. 222–3.)

756 *Saint Michael*: one of the greatest angels, and a leader of the heavenly host.

766–71 *who distinguishes | 'Twixt Saul and Nahash . . . Alaric as well as Charlemagne*: three examples of the difficulty of distinguishing immediately between contrasting types: Saul and the Ammonite King Nahash, whom he defeated (1 Samuel 11: 1–11); Saul and David, of whom he was jealous (his sin) and who succeeded him as King of Israel (1 and 2 Samuel); the Visigoth conqueror Alaric (*c*.370–410) and Charlemagne (*c*.742–814), Roman emperor and King of the Franks.

772 *wizards*: 'prophets' in first edition.

787–8 'defaming human nature—mesmerising' in Wellesley MS.

807 *Pure reason stronger than bare inference*: the distinction, taken over from German Idealism, is between two mental faculties: pure reason or 'spirit-insight' (l. 818) deals with supersensible concepts such as God; the empirically grounded understanding is dependent on sense experience, and must infer rather than intuit.

825 *clean white paper*: empirical philosophers maintained that the mind was essentially passive, a *tabula rasa* or blank slate on which sense-derived impressions came to be inscribed.

826 *palimpsest*: manuscript written upon more than once, the earlier writing having been wholly or partially erased to create space for new inscriptions. Thomas De Quincey's essay 'The Palimpsest of the Human Brain' was first published in 1845.

holograph: manuscript written in the hand of its author.

828 *Longus*: third-century AD author of the Greek pastoral romance *Daphnis and Chloe*. Its subject is the erotic awakening of the title characters, whose physical relations are suggestively described; Daphnis' sexual education includes the importunings of a pederast as well as the attentions of a married woman, who shows him how his physical desires can be satisfied.

828–31 *apocalypse ... alpha and omega*: the Book of Revelation or Apocalypse, which concludes the New Testament, was written in Greek, in which alpha and omega are the first and last characters of the alphabet. In Revelation 1: 8 the Lord says: 'I am Alpha and Omega, the beginning and the ending.'

868–9 *says | The apostle*: Revelation 21: 17.

870 *Lay telegraphs*: 'Build pyramids' in first edition.

872 *president*: 'senators' in first edition.

919–29 *My eagle ... Heré's foot*: Zeus sent an eagle to abduct Ganymede, and installed the beautiful youth on Mount Olympus as the gods' cup-bearer. Heré (Hera): wife of Zeus.

938 *imposthumes*: swellings.

941 *Bourbon*: royal family that long held the thrones of France and Spain.

964 *Term*: Roman god of boundaries and frontiers.

978 *phorminx*: lyre.

989–90 'And pastorals which no morning mist makes wet' in Wellesley MS.

1002 *old bottles ... new wine*: recalling Matthew 9: 17.

1003–6 *Keats's soul ... twenty perfect years*: the hyperbole is patent. Keats, for example, was in his twenty-sixth year at the time of his death in 1821.

1013–14 *Pope ... Byron*: Alexander Pope (1688–1744) and Lord Byron (1788–1824) both wrote imitative verse at an early age.

1035 *saltpetre*: chief constituent of gunpowder.

1097–9 *he holds ... first Master*: recalling the aesthetic of the speaker of Robert Browning's 1855 poem, 'Fra Lippo Lippi'.

1141 *In the beginning ... all good*: Genesis 1: 1, 31.

1145 *Deliver us from evil*: Matthew 6: 13.

Book II

12 *calyx*: whorl of leaves forming the outer covering of a budding flower.

38–40 *no bay ... Nor myrtle*: leaves from the bay (a kind of laurel) were associated with poetic achievement; myrtle was sacred to Venus, goddess of love.

52 *thyrsus*: staff carried by Bacchus, god of wine.

61 *caryatid*: sculpted female figure used as a supporting column.

76–7 *lady's Greek | Without the accents*: girls who learned Greek did so for the sake of reading, while boys had to pass examinations in the subject.

83 *The Oread . . . has a Naiad's heart*: naiads were river nymphs, unlike the land-based oreads.

110 *balsams*: balms.

140 *baldaquins*: altar canopies.

151–2 *minnow gods . . . have gone out in God*: i.e. a polytheistic conception of the world, which included inferior deities like nymphs and tritons, has been superseded by Christian monotheism.

167 *six thousand years*: 4004 BC was a traditional date for the creation of the world.

171–2 *When Egypt's slain . . . Before—where's Moses?*: i.e. the times need leaders, not poets. Miriam danced with timbrels and sang after the horsemen and chariots of Pharaoh had drowned in the Red Sea, which assured the Israelites' deliverance from Egyptian bondage (Exodus 15: 20–1).

173–4 *Moses . . . in the bulrushes*: Exodus 2: 1–6.

176 *sounding brass*: in 1 Corinthians 13: 1 sounding brass and a tinkling cymbal are figures for the worthlessness of a prophet whose qualities do not include charity.

202 *silks from Tarsus*: i.e. material luxuries.

209–10 *a tear | Wet as Cordelia's*: *King Lear* IV. vii. 71.

222 *perfect wives*: 'chaste wives' in first edition.

277–9 *the rich man . . . Abraham's bosom*: after their deaths, the beggar Lazarus was carried by angels to Abraham's bosom, while the rich man at whose gate he had lain went to hell (Luke 16: 19–26).

313–15 *statistical despairs . . . figures on a page*: early Victorian England was a period of unprecedented interest in economic and demographic data. Many statisticians were liberal reformers, and much of the published data called attention to the condition of the working classes.

324 *To draw me to this duty*: 'To give me my vocation' in Wellesley MS.

342 *white*: in archery, the central portion of the target (Reynolds).

413 *Do I look a Hagar, think you?*: 'Polygamy scarce suits me' in Wellesley MS. The barren wife of Abram gave her handmaid Hagar to her husband in order to obtain children through her (Genesis 16).

449 *oakum*: fibre obtained by picking apart old rope, the common task of prisoners and paupers.

483 *dust*: 'dunghill' in Wellesley MS.

     your Fouriers failed: i.e. socialists. Charles Fourier (1772–1837) was an influential French socialist writer. See iii. 585 n.

533–4 *the devil . . . on those mountain-peaks*: alluding to the second temptation of Christ (Luke 4: 5–8).

562 *dewlaps*: folds of skin hanging from the throats of animals.

622 *unchary*: uncaring.

679 *altar-horns*: for Old Testament Jews, the most sacred parts of the altar were the horns at its corners.

779–80 *Iphigenia bound | At . . . Aulis*: Artemis delayed the Greek fleet at Aulis with contrary winds until Agamemnon brought his daughter Iphigenia there and sacrificed her.

793 *Griseld*: the type of patient, long-suffering wife. To test her obedience, her husband pretended to have their children put to death.

795 *Ragged Schools*: supported by public charity and largely staffed by middle- and upper-class volunteers, these schools attempted to provide a rudimentary education for children so disadvantaged and brutalized that no other schools would accept them.

796 *Public Baths*: population growth and rapid urbanization created unprecedented problems of sanitation and public health in early Victorian England. Water-supply was a major concern, and by mid-century many urban areas had begun to establish public baths and wash-houses.

811–12 *Spanish monarch crowned the bones | Of his dead love*: according to legend, Pedro I, King of Portugal from

1357 to 1367, had clandestinely married Inês Pires de Castro, who bore him several children before she was murdered by the agents of Pedro's father. After he became king, Pedro is said to have had her remains exhumed, placed on a throne, and crowned Queen of Portugal. The Portuguese Pedro is here confused with his Spanish cousin, Pedro I, King of Castile and Léon from 1350 to 1366.

818 *Chaldean*: one skilled in occult learning; originally applied to Assyrian wise men, whose Semitic language was written from right to left.

854 *'Siste, viator'*: 'Pause, traveller'.

864–5 *asp | To Cleopatra's breast*: the means by which the Egyptian queen took her life.

870 *commination*: recital of threats against sinners in the Anglican liturgy.

890 *A Roman died so*: not identified.

898–9 *Who stands . . . nevermore*: Revelation 10: 1–6.

961 *Babylon or Balbec*: ancient cities built in or near the desert.

977 *Appian road*: the Via Appia was the first of the Roman highways, which were a technological achievement comparable to the railways of nineteenth-century Britain. Tombs and memorials to the dead were built along it. See ii. 853–4.

983 *three hundred pounds*: per annum.

989 *'testatrix'*: a female testator (one who has died and left a will).

1005 *glosing*: explaining away.

1037 *doit*: Dutch coin of little value.

1070 *Australian gold*: gold was first discovered in New South Wales and Victoria in 1851; heavy British investment followed.

1071–3 *a lottery . . . Some old Rhine tower or principality?*: Robert Browning to Elizabeth (15 Feb. 1846): 'Did you ever hear of the plain speaking of some of the continental lottery-projectors? An estate on the Rhine, for instance, is to be disposed of, and the holder of the lucky ticket will find himself suddenly owner of a mediaeval castle with an unlimited number of dependencies, vineyards, woods, pastures, and so forth.' (*Letters of Robert Browning and Elizabeth Barrett Barrett,*

1845–1846, ed. Elvan Kintner (Cambridge, Mass., 1969), i. 466.)

1149–51 *King Solomon . . . his holy ring | Charactered over with the ineffable spell*: Solomon was said to possess a signet-ring bearing the 'ineffable' name of God, which gave him miraculous powers.

1166 *Valdarno*: valley through which the Arno flows before reaching Florence.

1189 *the mother's 'tiring hand*: 'the mother's breast and milk' in Wellesley MS.

Book III

2 *goest where thou wouldest . . . said the Lord*: John 21: 18.

11 *the keys of heaven and earth*: in Matthew 16: 19 Jesus tells the apostle Peter that he will give him the keys of the kingdom of heaven.

48 *Ararat*: where God spoke to Noah (Genesis 8).

54 *Elisha*: when Elijah was taken up into heaven in a chariot of fire, Elisha picked up his cloak and thereby acquired the prophet's power (2 Kings 2: 1–15).

98 *A ninth seal*: facetious comparison of Aurora's letters to the book in Revelation 5–8 that was closed with seven seals; as each seal was opened, something direful occurred.

108 *phalansteries*: in the utopian scheme of Charles Fourier, society would be divided into units or phalanxes of 1,620 persons engaged in non-competitive, primarily agricultural effort.

122–33 *Danaë*: shut up in a chamber by her father to ensure that she remained intact, Danaë was visited by Zeus in the form of a shower of gold and impregnated by him.

172–5 *some Druidic idol's fiery brass . . . incarnadine the air*: in the nineteenth century information about the Druids was largely based on legendary sources. They are known to have filled huge wicker cages with human beings, animals, and combustible material and set them on fire. Compare the hollow bronze bull of Phalaris (viii. 388 n).

190–4 *No one sings . . . leave you dumb*: i.e. extraordinary vistas and visitations do not inspire the poet. Mount Sinai is where

Moses received the Ten Commandments; Parnassus is sacred to Apollo, god of poetry.

197–203 *Pharaoh's armaments . . . the song you choose*: Exodus 15: 19–21.

218 *'Collegisse juvat'*: 'it is pleasant to have gathered' (Horace, *Odes*, I. i).

249 *galvanic*: producing an electrical current.

252–3 *those hot fire-seeds of creation held | In Jove's clenched palm*: 'Not what man sees, but what God sees,—the *Ideas* of Plato, seeds of creation lying burningly on the Divine Hand' (Robert Browning, 'An Essay on Shelley', written in 1852).

295 *mattock*: pick-like agricultural tool.

318–20 *carved many an article . . . mallet-hand*: i.e. even in her short, ephemeral productions something of the artist's hand could be seen. A mallet is used to strike the chisel in stone- or wood-carving.

324 *Nephelococcygia*: 'Cloud-cuckoo-land' in Aristophanes' *Birds*.

340 *certes*: assuredly.

379–80 *blue . . . in stockings*: women having or affecting literary tastes were called bluestockings.

382 *the epic plunge*: the epic poet's beginning *in medias res*.

391 *Androcles*: the escaped slave who removed a thorn from a lion's paw and was recompensed when the beast spared his life during a subsequent encounter in the gladiators' ring.

409 *mulcted in*: deprived or divested of.

431 *to keep my booth in Mayfair*: i.e. to maintain my position in society.

   with the rest: 'or Vanity Fair' in Wellesley MS.

439 *derogate*: deviate from (socially) acceptable behaviour.

455 *there's the rub*: *Hamlet*, III. i. 65.

459 *Blowsalinda*: country girl in John Gay's *Shepherd's Week* (1714).

460 *Lyons' velvet*: the French city of Lyons was famous for the manufacture of silk, from which velvet is made.

471 *germane Wertherism*: in Goethe's novel *The Sorrows of Young Werther* (1774) the title character's chief tribulation is disappointment in love.

473 *A ghost . . . like Dido's*: during his visit to the Underworld, Aeneas met the shade of Dido, who had taken her own life when he deserted her (*Aeneid* vi).

478–9 'All genuine passion justifies itself' in Wellesley MS.

503–5 *play police . . . What may or may not pass*: a professional police force was established in London in 1829. Police attempts to regulate vehicular street traffic soon became a contentious issue, with many feeling that their freedom of movement was being restricted.

513–14 *that most perfect of antiques . . . the Genius of the Vatican*: also known as the contemplative Amor, the Eros of Centocelle, or Thanatos; thought to be a copy of a work by Praxiteles (Reynolds).

517 *Dancing*: 'Drunken' in first edition. The statue is in the Uffizi in Florence.

519 *Buonarroti's mask*: a detail in the figure of Night, one of the statues in the Medici Chapel in Florence executed by Michelangelo Buonarroti (1475–1564). The mask depicts a swinish male face.

544 *nominal*: in name only.

545 *proctors . . . gownsmen's wits*: at Oxford and Cambridge proctors are in charge of student discipline; a gownsman is a member of a university.

548 *Homer's ships*: the Greek ships that sailed to Troy are catalogued in *Iliad* ii.

549 *Melbourne's poor-bills, Ashley's factory bills*: the Poor Law Amendment Act of 1834 was passed during the ministry of Lord Melbourne. Lord Ashley, later Lord Shaftesbury, was closely associated with the legislation concerning factories passed by Parliament during the 1830s and 1840s.

550 *Aspasia*: in fifth-century BC Athens, Aspasia, the mistress of Pericles, was admired for her intellectual attainments, despite her equivocal social position.

556 *Dead Caesar who 'stops bungholes'*: Hamlet, v. i. 202–14.

585 *Proudhon, Considérant, and Louis Blanc*: three nineteenth-century French socialists who believed, with Fourier, that social arrangements based on individualism and competition should be replaced by a system based on principles of co-operation and allowing for the harmonious development of human nature. In *What is Property?* (1840) Pierre-Joseph Proudhon (1809–65) answered his title's question by affirming that 'property is theft'. He believed that capitalist society could be improved by self-help among the workers and through the financial assistance of the wealthy and of the government. Victor Considérant (1808–93) became the leader of the Fourierist movement after its founder's death. Louis Blanc (1811–82) attributed all social evils to competition. The remedy prescribed in his *Organization of Labour* (1839) was an equalization of wages, and social workshops in which workers in a given trade pooled their efforts for their common benefit.

596 *Sue*: the French novelist Eugène Sue (1804–57) was noted for his depictions of Parisian low life. In his books he did not attempt to hide his humanitarian views and ideas for social reform.

600–1 *the impossible . . . such as wearing gowns | Provided by the Ten Hours' movement*: factory workers in the textile industry had long demanded a ten-hour working day for women and young persons. After much controversy over a sixteen-year period, the Ten Hours Bill was passed by Parliament in 1847. Lady Waldemar's gowns would have been made from imported fabrics like velvet (iii. 460) or silk (iv. 18, 27).

603 *Indian tortoise*: in Hindu mythology the world is said to rest on a great tortoise swimming in the primeval ocean.

641 *patent*: officially sanctioned.

650 *more fantasy*: 'more appetite' in first edition.

667 *guerdon*: reward.

706 *Medicean Venus*: classical statue of Venus once in the possession of the Medici family.

738 *Oppressed in my deliverance*: 'As hard as in a sick room' in first edition.

755 *proclive*: inclining forward, precipitating.

831   *Malvern Hill*: in Herefordshire.

952   *scroll-finis*: ornamental design at the end of a text.

974   *Thomson's Seasons*: James Thomson's book-length poem *The Seasons* (1730).

979–80 *that small Ruth's | Small gleanings*: her family having been ruined by famine, the title character of the Book of Ruth went behind the harvesters in the fields and picked up what was left.

981   *Churchyard Elegies and Edens Lost*: Thomas Gray's *Elegy Written in a Country Churchyard* (1751) and John Milton's *Paradise Lost* (1667).

982   *Burns, and Bunyan, Selkirk, and Tom Jones*: the poet Robert Burns (1759–96); John Bunyan (1628–88), author of *The Pilgrim's Progress*; the adventures of Alexander Selkirk (1676–1721) formed the basis of Defoe's *Robinson Crusoe* (1719); *Tom Jones* (1749) is the best-known novel of Henry Fielding (1707–54).

1019–20 *ringing circles of ecstatic tune | Beneath the moistened finger*: when rubbed in a certain manner, musical glasses respond like the strings of a bowed instrument.

1053 *stertorous*: heavy snoring sound.

1160 *backbiting*: 'those scandalous' in first edition.

1174 *As seraphs might the making of the sun*: see *Paradise Lost*, vii. 346–56.

1207–8 *where John was laid | While Jesus loved him*: in John 13: 23–5 a disciple whom Jesus loved is said to be lying close to his breast during the Last Supper.

1222–3 *ointment-box ... nard*: in John 12: 3 Mary, the sister of Lazarus, anoints the feet of Jesus with ointment of spikenard; in Luke 7: 37–9 a woman who has sinned waters the feet of Jesus with her tears and anoints them with ointment.

1231–2 *sempstress-house | Far off in London*: at mid-century over 15,000 women worked in London as dressmakers or milliners. Of these, some 6,000 were engaged in the better class of establishments in the West End. Since it did not involve factory work, the needlework trade was considered a relatively genteel occupation; and there was the chance of advancement.

But the term of apprenticeship was at least two years, during which no wages were paid; if the apprentice lodged and boarded in the establishment, a premium had to be paid; and working conditions—long hours, overcrowding, poor ventilation, and inadequate lighting—were not infrequently injurious to health.

Book IV

55 *unlicensed*: underprivileged.

147 *putting out his hand to touch this ark*: 2 Samuel 6: 6–7.

190 *Rialto-prices*: i.e. market value; the Rialto was the commercial centre of Venice.

196 *as Indian widows do*: referring to the Hindu custom of suttee, the self-immolation of widows on their husbands' funeral pyres.

298 *signory*: i.e. lineage.

307 *obolus*: small coin.

309–12 *those sublime Vandykes ... (now the ruffs are off their necks)*: as court painter to Charles I during the 1630s, Anthony Van Dyck painted numerous portraits of the English aristocracy. The broad collars or ruffs with deeply cut edges often worn by his subjects came to be called 'vandykes'.

341 *the Trenton*: the Trenton Falls in upstate New York descend for two miles in a series of cataracts.

356 *indurate*: make hard or unfeeling.

370 *Austria's daughter*: Marie Louise, the Austrian princess who married Napoleon I in 1810.

373 *Saint James's*: fashionable parish church in Saint James's Square, Westminster.

380 *cothurn*: thick-soled shoe worn by Athenian tragic actors.

383–4 *Athenian wives | Who shrieked ... at the Eumenides*: Athenian women were said to have fainted when the Furies pursued Orestes during performances of Aeschylus' *Eumenides*.

388 *burr*: speak indistinctly.

399 *Spanish marriage-schemes*: political marriages involving the royal families of Spain and France.

402   *Guizot*: François Pierre Guillaume Guizot (1787–1874), French statesman.

403–4 *has Dickens turned his hinge . . . upon the fingers of the great*: Charles Dickens (1812–70) was tirelessly active as a social reformer and critic.

      potatoes: the Irish potato crop failed in 1845 and successive years to the end of the decade, causing hundreds of thousands of deaths and mass emigration.

406   *moly*: magical plant that helped Odysseus withstand the enchantments of Circe.

468   *keeper to our brother*: Genesis 4: 9.

481   *said Jesus Christ*: Matthew 19: 17.

483   *Called creatures good*: Genesis 1: 21, 25.

491   *bohea*: kind of tea.

493   *As chaste . . . as Potiphar's*: when Joseph resisted the sexual advances of the wife of his Egyptian master Potiphar, she claimed that he had tried to ravish her and caused him to be imprisoned (Genesis 39).

518   *vans*: vanes.

538   *Saint Giles*: 'St Giles is in the midst of the most populous part of the town, surrounded by broad, splendid avenues in which the gay world of London idles about, in the immediate neighbourhood of Oxford Street, Regent Street, of Trafalgar Square and the Strand. It is a disorderly collection of tall, three- or four-storied houses, with narrow, crooked, filthy streets . . . The houses are occupied from cellar to garret, filthy within and without . . . But all this is nothing in comparison with the dwellings in the narrow courts and alleys between the streets . . . in which the filth and tottering ruin surpass all description . . . Here live the poorest of the poor, the worst-paid workers with thieves and the victims of prostitution indiscriminately huddled together, the majority Irish, or of Irish extraction.' (Friedrich Engels, 'The Great Towns', in *The Condition of the Working Class in England* (1845).)

538–9 *in frieze . . . in cloth of gold*: at the time of his marriage to Mary Tudor, sister of Henry VIII and widow of Louis XII of France, the commoner Charles Brandon (who had become

Duke of Suffolk) appeared at a tournament on a horse whose
cloth of half frieze (coarse wool) and half gold bore the motto:

> Cloth of gold, do not thou despise
> Though thou be matched with cloth of frize:
> Cloth of frize, be not thou too bold
> Though thou be matched with cloth of gold.

(*Letters of Elizabeth Barrett Browning to Mary Russell Mitford,
1836–1854*, ed. Meredith B. Raymond and Mary Rose
Sullivan (Winfield, Kan., 1983), i. 50 n.)

550 *moil*: mire.

563 *moiré*: having a wavy or watered pattern.

595 *Raffael's mild Madonna of the Bird*: Raphael's *Madonna of the
Goldfinch* (1506).

627 *the Division*: the taking of a vote in one of the houses of
Parliament.

630 *Liverpool*: 'Manchester' in Wellesley MS.

651 *methodised*: 'organised' in first edition.

665 *Prince Albert's model lodging-house*: Prince Albert was president
of the Society for Improving the Condition of the Labouring
Classes (founded in 1844), and took an active interest in its
affairs. The society was interested in urban problems, including housing for families and lodging-houses. They commissioned designs for sanitary dwellings of both kinds that could
be built cheaply and arranged for the construction of models,
which came to be associated with the name of the prince
consort.

674 *Damiens' trunk and limbs*: in 1757 Robert François Damiens
attempted to assassinate Louis XV. He was condemned as a
regicide and sentenced to be torn to pieces by horses in a
public place.

749 *acts a play with it, as Hamlet did*: i.e. as Hamlet used a play
within Shakespeare's play to determine the guilt of his uncle
the king, so Romney is using his marriage to Marian Erle to
make his social equals aware of their responsibility to the
lower classes.

773 *liken to a brutalised King Lear*: the common people in the
church are now compared to Shakespeare's Lear, reduced to

powerlessness and poverty by his hard-hearted daughters Regan and Goneril, to whom the privileged members of society are likened.

991 *Hydra*: many-headed snake.

1066–7 'As heavens behind the furnace smoke' in Wellesley MS.

1100–2 *some chromatic sequence ... harmony of truth*: a musical metaphor: modulations of key through a chromatic progression of chords lead to a final harmony in an unanticipated key.

1120 *Vaucluse*: region of France.

1133 *Tossed out as straw before sick houses*: to muffle the noise of traffic, straw was sometimes put on the street in front of houses containing a seriously ill person.

1137 *torn*: 'bleeding' in first edition.

1150 *poet of Vaucluse*: Petrarch (1304–74).

1164 *poll-tax*: 'head-tax' in first edition.

1176–7 *Not a stone | But cries behind us, every weary step*: in the *Arabian Nights* tale of 'The Sisters Who Envied their Younger Sister', 'the Princess Parizade's [two] brothers ... try to get her the speaking bird, the singing tree, and the golden water, but each is turned aside by curses and execrations howled by the black stones that cover the hill and thereupon becomes himself a black stone. Parizade finally succeeds in the quest by stuffing her ears, and sets her brothers free' (*Letters of ... Elizabeth Barrett Barrett*, ii. 791 n).

1185 *stews*: brothels.

1186 *mow*: derisive grimace.

Book V

3 *lymph*: pure water, a stream; also the sap in plants.

30 *theurgic*: of, or pertaining to, the operation of a divine agency in human affairs.

75 *'Let no one be called happy till his death'*: closing lines of Sophocles' *Oedipus the King*.

83–4 'The forms of poems are the life that moves' in Wellesley MS.

87 *Atlas*: the Titan who supported the world on his shoulders.

104 *fakir*: one group of Hindu fakirs practise extreme austerities, including forms of self-torture.

113 *Panomphaean*: author of oracles.

116–17 'The great material nature skin of our skin' in Wellesley MS.

121–3 *allied | By issue and symbol, by significance | And correspondence, to that spirit-world*: in a letter of 23 August 1853 Barrett Browning commented on the doctrine of correspondences in the theosophic system of 'the Swedish seer' Emanuel Swedenborg (1688–1772): 'He is wonderful, it seems to me—his scheme of the natural and spiritual worlds and natures appears to me, in an internal light of its own, divine and true ... I receive it as a self-evident verity of which one wonders, "Why did I not think of that before?".' (Edward C. McAleer, 'New Letters from Mrs Browning to Isa Blagden', *PMLA* 66 (1951), 596.)

129 *cowslip*: wild flower.

142–5 *Payne Knight ... the mythic mountaineer ... Discoursing of an image seen through fog*: Richard Payne Knight (1750–1824) was well known in his day for his views on classical mythology, art, and literature. His *Discourse on the Worship of Priapus* (1786) proposed that all mythology and theology (including Christian theology) ultimately derived from primitive fertility cults in which the male and female genitalia were the symbols through which the procreative power was worshipped. His vociferous denial of the authenticity of the Elgin Marbles (purchased by the British government in 1816), and the peculiarities of his edition of Homer with prolegomena (1820) added to his reputation for dilettante capriciousness.

goitre: neck swelling due to over-activity of the thyroid gland can result from iodine deficiency. Regions where this element is naturally lacking include some of the Alpine valleys of Switzerland.

146 *Homer's heroes measured twelve feet high*: alluding to Payne Knight's view that Greek visual and literary art depicted abstract, idealized human types.

148 *front*: false hair worn by women over the forehead.

149 *Hector's infant whimpered at a plume*: when Hector reached out to embrace his infant son Astyanax, the child was frightened by the bronze and the horsehair crest of his father's war helmet (*Iliad* vi).

whimpered: 'blubbered' in first edition.

151 *All actual heroes are essential men*: not in first edition.

152 *all men*: 'Shandys' in Wellesley MS.

155 *epos*: epic poem.

156 *(ask Carlyle)*: Thomas Carlyle's *On Heroes, Hero-Worship, and the Heroic in History* was published in 1841. Robert Browning to Elizabeth (17 May 1846): 'All that you write about Art is most true. Carlyle has turned and forged, reforged on his anvil the fact that "no age ever appeared heroic to itself" ... and so, worthy of reproduction in Art by itself ... I thought after Carlyle's endeavours nobody could be ignorant of that.' (*Letters of ... Elizabeth Barrett Barrett*, ii. 710.)

158 *scout*: ridicule.

169–70 *Mount Athos carved, as Alexander schemed,* | *To some colossal statue of a man*: in his life of Alexander, Plutarch reports that the sculptor and architect Stasicrates (called Dinocrates in other sources) once told Alexander that 'of all the mountains he knew, that of Athos in Thrace was the most capable of being adapted to represent the shape and lineaments of a man; that if he pleased to command him, he would make it the noblest and most durable statue in the world, which in its left hand should hold a city of ten thousand inhabitants, and out of its right should pour a copious river into the sea.' (*Lives of the Noble Grecians and Romans*, trans. John Dryden (New York [1957]), 852.)

207 *Roland with his knights at Roncesvalles*: the eleventh-century heroic poem *The Song of Roland* recounts the death of the title character, Charlemagne's greatest knight, at the battle of Roncesvalles in 778.

213 *Fleet Street*: 'Regent Street' in first edition.

216 *double-breasted Age*: recalling the 'wondrous Mother-Age' of Tennyson's 'Locksley Hall,' l. 108.

240 *Jacob's white-peeled rods*: Genesis 30: 37–42.

246–7 *Shakespeare's ghost ... plead | Against our just damnation*: alluding to *Macbeth*, I. vii. 19–20.

250 *a wigless Hamlet*: in the eighteenth century Shakespearean actors usually wore contemporary dress and hairstyles, as in the frontispiece to Rowe's 1709 edition of the plays, which shows a Hamlet in knee-breeches and full wig.

289 *King Saul's father's asses*: 1 Samuel 9–10.

293 *Sicilian shores*: Aeschylus was in self-exile in Sicily at the time of his death.

298 *Hyblan bee*: poetaster (Mount Hybla was famous for its honey).

310 *crucial*: 'plastic' in Wellesley MS.

315 *greeting*: 'kiss' in first edition.

316 *Imogen and Juliet*: the heroines respectively of Shakespeare's *Cymbeline* and *Romeo and Juliet*.

320 *sacrificial goat, for Bacchus slain*: dithyrambic religious rite from which Greek drama evolved.

326 *Themis' son*: Prometheus.

354 *blue vein a-throb on Mahomet's brow*: 'I somehow like too that vein on the brow, which swelled-up black when he was in anger ... It was a kind of feature in the Hashem family, this black swelling of the brow; Mahomet had it prominent.' (Thomas Carlyle, 'The Hero as Prophet', in *Heroes and Hero-Worship*.)

361–4 *Saint Preux ... Julie's drooping eyelid*: hero and heroine of Jean-Jacques Rousseau's epistolary novel, *Julie, ou la nouvelle Héloïse* (1761).

400 *Pygmalion*: sculptor who fell in love with the image of a perfect woman that he had created. Aphrodite (Venus) brought the image to life.

414 *Phoebus Apollo*: god of poetry.

478 *a man said that*: see Robert Browning, *Colombe's Birthday* (1844), iv. 412–13.

494 *if Ugolino's full*: in Dante's *Inferno*, Cantos xxxii–xxxiii, Count Ugolino is found ceaselessly gnawing the head of the person

who had imprisoned him and his sons without food, ultimately forcing Ugolino to eat the bodies of his dead children.

506 *smutch*: smudge.

516 *Plotinus*: third-century AD Neoplatonic philosopher, who held that all modes of being, including material being, were the outflowings of a single immaterial power that was the ground of all existence and the source of all value.

554 *those at Babel*: the builders of the tower of Babel were struck by God with a confusion of tongues and scattered over the earth (Genesis 11: 1–9).

559–60 *Sparrows five | For just two farthings*: paraphrasing Luke 12: 6.

563–70 *I've seen some men ... From possible communion*: spiritualism, the phenomenon whereby spirits of the dead appear to communicate with the living through a medium, was introduced into England from America in 1852. The claims of its practitioners, and the aural and visual phenomena occurring during seances, became subjects of heated controversy. 'There is one reference [in *Aurora Leigh*] to the spirits, but nobody will be offended by it as Robert isn't.' (*Letters to her Sister, 1846–1859*, ed. Leonard Huxley (London, 1929), 250.)

592 *outriders*: mounted attendants.

600 *Some Scandinavian myth of Lemures*: i.e. the talk was incomprehensible to Lady Howe. Lemures belong to Roman mythology; they were evil spirits of the dead who wandered the earth and afflicted the living.

605 *the Leeds mesmerist*: The Viennese physician Franz Anton Mesmer (1734–1815) posited a mutual magnetic influence between heavenly bodies, the earth, and animal bodies that could be manipulated to produce hypnotic states in individuals during which clairvoyant experiences and physical changes could take place. Interest in mesmerism, or animal magnetism, was widespread in England from its introduction in the late 1830s until the early 1850s. Information about the subject and demonstrations of its power were provided by itinerant lecturers/performers who tended to be from socially marginal

backgrounds, though their London audiences included West End society.

607   the *'Woman's question'*: this was the name given to the proliferation of debate concerning the position of women in Victorian society. At mid-century the central issues in the feminist controversy were education, working conditions and employment opportunities, and inequalities in the marital relationship and in matrimonial law.

627   *aspectable*: agreeable to look upon.

663–5   *'A flower ... falling off'*: ironic allusion to Christ's words: 'And why take ye thought for raiment? Consider the lilies of the field, how they grow; they toil not, neither do they spin: And yet I say unto you, That even Solomon in all his glory was not arrayed like one of these.' (Matthew 6: 28–9.)

677   *Styrian*: Styria is a Roman Catholic region of Austria.

684   *Saint Lucy*: a saint who plucked out her eyes, her most beautiful feature, to help ensure her virginity.

696   *swear*: 'curse' in first edition.

704   *rushlight*: light from a rush candle; figuratively, a feeble glimmer of intelligence.

730   *Pisgah-hill*: from which Moses beheld the promised land (Deuteronomy 3: 27).

737   *Christian socialist*: active between 1848 and 1854, the Christian Socialists were a group of upper- and middle-class persons, including F. D. Maurice (1805–72) and Charles Kingsley (1819–75), who were concerned with the condition of the working classes and thought that the key to their improvement lay in the compatibility of Christianity and Socialism. They were influenced by the liberal theology of Maurice's *Kingdom of Christ* (1838), which emphasized social rather than individual salvation. Politics and religion were inseparable, Maurice argued, and it was the responsibility of the Church to make the divine order manifest in the world by addressing social questions.

740   *women-fishes*: mermaids.

747 *The catholic, apostolic, mother-church*: the Roman Catholic
     Church. Sir Blaise is ostentatiously Catholic in his dress,
     manner, and opinions.

756 *Göttingen*: its university made Göttingen one of the intellec-
     tual centres of Germany. In 'Christmas-Eve' (1850), Robert
     Browning's presentation of three distinctive points of view
     concerning Christianity, the speaker who puts the position of
     German rationalist thinkers is a professor at Göttingen.

765 *Meretrix*: harlot.

799 *Pallas*: Athene.

821 *Chipewa*: region of Wisconsin.

823 *Queen Pomare's and Emperor Soulouque's*: in 1843 Pomare IV
     of Tahiti was forced to accept a French protectorate and then
     to abdicate, despite her pleas to the British for help. She was
     reinstated in 1847. Faustin Elie Soulouque was elected
     president of Haiti in 1847; he made himself emperor two
     years later, ruling until 1859.

829 *an epic in twelve parts*: entitled 'Bunker Hill' in Wellesley MS.

911–13 *the holy ox | On Memphis-highway ... Our Apis-public
     lowing*: Apis, the bull of Memphis, was worshipped by the
     ancient Egyptians as an avatar of Osiris.

918 *says a Book I've read*: Revelation 8: 10–11.

940–3 *some golden tripod ... At Delphi*: the oracles of Apollo in
     the temple at Delphi uttered prophecies while seated on a
     tripod made of gold.

968 *bate*: subtract.

989 *'tiring glass*: mirror.

1045 *housewife*: case for needles.

1096 *My woodland sister, sweet maid Marian*: alluding to the Marian
     of the Robin Hood legends.

1183–4 *gall | And potash*: i.e. black and white.

1204 *Faustus*: the powers that the legendary Faustus acquired as a
     result of his pact with the Devil included the ability to turn
     base metals into gold.

1205 *'Leave my Job,' said God*: i.e. poets are afflicted with poverty
     as Job was afflicted by God with misfortunes.

1218 *Elzevirs*: books printed by the celebrated Elzevir family of Dutch printers during the late sixteenth and seventeenth centuries.

1222 *'conferenda haec cum his'*: 'compare this with that'.

1223 *'corruptè citat—lege potiùs'*: 'quoted inaccurately—read preferably'.

1228 *Proclus*: Neoplatonic philosopher of the fifth century AD.

1246–57 *the kissing Judas, Wolff . . . for the universe*: in his *Prolegomena ad Homerum* (1795) the German classical scholar Friedrich Augustus Wolf provoked a long-lasting controversy by arguing that the *Iliad* was a work of composite authorship, the various parts of which had been finally collected and collated in the sixth century BC. Wolf's methods and the kinds of questions he posed resembled those of contemporary German biblical scholars who were beginning to concern themselves with the historicity of the Scriptures. Because of this similarity in method and national origin, in England Wolf's views on the Homeric poems and German biblical criticism tended to be perceived as interconnected, with the former being regarded as subversive of traditional Christian beliefs.

1250–4 *Who floats in cream . . . Proclaims them bastards*: the ends of the Homeric hexameter lines on the white page are likened to the mouths of infants sucking at the breast.

Book VI

67–73 *a great man's face . . . democracy*: Louis Napoleon was elected president of the French Republic in 1848. He carried out a *coup d'état* in 1851, and immediately held a presidential election, which he won by another overwhelming majority. A year later he proclaimed himself Napoleon III, Emperor of the French.

91 *bosky*: wooded.

110–13 *the old Tuileries . . . a new fair face*: the Tuileries was the palace of the French kings. The new face is the Empress Eugénie, who did not come from royal stock. At the time of her marriage to Napoleon III in 1853, she was 26 and at the height of her beauty.

126 *dentist's teeth*: sets of false teeth displayed under a glass case indicated the shop of a surgeon-dentist (Reynolds).

129–30 *the first Napoleon's bones . . . 'neath the golden dome*: in 1840 the remains of Napoleon I were removed from Saint Helena and placed in a mausoleum under the gilded dome of the Hôtel des Invalides.

131–2 *'Shall | These dry bones live'*: Ezekiel 37: 1–10.

132–3 *thought Louis Philippe once, | And lived to know*: Louis Philippe, King of France from 1830 to 1848, was deposed by the Revolution of 1848, which brought to power Louis Napoleon, the nephew of Napoleon I.

152 *resumed*: recapitulated.

166 *track old Nilus to his silver roots*: in the early 1850s, missionary reports from eastern central Africa of vast inland lakes reached Europe and intensified interest in the question of the source of the Nile. In 1854 and 1856 Richard Burton and John Henning Speke led expeditions into the interior. In 1858 Speke finally discovered the source he named Lake Victoria.

167–70 *changes of the moon . . . Thessaly . . . many a witch*: in antiquity the people of Thessaly, a mountainous region of Greece, were reputed to be superstitious and addicted to the study of magic.

172 *osteologists*: scientists specializing in bones.

211 *civil conscriptions and lay monasteries*: pejorative allusions to the regimented and authoritarian features of socialist schemes.

213 *The bread of man . . . made all his life*: ironically recalling Matthew 4: 4 and Luke 4: 4.

214 *washing seven times*: Naaman cured his leprosy by bathing seven times in the Jordan (2 Kings 5: 1–14).

264 *the Institute*: the highest institution of learning in France is the Institut de France, which is composed of five academies, including the Académie Française, which deals with language and literature.

273 *Dumas*: Alexandre Dumas, either *père* (1802–70) or *fils* (1824–95); both were novelists and dramatists.

278 *Revolving pistols*: a handgun with a revolving cylinder was invented by Samuel Colt in 1830.

424 *the Market-place of Flowers*: the Marché aux Fleurs on the Quai Desaix; inexpensive flowers were sold during the morning hours.

438 *flowering mountain-gorse*: see iii. 884–6.

572–3 *hot and scarlet as the first live rose | The shepherd's heart-blood ebbed away into*: the shepherd Adonis was wounded in the thigh by a boar. As he lay dying, Aphrodite turned drops of his blood into roses.

669 *loathed . . . by*: 'stink . . . for' in Houghton MS.

713–15 *New Jerusalem . . . twelve stones*: see Revelation 21.

750 *oriflamme*: sacred banner.

762 *paltered*: trifled.

808 *madrepores*: coral-building animals. 'And I was at the lowest point of created life: a madrepore rooted to the rock, fathoms below the tide-mark; and worst of all, my individuality was gone.' (Charles Kingsley, *Alton Locke* (1850), ch. 36.)

1049 *pale*: boundary.

1176 *Along the swine's road, down the precipice*: alluding to the Gadarene swine possessed by unclean spirits in Mark 5: 11–13.

1273–4 *stone upon my sepulchre . . . roll away*: Matthew 28: 2.

Book VII

7 *chink*: make the sound produced by shaking coins together.

   naughty uses: 'filthy uses' in Wellesley MS.

10 *right damnable*: 'unmerciful' in first edition.

92 *crooked*: 'hump-backed' in Wellesley MS.

226–7 *if Cervantes . . . made his Don a Donna*: i.e. if the Spanish author of *Don Quixote* (1605, 1615), the story of the adventures of a knight-errant who is one of the last upholders of the chivalric tradition, had possessed the same ability to create female characters as his English contemporary, he would have made his title character female.

238 *flagitious*: villainous.

265 *hoggery*: hogs or swine collectively.

267 *thieving god*: Hermes (Mercury).

292–3 *I never did ... presently*: 'I took the wind-side of your leprosy | And drew my garments round me—I'm not proud' in Wellesley MS.

300–1 *gambled deep | As Lucifer, and won the morning-star*: see Revelation 2: 24–8.

308–9 *tares and wheat ... fire*: Matthew 13: 36–43.

342–3 *For which inheritance ... You sold that ... porridge*: In Genesis 25: 29–34 Esau sells his birthright to Jacob for a mess of pottage.

349 *it was writ of old*: in Deuteronomy 22: 10.

432 *Thor-hammers*: the Norse god of thunder and lightning possessed a hammer that could smash rock.

439 *Titans underneath the pile*: after their overthrow by the Olympians, the Titans were hurled into a dark region beneath the earth's surface and imprisoned there for ever.

470 *Odyssean ghosts*: during Odysseus' visit to the Underworld, lifeless phantoms of the dead gathered around him to drink the blood of the animals he had sacrificed and so get strength enough to speak to him (*Odyssey* xi).

473 *Tyrian*: purple.

566 *od-force of German Reichenbach*: in 1845 the German chemist Baron Karl von Reichenbach (1788–1869), discoverer of paraffin and creosote, announced the discovery of a mesmeric 'influence' termed *odyl*, claiming that it was present in some crystals, in magnets, and in those gifted as mesmerists. It was also said to be visible to some as an effluence of light. Elizabeth to Robert Browning (21 Apr. 1846): '*Love*, I have learnt to believe in. I see the new light which Reichenbach shows pouring forth visibly from these crystals tossed out.' (*Letters of ... Elizabeth Barrett Barrett*, ii. 640.)

647–8 'In spite of childish scrawls on tighter cards' in Wellesley MS.

662 *persiani*: curtains made of slats.

679 *nepenthe*: drug causing forgetfulness of grief.

746 *Phaedons*: i.e. speculations and beliefs concerning death and the immortality of the soul. Plato's *Phaedo* narrates the last hours of Socrates, which were spent in discussion of these subjects.

771 *fitted Venus' hand*: alluding to the golden apple inscribed 'for the fairest' which Paris awarded to Venus.

787 *Antinous*: this beautiful youth, the favourite of the Roman emperor Hadrian, was commemorated by statues after his early death. The statue called the Belvedere Antinous is in the Vatican Museum.

793 *empyreal*: celestial.

798 *conterminous*: coextensive.

805–6 *cup, column, or candlestick ... in the Mount*: alluding to God's detailed instructions to Moses on Mount Sinai concerning the construction and appointments of the Tabernacle (Exodus 25–31).

810 *said a poet of our day*: Robert Browning, in *Pippa Passes* (1841), Introduction, ll. 190–201.

822 *bush afire with God*: Exodus 3: 2–5.

830 *as Jove did Io*: Jove (Zeus) changed Io into a heifer to conceal her from his wife, who sent a gadfly to torment Io and pursue her throughout the world.

849 *audient*: listening.

865–6 *all the towns | Make offal of their daughters for its use*: prostitution.

887 *digamma*: vestigial letter of the Greek alphabet.

902 *Medaean boil-pot*: the sorceress Medea filled her cauldron with a variety of animal and vegetable materials.

915 *lawn*: fine-woven linen or cotton.

917 *Samminiato*: hill southeast of Florence

935–6 *Dante's purple lilies ... his prophet breath*: see *Purgatorio*, xxxii. 52–60.

942 *ichor*: blood-like fluid in the veins of gods.

965 *'I'd be a butterfly,'* or *'C'est l'amour'*: both songs enjoyed the height of their popularity during the 1820s, when they were

launched in theatre pieces and then sold as sheet music. 'C'est l'amour qui fait le monde' went through seven editions between 1821 and 1825; 'I'd be a Butterfly', with words and music by Thomas Haynes Bayly (1797–1839), was even more successful.

969 *ritournelle*: recurring passage in a song or other musical composition.

986 *like Alaric*: after his death in Italy in 410, the followers of Alaric diverted the course of a river, buried their leader with his most precious spoils in the river-bed, and then returned the water to its former channel.

1021 *auto-vestments*: garments in which heretics and unbelievers were burned at the climax of the *auto-da-fé*, when the sentence of the Spanish Inquisition was executed.

1023 *There are, too, who believe in heaven, and fear*: not in first edition.

1026 *oyster's part*: 'beast's part' in first edition.

1036 *the way, the truth, the life*: John 14: 6.

1095 *grillino*: cricket.

1174 *festa*: festival.

1176 *'issimo' and 'ino'*: Italian inflections for the superlative and diminutive degrees.

1181 *Donay's*: Florentine café.

1198 *Like grasshoppers at Athens*: Athenians supposed grasshoppers to be sprung from the ground, and themselves to be the most ancient people in Greece. Thus they were sometimes referred to as 'grasshoppers', and sometimes wore golden grasshoppers in their hair as badges of honour.

1248 *tern*: prize.

1256 *'Benigna sis'*: 'Be thou blessed'.

1261 *written in the Book*: Psalms 147: 9.

1303 *bells upon my robe*: recalling Aaron's robe in Exodus 28: 33–4.

1309 *oenomel*: mixture of wine and honey.

Book VIII

21–2 *Boccaccio's tale, | The Falcon's*: Decameron, v. ix.

33 *Poggio*: Florentine avenue.

44 *duomo-bell*: cathedral bell.

54 *Buonarroti's Bride*: the church of Santa Maria Novella, the façade of which is here described, was much admired by Michelangelo.

65 *empery*: dominion.

100–7 *since the Austrian boar . . . with all his swine*: Lombardy had belonged to the Austrian Empire since 1814. In 1849 Austrian troops entered Tuscany to support the regime of Grand Duke Leopold II, remaining in occupation until 1855.

149 *crossed*: making the sign of the cross as well as deleting.

151 *pauls*: Italian coins.

185 *Chianti*: common red wine of Tuscany.

187 *cockchafer*: nocturnal beetle.

334 *my Miriam*: see ii. 171–2 n.

388 *that Phalarian bull, society*: Phalaris, a Greek tyrant of the sixth century BC, was notorious for his cruelty, especially for the hollow bronze bull in which victims were confined and roasted alive. 'I will venture to believe that in no time, since the beginnings of Society, was the lot of those same dumb millions of toilers so entirely unbearable as it is even in the days now passing over us . . . it is to die slowly all our life long, imprisoned in a deaf, dead, Infinite Injustice, as in the accursed iron belly of a Phalaris' Bull.' (Thomas Carlyle, *Past and Present* (1842), III. xiii.)

414 *eighty thousand women*: contemporary estimates of the number of prostitutes in mid-nineteenth-century London varied greatly. The figure of 80,000 was cited by the Bishop of Exeter and by James Beard Talbot, author of *The Miseries of Prostitution* (1844), and was accepted by Bracebridge Hemyng in his contribution to Henry Mayhew's *London Labour and the London Poor* (London, 1861–2), iv. 213.

427–36 *'You will not compass . . . develops from within'*: repeated from ii. 476–85.

507 *Ulysses' dog*: in *Odyssey* xvii, the aged dog Argus, who had been trained as a puppy by Odysseus (Ulysses) twenty years

before, recognizes the voice of his disguised master, wags his tail, and dies.

646 *clay Christ laid upon their eyelids*: John 9: 1–7.

653–4 *Saint Paul | Has promised*: 1 Corinthians 15: 42–50.

658 *wards*: parts of the mechanism of a lock.

672 *bruit*: spread rumour.

680 *doxology*: liturgical praise to God; here used ironically.

711 *cashiered*: dismissed from service.

734–41 *employ | Seven men . . . to make a perfect pin . . . and not a man too much*: in book 1, chapter 1 of *The Wealth of Nations* the trade of pin-making is Adam Smith's example of 'the effects of the division of labour' on 'the productive powers of labour' (4th edn. (Edinburgh, 1850), 2–3).

769 *Whatever may be lacking on the Mount*: Mount Sinai, where God gave Moses a detailed 'pattern' for building the Tabernacle (Exodus 25–31).

795–6 *when the prophet beats the ass, | The angel intercedes*: Numbers 22: 21–34.

843 *leech*: physician.

904 *'the frogs'*: see Revelation 16: 13.

984 *'vale et plaude'*: 'farewell and be praised'.

1113 *metaphrase*: reformulated phrase; also translation into metrical form.

1114–15 *carve . . . white Loves out of snow, | As Buonarroti*: Michelangelo is said to have made a statue of snow at the request of Piero de Medici.

1136–8 *cup at supper . . . vinegar and gall*: the cup of wine that Christ shared with his apostles at the Last Supper (Luke 22: 20), in contrast to the sponge soaked in vinegar that was put to his mouth on the Cross (John 19: 29–30).

1216 *arrogance of nature*: 'manly arrogance' in Wellesley MS.

Book IX

53 *its hooks of rhyme*: 'rhyme's golden hooks' in first edition.

103 *Saint Sophia's dome*: in Constantinople.

154 *'fox and goose'*: board-game resembling checkers/draughts, played with seventeen pieces called geese and one fox.

224 *aftermath*: second crop.

253–4 *Aaron's priestly robe . . . when he took it off to die*: Numbers 20: 26–8.

321 *I am grown so proud with grief*: 'Marian had to be dragged through the uttermost debasement of circumstances to arrive at the sentiment of personal dignity. I am sorry, but indeed it seemed necessary.' (*Letters*, ed. Frederic G. Kenyon (London, 1898), ii. 242.)

393 *chin-cloth*: chin-band; see i. 178 n.

395 *withes*: flexible branches used for tying or binding.

431 *dandle*: to dance an infant on one's knees or in one's arms.

469 *impuissance*: powerlessness.

493 *the great Taskmaster*: recalling Milton's 'How Soon Hath Time', l. 14.

564 *mulcted*: penalized or punished.

570–2 *blind . . . in the blaze of day . . . As dark*: recalling Milton's *Samson Agonistes*, l. 80.

579 *The visual nerve is withered to the root*: 'the only injury received by Romney in the fire was from a blow and from the emotion produced by the *circumstances* of the fire. Not only did he *not* lose his eyes in the fire, but he describes the ruin of his house as no blind man could. He was standing there, a spectator. Afterwards he had a fever, and the eyes, the visual nerve, perished, showing no external stain—perished as Milton's did. I believe that a great shock on the nerves might produce such an effect in certain constitutions, and the reader on referring as far back as Marian's letter (when she avoided the marriage) may observe that his eyes had never been strong, that her desire had been to read his notes at night, and save them. For it was necessary, I thought, to the bringing-out of my thought, that Romney should be mulcted in his natural sight.' (*Letters*, ii. 246.)

643 *all the high necessities of Art*: 'all the ministry of holy Art' in Houghton MS.

667 *'in leone'*: in the constellation of Leo, the fifth sign of the zodiac.

702 *My Cloud*: a pillar of cloud led the Israelites through the desert by day (Exodus 13: 21).

845 *the old Jewish temple's Selah-pause*: in a note on her use of *Selah* in *An Essay on Mind* (1826), Barrett Browning wrote: 'Respecting this Hebrew word, which is found "seventy times in the Psalms, and three times in Habakkuk", Calmet observes—"One conjecture is, that it means the end or a pause, and that the ancient musicians put it occasionally in the margin of their psalters, to shew where a musical pause was to be made, and where the tune ended".' (*Complete Works*, ed. Charlotte Porter and Helen A. Clarke (New York, 1900), i. 268–9.) See Augustin Calmet's *Dictionnaire . . . de la Bible* (Paris, 1730), iii. 512–13.

857 *humbleness . . . made me great*: see Luke 14: 11; 18: 14.

868 *Fourier's void*: 'I love liberty so intensely that I hate Socialism. I hold it to be the most desecrating and dishonouring to humanity of all creeds. I would rather (for *me*) live under the absolutism of Nicholas of Russia than in a Fourier machine, with my individuality sucked out of me by a social air-pump . . . If Fourierism could be realised (which it surely cannot) out of a dream, the destinies of our race would shrivel up under the unnatural heat.' (*Letters*, i. 452, 467.)

869 *Comte absurd*: 'Comte is dwarfed' in first edition. Auguste Comte (1798–1857), French positivist philosopher and social thinker, held that all valid knowledge was experientially derived and that in the nineteenth century the social sciences had begun to yield verifiable information that would serve as the basis of a 'Religion of Humanity' which would supersede Christianity. In his later writings Comte elaborated his plan for social reorganization with a prescriptive specificity and a mania for regulation that even appalled admirers of his earlier work.

Cabet puerile: Étienne Cabet (1788–1856) was a French Communist whose utopian romance, *Voyage en Icarie* (1840), was influenced by the ideas of Robert Owen and Fourier and contained a scathing criticism of the existing social order. In the 1840s he promoted the establishment of communistic communities in the United States. The first attempt, made in Texas in 1848, ended in disaster. The next year Cabet led a group to Illinois, where a community was established from which he was formally expelled in 1856 for refusing to accept the result of a democratic election.

885–6 *Sharon gave | A name to*: Song of Solomon 2: 1.

913 *inscient*: inwardly knowing.

915 *Art's a service*: 'Art's a priesthood' in Houghton MS.

932 *level as Jericho's*: Joshua 6: 1–20.

949 *HE shall make all new*: 'Behold, I make all things new' (Revelation 21: 5).

962–4 *Jasper ... amethyst*: part of John's vision of the New Jerusalem descending out of heaven from God (Revelation 21: 18–20).

THE WORLD'S CLASSICS

A Select List

JANE AUSTEN: Emma
Edited by James Kinsley and David Lodge

J. M. BARRIE: Peter Pan in Kensington Gardens & Peter and Wendy
Edited by Peter Hollindale

WILLIAM BECKFORD: Vathek
Edited by Roger Lonsdale

JOHN BUNYAN: The Pilgrim's Progress
Edited by N. H. Keeble

THOMAS CARLYLE: The French Revolution
Edited by K. J. Fielding and David Sorensen

GEOFFREY CHAUCER: The Canterbury Tales
Translated by David Wright

CHARLES DICKENS: Christmas Books
Edited by Ruth Glancy

MARIA EDGEWORTH: Castle Rackrent
Edited by George Watson

ELIZABETH GASKELL: Cousin Phillis and Other Tales
Edited by Angus Easson

THOMAS HARDY: A Pair of Blue Eyes
Edited by Alan Manford

HOMER: The Iliad
Translated by Robert Fitzgerald
Introduction by G. S. Kirk

HENRIK IBSEN: An Enemy of the People, The Wild Duck,
Rosmersholm
Edited and Translated by James McFarlane

HENRY JAMES: The Ambassadors
Edited by Christopher Butler

JOCELIN OF BRAKELOND:
Chronicle of the Abbey of Bury St. Edmunds
Translated by Diana Greenway and Jane Sayers

BEN JONSON: Five Plays
Edited by G. A. Wilkes

LEONARDO DA VINCI: Notebooks
Edited by Irma A. Richter

HERMAN MELVILLE: The Confidence-Man
Edited by Tony Tanner

PROSPER MÉRIMÉE: Carmen and Other Stories
Translated by Nicholas Jotcham

EDGAR ALLAN POE: Selected Tales
Edited by Julian Symons

MARY SHELLEY: Frankenstein
Edited by M. K. Joseph

BRAM STOKER: Dracula
Edited by A. N. Wilson

ANTHONY TROLLOPE: The American Senator
Edited by John Halperin

OSCAR WILDE: Complete Shorter Fiction
Edited by Isobel Murray

VIRGINIA WOOLF: Mrs Dalloway
Edited by Claire Tomalin

A complete list of Oxford Paperbacks, including The World's Classics, OPUS, Past Masters, Oxford Authors, Oxford Shakespeare, and Oxford Paperback Reference, is available in the UK from the Arts and Reference Publicity Department (BH), Oxford University Press, Walton Street, Oxford OX2 6DP.

In the USA, complete lists are available from the Paperbacks Marketing Manager, Oxford University Press, 200 Madison Avenue, New York, NY 10016.

Oxford Paperbacks are available from all good bookshops. In case of difficulty, customers in the UK can order direct from Oxford University Press Bookshop, Freepost, 116 High Street, Oxford, OX1 4BR, enclosing full payment. Please add 10 per cent of published price for postage and packing.